Proceedings of the Shared Task: Modeling Multilingual Unrestricted Coreference in OntoNotes

Held at EMNLP-CoNLL 2012

Jeju Island, Korea
13 July 2012

ISBN: 978-1-62748-404-6

Printed from e-media with permission by:

Curran Associates, Inc.
57 Morehouse Lane
Red Hook, NY 12571

Some format issues inherent in the e-media version may also appear in this print version.

Printed by Curran Associates, Inc. (2013)

For permission requests, please contact the Association for Computational Linguistics at the address below.

Association for Computational Linguistics
209 N. Eighth Street
Stroudsburg, Pennsylvania 18360

Phone: 1-570-476-8006
Fax: 1-570-476-0860

acl@aclweb.org

Additional copies of this publication are available from:

Curran Associates, Inc.
57 Morehouse Lane
Red Hook, NY 12571 USA
Phone: 845-758-0400
Fax: 845-758-2634
Email: curran@proceedings.com
Web: www.proceedings.com

EMNLP-CoNLL 2012

Joint Conference on Empirical Methods in Natural Language Processing and Computational Natural Language Learning

Proceedings of the Shared Task: Modeling Multilingual Unrestricted Coreference in OntoNotes

July 13, 2012

We wish to thank our sponsor: ETERNALS
https://www.eternals.eu/

Introduction

This volume contains a description of the CoNLL-2012 Shared Task and the participating systems. The CoNLL-2012 shared task was on modeling multilingual unrestricted coreference in the OntoNotes data. This was an extension of the CoNLL-2011 shared task and involved automatic anaphoric mention detection and coreference resolution across three languages – English, Chinese and Arabic – using the OntoNotes 5.0 corpus, given predicted information on the syntax, proposition, word sense and named entity layers as input. The goal was to identify anaphoric mentions – both entities and events – and perform coreference resolution to create clusters of mentions representing the same entity or event in the text. The English and Chinese language portion of the OntoNotes data comprises roughly one million words per language from newswire, magazine articles, broadcast news, broadcast conversations, web data and conversational speech. The English corpus also contains a further 200k of the English translation of the New Testament. The Arabic portion is smaller, comprising 300k of newswire articles. One of the challenges for the shared task participants (though they were limited by the time constraints of the task) and also for continuing research going forward was to find effective ways to bring these multiple layers of information to bear on the coreference task to improve upon the current state of the art. An additional challenge for participants of this year's shared task was to develop systems that perform well across languages. We were happy to see many competitive systems in both English and Chinese. The results for Arabic are encouraging as well, in spite of the smaller data set.

As is traditional with CoNLL, we had two tracks – an open and a closed track. Since world knowledge is an important factor in coreference resolution, even in the closed task participants were allowed to use some limited, outside sources, including WordNet and a pre-computed table predicting number and gender information for noun phrases for the English task. This information is not available for Chinese and for Arabic due to lack of similar resources. For the open task, as usual, participants were allowed to use any other source of information, such as Wikipedia, gazetteers, etc., that did not violate the evaluation criteria designed to protect the test set. A total of 17 participants submitted system outputs and one participant withdrew because they found a bug in their system. Among the remaining 16 participants, 15 submitted system description papers. All 16 systems participated in the English task, 15 systems participated in the Chinese task and 8 systems participated in the Arabic task. There were 15 entries in the closed track and 3 in the open track. We hope that the data set of this year's shared task will provide a useful benchmark and spur further research in this important sub-field of language processing.

Sameer Pradhan, Alessandro Moschitti and Nianwen Xue
Organizers of the CoNLL-2012 Shared Task

Organizers:

Sameer Pradhan, Raytheon BBN Technologies
Alessandro Moschitti, University of Trento
Nianwen Xue, Brandeis University

Advisory Committee:

Mitchell Marcus, University of Pennsylvania
Martha Palmer, University of Colorado
Lance Ramshaw, Raytheon BBN Technologies
Ralph Weischedel, Raytheon BBN Technologies

Program Committee:

Jie Cai, HITS gGmbH
Kadri Hacioglu, Rosetta Stone
Veŕonique Hoste, University College Ghent
Dan Jurafsky, Stanford University
Sandra Kubler, Indiana University
Heeyoung Lee, Stanford University
Xiaoqiang Luo, IBM Research
Mitchell Marcus, University of Pennsylvania
Alessandro Moschitti, University of Trento
Vincent Ng, University of Texas at Dallas
Pierre Nugues, Lund University
Simone Ponzetto, University of Rome
Marta Recasens, University of Barcelona
Dan Roth, University of Illinois at Urbana-Champaign
Michael Strube, HITS gGmbH
Olga Uryupina, University of Trento
Nianwen Xue, Brandeis University

Table of Contents

Conference Program

Friday, July 13, 2012

CoNLL-2012 Shared Task: Modeling Multilingual Unrestricted Coreference in OntoNotes

Sameer Pradhan
Raytheon BBN Technologies,
Cambridge, MA 02138
USA
pradhan@bbn.com

Alessandro Moschitti
University of Trento,
38123 Povo (TN)
Italy
moschitti@disi.unitn.it

Nianwen Xue
Brandeis University,
Waltham, MA 02453
USA
xuen@cs.brandeis.edu

Olga Uryupina
University of Trento,
38123 Povo (TN)
Italy
uryupina@gmail.com

Yuchen Zhang
Brandeis University,
Waltham, MA 02453
USA
yuchenz@brandeis.edu

Abstract

The CoNLL-2012 shared task involved predicting coreference in English, Chinese, and Arabic, using the final version, v5.0, of the OntoNotes corpus. It was a follow-on to the English-only task organized in 2011. Until the creation of the OntoNotes corpus, resources in this sub-field of language processing were limited to noun phrase coreference, often on a restricted set of entities, such as the ACE entities. OntoNotes provides a large-scale corpus of general anaphoric coreference not restricted to noun phrases or to a specified set of entity types, and covers multiple languages. OntoNotes also provides additional layers of integrated annotation, capturing additional shallow semantic structure. This paper describes the OntoNotes annotation (coreference and other layers) and then describes the parameters of the shared task including the format, pre-processing information, evaluation criteria, and presents and discusses the results achieved by the participating systems. The task of coreference has had a complex evaluation history. Potentially many evaluation conditions, have, in the past, made it difficult to judge the improvement in new algorithms over previously reported results. Having a standard test set and standard evaluation parameters, all based on a resource that provides multiple integrated annotation layers (syntactic parses, semantic roles, word senses, named entities and coreference) and in multiple languages could support joint modeling and help ground and energize ongoing research in the task of entity and event coreference.

1 Introduction

The importance of coreference resolution for the entity/event detection task, namely identifying all mentions of entities and events in text and clustering them into equivalence classes, has been well recognized in the natural language processing community.

Early work on corpus-based coreference resolution dates back to the mid-90s by McCarthy and Lenhert (1995) where they experimented with decision trees and hand-written rules. Corpora to support supervised learning of this task date back to the Message Understanding Conferences (MUC) (Hirschman and Chinchor, 1997; Chinchor, 2001; Chinchor and Sundheim, 2003). The de facto standard datasets for current coreference studies are the MUC and the ACE[1] (Doddington et al., 2004) corpora. These corpora were tagged with coreferring entities in the form of noun phrases in the text. The MUC corpora cover all noun phrases in text but are relatively small in size. The ACE corpora, on the other hand, cover much more data, but the annotation is restricted to a small subset of entities.

Automatic identification of coreferring entities and events in text has been an uphill battle for several decades, partly because it is a problem that requires world knowledge to solve and word knowledge is hard to define, and partly owing to the lack of substantial annotated data. Aside from the fact that resolving coreference in text is simply a very hard problem, there have been other hindrances that further contributed to the slow progress in this area:

(i) *Smaller sized corpora* such as MUC which covered coreference across all noun phrases. Corpora such as ACE which are larger in size, *but cover a smaller set of entities*; and

(ii) *low consistency in existing corpora* annotated with coreference — in terms of inter-annotator agreement (ITA) (Hirschman et al., 1998) — owing to attempts at covering multiple coreference phenomena that are not equally annotatable with high agreement which likely lessened the reliability of statistical evidence in the form of lexical coverage and semantic relatedness that could be derived from the data and

[1] http://projects.ldc.upenn.edu/ace/data/

used by a classifier to generate better predictive models. The importance of a well-defined tagging scheme and consistent ITA has been well recognized and studied in the past (Poesio, 2004; Poesio and Artstein, 2005; Passonneau, 2004). There is a growing consensus that in order to take language understanding applications such as question answering or distillation to the next level, we need more consistent annotation for larger amounts of broad coverage data to train better automatic models for entity and event detection.

(iii) *Complex evaluation* with multiple evaluation metrics and multiple evaluation scenarios, complicated with varying training and test partitions, led to situations where many researchers report results with only one or a few of the available metrics and under a subset of evaluation scenarios. This has made it hard to gauge the improvement in algorithms over the years (Stoyanov et al., 2009), or to determine which particular areas require further attention. Looking at various numbers reported in literature can greatly affect the perceived difficulty of the task. It can seem to be a very hard problem (Soon et al., 2001) or one that is relatively easy (Culotta et al., 2007).

(iv) *the knowledge bottleneck* which has been a well-accepted ceiling that has kept the progress in this task at bay.

These issues suggest that the following steps might take the community in the right direction towards improving the state of the art in coreference resolution:

(i) Create a *large corpus* with *high inter-annotator agreement* possibly by restricting the coreference annotating to phenomena that can be annotated with high consistency, and *covering an unrestricted set of entities and events*; and

(ii) Create a *standard evaluation scenario* with an official evaluation setup, and possibly several ablation settings to capture the range of performance. This can then be used as a standard benchmark by the research community.

(iii) Continue to *improve learning algorithms* that better incorporate world knowledge and jointly incorporate information from other layers of syntactic and semantic annotation to improve the state of the art.

One of the many goals of the OntoNotes project[2] (Hovy et al., 2006; Weischedel et al., 2011) was to explore whether it could fill this void and help push the progress further — not only in coreference, but with the various layers of semantics that it tries to capture. As one of its layers, it has created a corpus for general anaphoric coreference that covers entities and events not limited to noun phrases or a subset of entity types. The coreference layer in OntoNotes constitutes just one part of a multi-layered, integrated annotation of shallow semantic structures in text with high inter-annotator agreement. This addresses the first issue.

In the language processing community, the field of speech recognition probably has the longest history of shared evaluations held primary by NIST[3] (Pallett, 2002). In the past decade machine translation has been a topic of shared evaluations also by NIST[4]. There are many syntactic and semantic processing tasks that are not quite amenable to such continued evaluation efforts. The CoNLL shared tasks over the past 15 years have filled that gap, helping establish benchmarks and advance the state of the art in various sub-fields within NLP. The importance of shared tasks is now in full display in the domain of clinical NLP (Chapman et al., 2011) and recently a coreference task was organized as part of the i2b2 workshop (Uzuner et al., 2012). The computational learning community is also witnessing a shift towards joint inference based evaluations, with the two previous CoNLL tasks (Surdeanu et al., 2008; Hajič et al., 2009) devoted to joint learning of syntactic and semantic dependencies. A SemEval-2010 coreference task (Recasens et al., 2010) was the first attempt to address the second issue. It included six different Indo-European languages — Catalan, Dutch, English, German, Italian, and Spanish. Among other corpora, a small subset ($\sim$120K) of English portion of OntoNotes was used for this purpose. However, the lack of a strong participation prevented the organizers from reaching any firm conclusions. The CoNLL-2011 shared task was another attempt to address the second issue. It was well received, but the shared task was only *limited to the English portion of OntoNotes*. In addition, the coreference portion of OntoNotes did not have a concrete baseline prior to the 2011 evaluation, thereby making it challenging for participants to gauge the performance of their algorithms in the absence of established state of the art on this flavor of annotation. The closest comparison was to the results reported by Pradhan et al. (2007b) on the newswire portion of OntoNotes. Since the corpus also covers two other languages from completely different language families, Chinese and Arabic, it provided a great opportunity to have a *follow-on task in 2012 covering all*

[2]http://www.bbn.com/nlp/ontonotes

[3]http://www.itl.nist.gov/iad/mig/publications/ASRhistory/index.html

[4]http://www.itl.nist.gov/iad/mig/tests/mt/

three languages. As we will see later, peculiarities of each of these languages had to be considered in creating the evaluation framework.

The first systematic learning-based study in coreference resolution was conducted on the MUC corpora, using a decision tree learner, by Soon et al. (2001). Significant improvements have been made in the field of language processing in general, and improved learning techniques have pushed the state of the art in coreference resolution forward (Morton, 2000; Harabagiu et al., 2001; McCallum and Wellner, 2004; Culotta et al., 2007; Denis and Baldridge, 2007; Rahman and Ng, 2009; Haghighi and Klein, 2010). Researchers have continued to find novel ways of exploiting ontologies such as WordNet. Various knowledge sources from shallow semantics to encyclopedic knowledge have been exploited (Ponzetto and Strube, 2005; Ponzetto and Strube, 2006; Versley, 2007; Ng, 2007). Given that WordNet is a static ontology and as such has limitation on coverage, more recently, there have been successful attempts to utilize information from much larger, collaboratively built resources such as Wikipedia (Ponzetto and Strube, 2006). More recently researchers have used graph based algorithms (Cai et al., 2011a) rather than pair-wise classifications. For a detailed survey of the progress in this field, we refer the reader to a recent article (Ng, 2010) and a tutorial (Ponzetto and Poesio, 2009) dedicated to this subject. In spite of all the progress, current techniques still rely primarily on surface level features such as string match, proximity, and edit distance; syntactic features such as apposition; and shallow semantic features such as number, gender, named entities, semantic class, Hobbs' distance, etc. Further research to reduce the knowledge gap is essential to take coreference resolution techniques to the next level.

The rest of the paper is organized as follows: Section 2 presents an overview of the OntoNotes corpus. Section 3 describes the range of phenomena annotated in OntoNotes, and language-specific issues. Section 4 describes the shared task data and the evaluation parameters, with Section 4.4.2 examining the performance of the state-of-the-art tools on all/most intermediate layers of annotation. Section 5 describes the participants in the task. Section 6 briefly compares the approaches taken by various participating systems. Section 7 presents the system results with some analysis. Section 8 compares the performance of the systems on the a subset of the Engish test set that corresponds with the test set used for the CoNLL-2011 evaluation. Section 9 draws some conclusions.

2 The OntoNotes Corpus

The OntoNotes project has created a large-scale corpus of accurate and integrated annotation of multiple levels of the shallow semantic structure in text. The English and Chinese language portion comprises roughly one million words per language of newswire, magazine articles, broadcast news, broadcast conversations, web data and conversational speech data. The English subcorpus also contains an additional 200K words of the English translation of the New Testament as Pivot Text. The Arabic portion is smaller, comprising 300K words of newswire articles. The hope is that this rich, integrated annotation covering many layers will allow for richer, cross-layer models and enable significantly better automatic semantic analysis. In addition to coreference, this data is also tagged with syntactic trees, propositions for most verb and some noun instances, partial verb and noun word senses, and 18 named entity types. Manual annotation of a large corpus with multiple layers of syntax and semantic information is a costly endeavor. Over the years in the development of this corpus, there were various priorities that came into play, and therefore not all the data in the corpus could be annotated with all the different layers of annotation. However, such multi-layer annotations, with complex, cross-layer dependencies, demands a robust, efficient, scalable storage mechanism while providing efficient, convenient, integrated access to the the underlying structure. To this effect, it uses a relational database representation that captures both the inter- and intra-layer dependencies and also provides an object-oriented API for efficient, multi-tiered access to this data (Pradhan et al., 2007a). This facilitates the extraction of cross-layer features in integrated predictive models that will make use of these annotations.

OntoNotes comprises the following layers of annotation:

- **Syntax** — A layer of syntactic annotation for English, Chinese and Arabic based on a revised guidelines for the Penn Treebank (Marcus et al., 1993; Babko-Malaya et al., 2006), the Chinese Treebank (Xue et al., 2005) and the Arabic Treebank (Maamouri and Bies, 2004).
- **Propositions** — The proposition structure of verbs based on revised guidelines for the English PropBank (Palmer et al., 2005; Babko-Malaya et al., 2006), the Chinese PropBank (Xue and Palmer, 2009) and the Arabic PropBank (Palmer et al., 2008; Zaghouani et al., 2010).
- **Word Sense** — Coarse-grained word senses are tagged for the most frequent polysemous verbs and nouns, in order to maximize token

coverage. The word sense granularity is tailored to achieve 90% inter-annotator agreement as demonstrated by Palmer et al. (2007). These senses are defined in the sense inventory files. In case of English and Arabic languages, the sense-inventories (and frame files) are defined separately for each part of speech that is realized by the lemma in the text. For Chinese, however the sense inventories (and frame files) are defined per lemma — independent of the part of speech realized in the text. For the English portion of OntoNotes, each individual sense has been connected to multiple WordNet senses. This provides users direct access to the WordNet semantic structure. There is also a mapping from the OntoNotes word senses to PropBank frames and to VerbNet (Kipper et al., 2000) and FrameNet (Fillmore et al., 2003). Unfortunately, owing to lack of comparable resources as comprehensive as WordNet in Chinese or Arabic, neither language has any inter-resource mappings available.

- **Named Entities —** The corpus was tagged with a set of 18 well-defined proper named entity types that have been tested extensively for inter-annotator agreement by Weischedel and Burnstein (2005).
- **Coreference —** This layer captures general anaphoric coreference that covers entities and events not limited to noun phrases or a limited set of entity types (Pradhan et al., 2007b). It considers all pronouns (PRP, PRP$), noun phrases (NP) and heads of verb phrases (VP) as potential mentions. Unlike English, Chinese and Arabic have dropped subjects and objects which were also considered during coreference annotation[5]. We will take a look at this in detail in the next section.

3 Coreference in OntoNotes

General anaphoric coreference that spans a rich set of entities and events — not restricted to a few types, as has been characteristic of most coreference data available until now — has been tagged with a high degree of consistency in the OntoNotes corpus. Two different types of coreference are distinguished: Identity (IDENT), and Appositive (APPOS). Identity coreference (IDENT) is used for anaphoric coreference, meaning links between pronominal, nominal, and named mentions of specific referents. It does not include mentions of generic, underspecified, or abstract entities. Appositives (APPOS) are treated separately because they function as attributions, as described further below. Coreference is annotated for all specific entities and events. There is no limit on the semantic types of NP entities that can be considered for coreference, and in particular, coreference is not limited to ACE types. The guidelines are fairly language independent. We will look at some salient aspects of the coreference annotation in OntoNotes. For more details, and examples, we refer the reader to the release documentation. We will primarily use English examples to describe various aspects of the annotation and use Chinese and Arabic examples especially to illustrate phenomena not observed in English, or that have some language specific peculiarities.

3.1 Noun Phrases

The mentions over which IDENT coreference applies are typically pronominal, named, or definite nominal. The annotation process begins by automatically extracting all of the NP mentions from parse trees in the syntactic layer of OntoNotes annotation, though the annotators can also add additional mentions when appropriate. In the following two examples (and later ones), the phrases in bold form the links of an IDENT chain.

(1) She had **a good suggestion** and **it** was unanimously accepted by all.

(2) **Elco Industries Inc.** said **it** expects net income in the year ending June 30, 1990, to fall below a recent analyst's estimate of $ 1.65 a share. **The Rockford, Ill. maker of fasteners** also said **it** expects to post sales in the current fiscal year that are "slightly above" fiscal 1989 sales of $ 155 million.

Noun phrases (NPs) in Chinese can be complex noun phrases or bare nouns (nouns that lack a determiner such as "the" or "this"). Complex noun phrases contain structures modifying the head noun, as in the following examples:

(3) (他担任 总统 任内 最后 一 次 的 (亚 太 经 济 合作 会议 (高峰会))).
((His last APEC (summit meeting)) as the President)

(4) (越南 统一 后 (第一 位 前往 当地 访问 的 (美国 总统)))
((The first (U.S. president)) who went to visit Vietnam after its unification)

In these examples, the smallest phrase in parentheses is the bare noun. The longer phrase in parantheses includes modifying structures. All the expressions in the parantheses, however, share the same head noun, i.e., "高峰会 (summit meeting)", and "美国总统 (U.S. president)" respectively. Nested noun phrases, or nested NPs, are contained within

[5] As we will see later these are not used during the task.

longer noun phrases. In the above example, "summit meeting" and "U.S. president" are nested NPs. Wherever NPs are nested, the largest logical span is used in coreference.

3.2 Verbs

Verbs are added as single-word spans if they can be coreferenced with a noun phrase or with another verb. The intent is to annotate the VP, but the single-word verb head is marked for convenience. This includes morphologically related nominalizations as in (5) and noun phrases that refer to the same event, even if they are lexically distinct from the verb as in (6). In the following two examples, only the chains related to the *growth* event are shown in bold. The Arabic translation of the same example identifies mentions using parantheses.

(5) The European economy **grew** rapidly over the past years, **this growth** helped raising ....

لقد (نما) الإقتصاد الأوروبي بسرعة خلال السنوات الماضية، (هذا النمو) ساهم في رفع ...

(6) Japan's domestic sales of cars, trucks and buses in October **rose** 18% from a year earlier to 500,004 units, a record for the month, the Japan Automobile Dealers' Association said. The strong **growth** followed year-to-year increases of 21% in August and 12% in September.

3.3 Pronouns

All pronouns and demonstratives are linked to anything that they refer to, and pronouns in quoted speech are also marked. Expletive or pleonastic pronouns (*it, there*) are not considered for tagging, and generic *you* is not marked. In the following example, the pronoun *you* and *it* would not be marked. (In this and following examples, an asterisk (*) before a boldface phrase identifies entity/event mentions that would *not* be tagged in the coreference annotation.)

(7) Senate majority leader Bill Frist likes to tell a story from his days as a pioneering heart surgeon back in Tennessee. A lot of times, Frist recalls, ***you'd** have a critical patient lying there waiting for a new heart, and ***you'd** want to cut, but ***you** couldn't start unless ***you** knew that the replacement heart would make ***it** to the operating room.

In Chinese, all the following pronouns — 你，我，他，她，它， 你们，我们，他们，它们，我，您，咱们 (*you, me, he, she*, and so on), and demonstrative pronouns — 这个，那个， 这些，那些 (*this, that, these, those*) in singular, plural or possessive forms are linked to anything they refer to.

Pronouns from classical Chinese such as 其中 (*among which*), 其 (*he/she/it*), 之 (*he/she/it*) are also linked with other mentions to which they refer.

In Arabic, the following pronouns are coreferenced – nominative personal pronouns (subject) and demonstrative pronouns which are detached. Subject pronouns are often null in Arabic; overt subject pronouns are rare, but do occur.

هما / هم / هن / نحن / انتما / انتم / انتن
(*We, you, they*)

انا / انت / هو / هي
(*I, you, she, he*)

Object pronouns are attached to the verb (direct objects) or preposition (indirect objects)

ي / ك / ـه / ها
(*Me, you, him, her*)

نا / كُم / كُن / كُما / هُم / هُن
(*Us, you, them*)

and, possessive (adjectival) pronouns are identical to object pronouns, but are attached to nouns.

ي / ك / ـه / ها
(*My, your, his, her*)

نا / كُم / كُن / كُما / هُم / هُن
(*Our, your, their*)

Pronouns such as 你，您，你们，大家，各位 can be considered generic. In this case, they are not linked to other generic mentions in the same discourse. For example,

(8) 请 ***大家** 带好自己的随身物品。***大家** 请下车。
Please take your belongings with ***you**. Please get off the train, ***everyone**.

In Chinese, if the subject or object can be recovered from the context, or if it is of little interest for the reader/listener to know, it can be omitted. In the Chinese Treebank, a small *pro* in inserted in positions where the subject or object is omitted. A *pro* can be replaced by overt NPs if they refer to the same entity or event, and the *pro* and its overt NP antecedent do not have to be in the same sentence. Exactly what *pro* stands for is determined by the linguistic context in which it appears.

(9) 吉林省主管经贸工作的副省长全哲洙说："**(*pro*)** 欢迎国际社会同**(我们)** 一道，共同推进图门江开发事业， 促进区域经济发展，造福东北亚人民。
Quan Zhezhu, Vice Governor of Jinlin Province who is in charge of economics and trade, said: "**(*pro*)** Welcome international societies to join **(us)** in the development of Tumen Jiang, so as to promote regional economic development and benefit people in Northeast Asia.

Sometimes, *pro*s cannot be recovered in the text—i.e., an overt NP cannot be identified as their antecedent in the same text — and therefore they are not linked. For instance, the *pro* in existential sentences usually cannot be recovered or linked in the annotation, as in the following example:

(10) **(*pro*)** 有二十三项高新技术项目进区开发。
There are 23 high-tech projects under development in the zone.

Also, if *pro* does not refer to a specific entity or event, it is considered generic *pro* and not linked as in (11).

(11) 肯德基 、 麦当劳 等 速食店 全 大陆 都 推出 了 **(*pro*)** 买 套餐赠送 布质 或 棉质 圣诞 老人 玩具 的 促销.
In Mainland China, fast food restaurants such as Kentucky Fried Chicken and McDonald's have launched their promotional packages by providing free cotton Santa toys for each combo **(*pro*)** purchased.

Finally, *pro*s in idiomatic expressions are not linked. Similar to Chinese, Arabic null subjects and objects are also eligible for coreference and treated similarly. In the Arabic Treebank, these are marked with just an "*". There exists few of these instances in English — marked (yet differently) with a *PRO* in the treebank and which are connected in PropBank annotation but not in coreference.

3.4 Generic mentions

Generic nominal mentions can be linked with referring pronouns and other definite mentions, but not with other generic nominal mentions.

This would allow linking of the bolded mentions in (12) and (13), but not in (14).

(12) **Officials** said **they** are tired of making the same statements.

(13) **Meetings** are most productive when **they** are held in the morning. **Those meetings**, however, generally have the worst attendance.

(14) Allergan Inc. said it received approval to sell the PhacoFlex intraocular lens, the first foldable silicone lens available for ***cataract surgery**. The lens' foldability enables it to be inserted in smaller incisions than are now possible for ***cataract surgery**.

Bare plurals, as in (12) and (13), are always considered generic. In example (15) below, there are three generic instances of *parents*. These are marked as distinct IDENT chains (with separate chains distinguished by subscripts X, Y and Z), each containing a generic and the related referring pronouns.

(15) **Parents**$_X$ should be involved with **their**$_X$ children's education at home, not in school. **They**$_X$ should see to it that **their**$_X$ kids don't play truant; **they**$_X$ should make certain that the children spend enough time doing homework; **they**$_X$ should scrutinize the report card. **Parents**$_Y$ are too likely to blame schools for the educational limitations of **their**$_Y$ children. If **parents**$_Z$ are dissatisfied with a school, **they**$_Z$ should have the option of switching to another.

In (16) below, the verb "halve" cannot be linked to "a reduction of 50%", since "a reduction" is indefinite.

(16) Argentina said it will ask creditor banks to ***halve** its foreign debt of $64 billion — the third-highest in the developing world . Argentina aspires to reach ***a reduction of 50%** in the value of its external debt.

3.5 Pre-modifiers

Proper pre-modifiers can be coreferenced, but proper nouns that are in a morphologically adjectival form are treated as adjectives, and are not coreferenced. For example, adjectival forms of GPEs such as *Chinese* in "the Chinese leader", would not be linked. Thus we could coreference *United States* in "the United States policy" with another referent, but not *American* in "the American policy." GPEs and Nationality acronyms (e.g. *U.S.S.R.* or *U.S.*). are also considered adjectival. Pre-modifier acronyms can be coreferenced unless they refer to a nationality. Thus in the examples below, *FBI* can be coreferenced to other mentions, but *U.S.* cannot.

(17) **FBI** spokesman

(18) ***U.S.** spokesman

In Chinese adjectival and nominal forms of GPEs are not morphologically distinct, and in such cases the annotator decides whether it is an adjectival usage. Usually if something is tagged as NORP then it is not considered as a mention.

Dates and monetary amounts can be considered part of a coreference chain even when they occur as pre-modifiers.

(19) The current account deficit on France's balance of payments narrowed to 1.48 billion French francs ($236.8 million) in August from a revised 2.1 billion francs in **July**, the Finance Ministry said. Previously, the **July** figure was estimated at a deficit of 613 million francs.

(20) The company's **$150** offer was unexpected. The firm balked at **the price**.

3.6 Copular verbs

Attributes signaled by copular structures are not marked; these are attributes of the referent they modify, and their relationship to that referent will be captured through word sense and proposition annotation.

(21) **John**$_X$ is a linguist. **People**$_Y$ are nervous around **John**$_X$, because **he**$_X$ always corrects **their**$_Y$ grammar.

Copular (or 'linking') verbs are those verbs that function as a copula and are followed by a subject complement. Some common copular verbs are: *be, appear, feel, look, seem, remain, stay, become, end up, get*. Subject complements following such verbs are considered attributes and are not linked. Since *Called* is copular, neither IDENT nor APPOS coreference is marked in the following case.

(22) Called Otto's Original Oat Bran Beer, the brew costs about $12.75 a case.

Some examples of copular verbs in Chinese are 是 (*to be*) and 为 (*to be, to serve as*). In addition, other verbs (particularly so-called *light verbs*) that trigger an attributive reading on the following NP: 成为 (*become*), (当)选为 (*is elected*), 称为 (*is called*), (好)像 (*looks like*), 叫做 (*is called*), etc.

(23) (上海)是*(中国最大的城市)。(上海)发展得很快。
(Shanghai) is ***(the largest city in China)**.
(Shanghai) develops fast.

In the above example, the two mentions of 上海 (*Shanghai*) co-refer with each other, but the entity does not co-refer with 中国最大的城 市 (*the largest city in China*).

3.7 Small clauses

Like copulas, small clause constructions are not marked as coreferent. The following example is treated as if the copula were present ("John considers Fred to be an idiot"):

(24) John considers ***Fred *an idiot**.

Note that the mention *Fred*, however, can be connected to other mentions of *Fred* in the text.

3.8 Temporal expressions

Temporal expressions such as the following are linked:

(25) John spent **three years** in jail. In **that time**...

Deictic expressions such as *now, then, today, tomorrow, yesterday*, etc. can be linked, as well as other temporal expressions that are relative to the time of the writing of the article, and which may therefore require knowledge of the time of the writing to resolve the coreference. Annotators were allowed to use knowledge from outside the text in resolving these cases. In the following example, *the end of this period* and *that time* can be coreferenced, as can *this period* and *from three years to seven years*.

(26) The limit could range **from three years to seven years**$_X$, depending on the composition of the management team and the nature of its strategic plan. At **(the end of (this period)**$_X$**)**$_Y$, the poison pill would be eliminated automatically, unless a new poison pill were approved by the then-current shareholders, who would have an opportunity to evaluate the corporation's strategy and management team at **that time**$_Y$.

In multi-date temporal expressions, embedded dates are not separately connected to other mentions of that date. For example in *Nov. 2, 1999*, *Nov.* would not be linked to another instance of *November* later in the text.

3.9 Appositives

Because they logically represent attributions, appositives are tagged separately from Identity coreference. They consist of a head, or referent (a noun phrase that points to a specific object/concept in the world), and one or more attributes of that referent. An appositive construction contains a noun phrase that modifies an immediately-adjacent noun phrase (separated only by a comma, colon, dash, or parenthesis). It often serves to rename or further define the first mention. Marking appositive constructions allows capturing the attributed property even though there is no explicit copula.

(27) **John**$_{head}$, **a linguist**$_{attribute}$

The head of each appositive construction is distinguished from the attribute according to the following heuristic specificity scale, in a decreasing order from top to bottom:

Type	Example
Proper noun	John
Pronoun	He
Definite NP	the man
Indefinite specific NP	a man I know
Non-specific NP	man

This leads to the following cases:

(28) **John**$_{head}$, **a linguist**$_{attribute}$

(29) **A famous linguist**$_{attribute}$, **he**$_{head}$ studied at ...

Type	Description
Annotator Error	An annotator error. This is a catch-all category for cases of errors that do not fit in the other categories.
Genuine Ambiguity	This is just genuinely ambiguous. Often the case with pronouns that have no clear antecedent (especially this & that)
Generics	One person thought this was a generic mention, and the other person didn't
Guidelines	The guidelines need to be clear about this example
Callisto Layout	Something to do with the usage/design of Callisto
Referents	Each annotator thought this was referring to two completely different things
Possessives	One person did not mark this possessive
Verb	One person did not mark this verb
Pre Modifiers	One person did not mark this Pre Modifier
Appositive	One person did not mark this appositive
Copula	Disagreement arose because this mention is part of a copular structure a) Either each annotator marked a different half of the copula b) Or one annotator unnecessarily marked both

Figure 1: Description of various disagreement types.

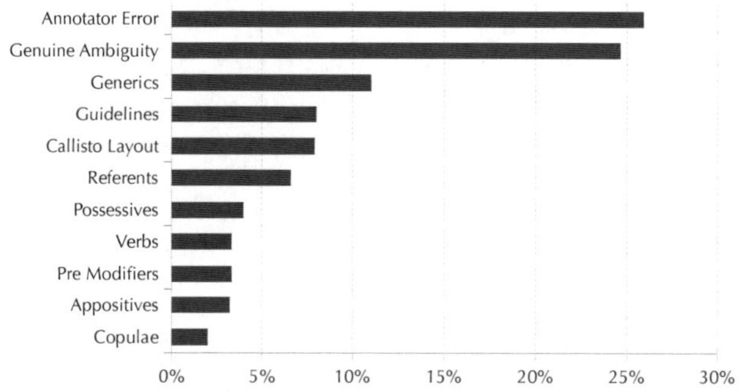

Figure 2: The distribution of disagreements across the various types in Table 1 for a sample of 15K disagreements in the English portion of the corpus.

(30) **a principal of the firm**$_{\text{attribute}}$, **J. Smith**$_{\text{head}}$

In cases where the two members of the appositive are equivalent in specificity, the left-most member of the appositive is marked as the head/referent. Definite NPs include NPs with a definite marker (*the*) as well as NPs with a possessive adjective (his). Thus the first element is the head in all of the following cases:

(31) The chairman, the man who never gives up

(32) The sheriff, his friend

(33) His friend, the sheriff

In the specificity scale, specific names of diseases and technologies are classified as proper names, whether they are capitalized or not.

(34) A dangerous bacteria, bacillium, is found

When the entity to which an appositive refers is also mentioned elsewhere, only the single span containing the entire appositive construction is included in the larger IDENT chain. None of the nested NP spans are linked. In the example below, the entire span can be linked to later mentions to *Richard Godown*.

The sub-spans are not included separately in the IDENT chain.

(35) **Richard Godown, president of the Industrial Biotechnology Association**

Ages are tagged as attributes (as if they were ellipses of, for example, *a 42-year-old*):

(36) **Mr.Smith**$_{\text{head}}$, **42**$_{\text{attribute}}$,

Similar rules apply for Chinese and Arabic. Unlike English, where most appositives have a punctuation marker, in Chinese that is not necessarily the frequent case. In the following example we can see an appositive construction without any punctuations between the head and the attribute.

(37) 上图 左 起 ： (无锡市市长)$_{\text{X[attribute]}}$ (王宏民)$_{\text{X[head]}}$， (副 市 长)$_{\text{Y[attribute]}}$ (洪锦 、 张怀西)$_{\text{Y[head]}}$， ...

Language	Genre	A1-A2	A1-ADJ	A2-ADJ
English	Newswire [NW]	80.9	85.2	88.3
	Broadcast News [BN]	78.6	83.5	89.4
	Broadcast Conversation [BC]	86.7	91.6	93.7
	Magazine [MZ]	78.4	83.2	88.8
	Weblogs and Newsgroups [WB]	85.9	92.2	91.2
	Telephone Conversation [TC]	81.3	94.1	84.7
	Pivot Text [PT] (New Testament)	89.4	96.0	92.0
Chinese	Newswire [NW]	73.6	84.8	75.1
	Broadcast News [BN]	80.5	86.4	91.6
	Broadcast Conversation [BC]	84.1	90.7	91.2
	Magazine [MZ]	74.9	81.2	80.0
	Weblogs and Newsgroups [WB]	87.6	92.3	93.5
	Telephone Conversation [TC]	65.6	86.6	77.1

Table 1: Inter Annotator (A1 and A2) and Adjudicator (ADJ) agreement for the Coreference Layer in OntoNotes measured in terms of the MUC score.

Figure above from left : **Wuxi Mayor**$_{\mathsf{X[attribute]}}$ **Wang Hongmin**$_{\mathsf{X[head]}}$, **Deputy Mayors**$_{\mathsf{Y[attribute]}}$ **Hong Jin, Zhang Huaixi**$_{\mathsf{Y[head]}}$, ...

3.10 Special Issues

In addition to the ones above, there are some special cases such as:

- No coreference is marked between an organization and its members.
- GPEs are linked to references to their governments, even when the references are nested NPs, or the modifier and head of a single NP.
- In extremely rare cases, metonymic mentions can be co-referenced. This is done only when the two mentions clearly and without a doubt refer to the same entity. For example:

  (38) In a statement released this afternoon, **10 Downing Street** called the bombings in Casablanca "a strike against all peace-loving people."

  (39) In a statement, **Britain** called the Casablanca bombings "a strike against all peace-loving people."

  In this case, it is obvious that "10 Downing Street" and "Britain" are being used interchangeably in the text. Again, if there is any ambiguity, however, these terms are not coreferenced with each other.
- In Arabic, verbal inflections are not considered pronominal and are not coreferenced. The portion marked with an * in the example below is an inflection and not a pronoun, and so should not be marked.

  (40) صرح (*ت) الناطقة ب آسم وزارة الخارجية السويسرية دانييلا ستوفل : آ إن (ها) ليست في برن و لا في جنيف

  The Swiss foreign ministry's spokeswoman announced the **(she)** is neither in Burne nor in Geneva Pronouns in quoted speech are also marked.

3.11 Annotator Agreement and Analysis

Table 1 shows the inter-annotator and annotator-adjudicator agreement on all the genres and languages of OntoNotes. A 15K disagreements in various parts of the English data was analyzed, and grouped into one of the categories shown in Figure 1. Figure 2 shows the distribution of these different types that were found in that sample. It can be seen that genuine ambiguity and annotator error are the biggest contributors — the latter of which is usually captured during adjudication, thus showing the increased agreement between the adjudicated version and the individual annotator version. Interestingly, this mirrors the annotator disagreement analysis on the MUC corpus provided by Hirschman et al. (1998).

4 CoNLL-2012 Coreference Task

The CoNLL-2012 shared task was held across all three languages — English, Chinese and Arabic — of the OntoNotes v5.0 data. The task was to automatically identify mentions of entities and events in text and to link the coreferring mentions together to form entity/event chains. The coreference decisions had to be made using automatically predicted information on other structural and semantic layers including the parses, semantic roles, word senses, and named entities. Given various factors, such as the lack of resources and state-of-the-art tools, and time constraints, we could not provide some layers of information for the Chinese and Arabic portion of the data.

The three languages are from quite different language families. The morphology of these languages is quite different. Arabic has a complex morphology, English has limited morphology, whereas Chinese has very little morphology. English word segmentation amounts to rule-based tokenization, and is close to perfect. In the case of Chinese and Arabic, although the tokenization/segmentation is not as good as English, the accuracies are in the high 90s. Syntactically, there are many dropped subjects and objects in Arabic and Chinese, whereas English is not a pro-drop language. Another difference is the amount of resources available for each language. English has probably the most resources at its disposal, whereas Chinese and Arabic lack significantly

— Arabic more so than Chinese. Given this fact, plus the fact that the CoNLL format cannot handle multiple segmentations, and that it would complicate scoring since we are using exact token boundaries (as discussed later in Section 4.5), we decided to allow the use of gold, treebank segmentation for all languages. In the case of Chinese, the words themselves are lemmas, so no additional information needs to be provided. For Arabic, by default written text is unvocalised, so we decided to also provide correct, gold standard lemmas, along with the correct vocalized version of the tokens. Table 2 lists which layers were available and quality of the provided layers (when provided.)

Layer	English	Chinese	Arabic
Segmentation	•	•	•
Lemma	√	—	•
Parse	√	√	√[6]
Proposition	√	√	×
Predicate Frame	√	×	×
Word Sense	√	√	√
Name Entities	√	×	×
Speaker	•	•	—

Table 2: Summary of predicted layers provided for each language. A "•" indicates gold annotation, a "√" indicates predicted, a "×" indicates an absence of the predicted layer, and a "—" indicates that the layer is not applicable to the language.

As is customary for CoNLL tasks, there were two *primary* tracks — *closed* and *open*. For the *closed* track, systems were limited to using the distributed resources, in order to allow a fair comparison of algorithm performance, while the *open* track allowed for almost unrestricted use of external resources in addition to the provided data. Within each *closed* and *open* track, we had an optional *supplementary* track which allowed us to run some ablation studies over a few different input conditions. This allowed us to evaluate the systems given: i) Gold mention boundaries (GB), ii) Gold mentions (GM), and iii) Gold parses (GS). We will refer to the main task – where no mention boundaries are provided – as NB.

4.1 Primary Evaluation

The primary evaluation comprises the *closed* and *open* tracks where predicted information is provided on all layers of the test set other than coreference. As mentioned earlier, we provide gold lemma and vocalization information for Arabic, and we use gold standard treebank segmentation for all three languages.

[6]The predicted part of speech for Arabic are a mapped down version of the richer gold version present in the treebank

4.1.1 Closed Track

In the *closed* track, systems were limited to the provided data. For the training and test data, in addition to the underlying text, *predicted* versions of all the supplementary layers of annotation were provided using off-the-shelf tools (parsers, semantic role labelers, named entity taggers, etc.) retrained on the training portion of the OntoNotes data — as described in Section 4.4.2. For the training data, however, in addition to predicted values for the other layers, we also provided manual, *gold-standard* annotations for all the layers. Participants were allowed to use either the gold-standard or predicted annotation to train their systems. They were also free to use the gold-standard data to train their own models for the various layers of annotation, if they judged that those would either provide more accurate predictions or alternative predictions for use as multiple views, or if they wished to use a lattice of predictions.

More so than previous CoNLL shared tasks, coreference predictions depend on world knowledge, and many state-of-the-art systems use information from external resources such as WordNet, which provides a layer of information that could help a system recognize semantic connections between the various lexicalized mentions in the text. Therefore, in the case of English, similar to the previous year's task, we allowed the use of WordNet in the closed track. Since word senses in OntoNotes are predominantly[7] coarse-grained groupings of WordNet senses, systems could also map from the predicted or gold-standard word senses to the sets of underlying WordNet senses. Another significant piece of knowledge that is particularly useful for coreference but that is not available in the layers of OntoNotes is that of *number* and *gender*. There are many different ways of predicting these values, with differing accuracies, so in order to ensure that participants in the *closed* track were working from the same data, thus allowing clearer algorithmic comparisons, we specified a particular table of number and gender predictions generated by Bergsma and Lin (2006), for use during both training and testing. Unfortunately neither Arabic, nor Chinese have comparable resources available that we could allow participants to use. Chinese, in particular, does not have number or gender inflections for nouns, but (Baran and Xue, 2011) look at a way to infer such information.

4.1.2 Open Track

In addition to resources available in the *closed* track, in the *open* track, systems were allowed to use

[7]There are a few instances of novel senses introduced in OntoNotes which were not present in WordNet, and so lack a mapping back to the WordNet senses

Algorithm 1 Procedure used to create OntoNotes training, development and test partitions.

Procedure: GENERATE_PARTITIONS(ONTONOTES) **returns** TRAIN, DEV, TEST

```
TRAIN ← ∅
DEV ← ∅
TEST ← ∅
for all SOURCE ∈ ONTONOTES do
  if SOURCE = WALL STREET JOURNAL then
    TRAIN ← TRAIN ∪ SECTIONS 02 – 21
    DEV ← DEV ∪ SECTIONS 00, 01, 22, 24
    TEST ← TEST ∪ SECTION 23
  else
    if Number of files in SOURCE ≥ 10 then
      TRAIN ← TRAIN ∪ FILE IDs ending in 1 – 8
      DEV ← DEV ∪ FILE IDs ending in 0
      TEST ← TEST ∪ FILE IDs ending in 9
    else
      DEV ← DEV ∪ FILE IDs ending in 0
      TEST ← TEST ∪ FILE ID ending in the highest number
      TRAIN ← TRAIN ∪ Remaining FILE IDs for the SOURCE
    end if
  end if
end for
return TRAIN, DEV, TEST
```

external resources such as Wikipedia, gazetteers etc. The purpose of this track is mainly to get an idea of the performance ceiling on the task at the cost of not being able to perform a fair comparison across all systems. Another advantage of the *open* track is that it might reduce the barriers to participation by allowing participants to field existing research systems that already depend on external resources — especially if there were hard dependencies on these resources — so they can participate in the task with minimal, or no modification to their existing system.

4.2 Supplementary Evaluation

In addition to the option of selecting between the primary *closed* or the *open* tracks, the participants also had an option to run their systems in the following ablation settings.

Gold Mention Boundaries (GB) In this case, we provided all possible correct mention boundaries in the test data. This essentially entails all NPs, and PRPs in the data extracted from the gold parse trees, as well as the mentions that do not align with any parse constituent, for example, non-existent constituents in the predicted parse owing to errors, some named entities, etc.

Gold Mentions (GM) In this dataset, we provided *only* and *all* the correct mentions for the test sets, thereby reducing the task to one of pure mention clustering, and eliminating the task of mention detection and anaphoricity determination[8]. These also include potential spans that do not align with any constituent in the predicted parse tree.

Gold Parses (GS) In this case, for each language, we replaced the predicted parses in the *closed* track data with manual, gold parses.

4.3 Train, Development and Test Splits

For various reasons, not all the documents in OntoNotes have been annotated with all the different layers of annotation, with full coverage.[9] There is a core portion, however, which is roughly 1.6M English words, 950K Chinese words, and 300K Arabic words which has been annotated with all the layers. This is the portion that we used for the shared task.

We used the same algorithm as in CoNLL-2011 to

[8]Mention detection interacts with anaphoricity determination since the corpus does not contain any singleton mentions.

[9]As mentioned earlier, large scale manual annotation of various layers of syntax and semantics is an expensive endeavor. Adding to this, the fact that word sense annotation is most efficiently done one lemma at a time, ideally all instances of the same across the entire corpus, or as large a portion as possible, full coverage across all lemma instances is hard to achieve given the long tail of low frequency lemmas with a Zipfian distribution. Similar issue affects PropBank annotation, but furthermore, currently it only covers mostly verb predicates, and a few eventive noun predicates.

[10]http://projects.ldc.upenn.edu/ace/data/

[11]These numbers are for the part of OntoNotes v5.0 that have all layers of annotation including coreferenced.

Corpora	Language	Words				Documents			
		Total	Train	Dev	Test	Total	Train	Dev	Test
MUC-6	English	25K	12K	13K		60	30	30	
MUC-7	English	40K	19K	21K		67	30	37	
ACE[10](2000-2004)	English	960K	745K	215K		-	-	-	
	Chinese	615K	455K	150K		-	-	-	
	Arabic	500K	350K	150K		-	-	-	
OntoNotes[11]	English	1.6M	1.3M	160K	170K	2,384 (3493)	1,940 (2,802)	222 (343)	222 (348)
	Chinese	950K	750K	110K	90K	1,729 (2,280)	1,391 (1,810)	172 (252)	166 (218)
	Arabic	300K	240K	30K	30K	447 (447)	359 (359)	44 (44)	44 (44)

Table 3: Number of documents in the OntoNotes v5.0 data, and some comparison with the MUC and ACE data sets. The numbers in parenthesis for the OntoNotes corpus indicate the total number of *parts* that correspond to the documents. Each part was considered a separate document for evaluation purposes.

create the train/development/test partitions for English, Chinese and Arabic. We tried to reuse previously established partitions for Chinese and Arabic, but either they were not in the selection used for OntoNotes, or were partially overlapping, or had a very small portion of OntoNotes covered in the test set. Unfortunately, unlike English WSJ partitions, there was no clean way of reusing those partitions. Algorithm 1 details this procedure. The list of training/development/test document IDs can be found on the task webpage[12]. Following the recent CoNLL tradition, participants were allowed to use both the training and the development data to train their final model(s).

The number of documents in the corpus for this task, for each of the different languages, and for each of the training/development/test portions, are shown in Table 3. For comparison purposes, it also lists the number of documents in the MUC-6, MUC-7, and ACE (2000-2004) corpora. The MUC-6 data was taken from the Wall Street Journal, whereas the MUC-7 data was from the New York Times. The ACE data spanned many different languages and genres similar to the ones in OntoNotes. In fact, there is some overlap between ACE and OntoNotes source documents.

4.4 Data Preparation

This section gives details of the different annotation layers including the automatic models that were used to predict them, and describes the formats in which the data was provided to the participants.

[12] http://conll.cemantix.org/2012/download/ids/

For each language there are two sub-directories — "all" contains more general lists which include documents that had at least one of the layers of annotation, and "coref" contains the lists that include document that have coreference annotation. The former were used to generate training/development/test sets for layers other than coreference, and the latter was used to generate training/development/test sets for the coreference layer used in this shared task.

4.4.1 Manual Annotation *Gold* Layers

Let us take a look at the manually annotated, or *gold* layers of information that were made available for the training data.

Coreference The manual coreference annotation is stored as chains of linked mentions connecting multiple mentions of the same entity. Coreference is the only document-level phenomenon in OntoNotes, and the complexity of annotation increases non-linearly with the length of a document. Unfortunately, some of the documents — especially the ones in the broadcast conversation, weblogs, and telephone conversation genre — are very long and that prohibited efficient annotation in their entirety. These had to be split into smaller parts. A few passes to join some adjacent parts were conducted, but since some documents had as many as 17 parts, there are still multi-part documents in the corpus. Since the coreference chains are coherent only within each of these document parts, for the purpose of this task, each such part is treated as a separate document. Another thing to note is that there were some cases of sub-token annotation in the corpus owing to the fact that tokens were not split at hyphens. Cases such as pro-WalMart had the sub-span WalMart linked with another instance of WalMart. The recent Treebank revision split tokens at *most* hyphens and made a majority of these sub-token annotations go away. There were still some residual sub-token annotations. Since subtoken annotations cannot be represented in the CoNLL format, and they were a very small quantity — much less than even half a percent — we decided to ignore them. Unlike English, Chinese and Arabic have coreference annotation on elided subjects/objects. Recovering these entities in text is a hard problem, and the most recently reported numbers in literature for Chinese are around a F-score of 50 (Yang and Xue, 2010; Cai et al., 2011b). For Arabic there have not been much studies on recovering these. A study by Gabbard (2010) shows that these can be recovered with an F-score of 55 with automatic parses and roughly 65 using gold parses[13]. Considering the level of prediction accuracy of these tokens, and the relative frequency of the same, plus the fact that the CoNLL tabular format is not amenable to a variable number of tokens, we decided not to consider them as part of the task. In other words, we removed the manually identified traces (***pro*** and *) respectively in Chinese and Arabic Treebanks. We also do not consider the links that are formed by these tokens in the gold evaluation key.

Tables 4 and 5 shows the distribution of mentions by the syntactic categories, and the counts of entities, links and mentions in the corpus respectively. Interestingly the mentions formed by these dropped pronouns total roughly about 11% for both Chinese and Arabic. All of this data has been Treebanked and PropBanked either as part of the OntoNotes effort, or some previous effort.

Language	Syntactic category	Train Count	Train %	Development Count	Development %	Test Count	Test %
English	Noun Phrase	61.8K	39.46	9.7K	45.57	9.2K	42.97
	Pronoun	66.7K	42.61	7.8K	36.66	8.2K	38.69
	Proper Noun	18.1K	11.60	2.2K	10.66	2.3K	10.96
	Dropped Pro.	-	-	-	-	-	-
	Other Noun	2.636	1.68	546	2.55	500	2.33
	Verb	2.522	1.61	299	1.40	342	1.60
	Other	4.761	3.04	676	3.16	738	3.45
Chinese	Noun Phrase	40.7K	34.23	5.4K	32.53	5.1K	35.31
	Pronoun	20.8K	17.50	3.3K	19.88	2.5K	17.65
	Dropped Pro.	13.5K	11.39	1.9K	12.04	1.5K	10.71
	Proper Noun	19.0K	15.96	2.8K	17.24	2.2K	15.54
	Other Noun	23.6K	19.88	2.8K	17.08	2.8K	19.71
	Verb	244	0.20	51	0.31	20	0.14
	Other	994	0.83	153	0.92	139	0.95
Arabic	Noun Phrase	10.8K	34.93	1.3K	35.02	1.3K	36.51
	Pronoun	8.9K	28.77	1.0K	28.33	1.1K	30.58
	Dropped Pro.	3.5K	11.52	477	12.57	429	11.78
	Proper Noun	4.0K	13.01	450	11.86	390	10.71
	Other Noun	3.3K	10.90	439	11.57	345	9.47
	Verb	25	0.08	4	0.11	0	0.00
	Other	247	0.79	21	0.55	35	0.96

Table 4: Distribution of mentions in the data by their syntactic category.

Parse Trees These represent the syntactic layer that is a revised version of the treebanks in English, Chinese and Arabic. Arabic treebank has probably seen the most revision over the past few years, in an effort to increase consistency. For purposes of this task, traces were removed from the syntactic trees, since the CoNLL-style data format, being indexed by tokens, does not provide any good means of conveying that information. As mentioned in the previous section, these include the cases of traces in Chinese and Arabic which are dropped subjects/objects that are legitimate targets for coreference annotation. Function tags were also removed, since the parsers that we used for the predicted syntax layer did not provide them. One thing that needs to be dealt with in conversational data is the presence of disfluencies (restarts, etc.). In the English parses of the OntoNotes, the disfluencies are marked using a special EDITED[14] phrase tag — as was the case for the Switchboard Treebank. Given the frequency of disfluencies and the performance with which one can identify them automatically,[15] a probable processing pipeline would filter them out before parsing. Since we did not have a readily available tagger for tagging disfluencies, we decided to remove them using oracle information available in the English Treebank, and the coreference chains were remapped to trees without disfluencies. Owing to various constraints, we decided to retain the disfluencies in the Chinese data. Since Arabic portion of the corpus is all newswire, this had no impact on it. However, for both Chinese and Arabic, since we remove trace tokens corresponding to dropped pronouns, all the other layers of annotation had to be remapped to the remaining sequence of tree tokens.

Language	Type	Train	Development	Test	All
English	Entities/Chains	35,143	4,546	4,532	44,221
	Links	120,417	14,610	15,232	150,259
	Mentions	155,560	19,156	19,764	194,480
Chinese	Entities/Chains	28,257	3,875	3,559	35,691
	Links	74,597	10,308	9,242	94,147
	Mentions	102,854	14,183	12,801	129,838
Arabic	Entities/Chains	8,330	936	980	10,246
	Links	19,260	2,381	2,255	23,896
	Mentions	27,590	3,313	3,235	34,138

Table 5: Number of entities, links and mentions in the OntoNotes v5.0 data.

Propositions The propositions in OntoNotes are PropBank-style semantic roles for English, Chinese and Arabic. Most of the verb predicates in the corpus have been annotated with their arguments. As part of the OntoNotes effort, some enhancements were made to the English PropBank and Treebank to make them synchronize better with each other (Babko-Malaya et al., 2006). One of the outcomes of this effort was that two types of LINKs that represent pragmatic coreference (LINK-PCR) and selec-

[13]These numbers are not in the thesis, but we received them in an email communication with the Ryan Gabbard.

[14]There is another phrase type — EMBED in the telephone conversation genre which is similar to the EDITED phrase type, and sometimes identifies insertions, but sometimes contains logical continuation of phrases by different speakers, so we decided not to remove that from the data.

[15]A study by Charniak and Johnson (2001) shows that one can identify and remove edits from transcribed conversational speech with an F-score of about 78, with roughly 95 Precision and 67 recall.

tional preferences (LINK-SLC) were added to PropBank. More details can be found in the addendum to the PropBank guidelines[16] in the OntoNotes v5.0 release. Since the community is not used to this representation which relies heavily on the trace structure in the Treebank which we are excluding, we decided to *unfold* the LINKs back to their original representation as in the PropBank 1.0 release. This functionality is part of the OntoNotes DB Tool.[17]

Word Sense Gold standard word sense annotation was supplied using sense numbers (along with the sense inventories) as specified in the OntoNotes list of senses for each lemma. The coverage of the word sense annotation varies among the languages. English has the most coverage, while coverage for Chinese and Arabic is more sporadic. Even for English, the coverage for word sense annotation is not complete. Only some of the verbs and nouns are annotated with word sense information.

Named Entities Named Entities in OntoNotes data are specified using a catalog of 18 Name types.

Other Layers Discourse plays a vital role in coreference resolution. In the case of broadcast conversation, or telephone conversation data, it partially manifests itself in the form of speakers of a given utterance, whereas in weblogs or newsgroups it does so as the writer, or commenter of a particular article or thread. This information provides an important clue for correctly linking anaphoric pronouns with the right antecedents. This information could be automatically deduced, but since it would add additional complexity to the already complex task, we decided to provide oracle information of this metadata both during training and testing. In other words, speaker and author identification was not treated as an annotation layer that needed to be predicted. This information was provided in the form of another column in the `.conll` file. There were some cases of interruptions and interjections that led to a sentence associated with two different speakers, but since the frequency of this was quite small, we decided to make an assumption of one speaker/writer per sentence.

4.4.2 Predicted Annotation Layers

The predicted annotation layers were derived using automatic models trained using cross-validation on other portions of OntoNotes v5.0 data. As mentioned earlier, there are some portions of the OntoNotes corpus that have not been annotated for coreference but that have been annotated for other layers. For training models for each of the layers, where feasible, we used all the data that we could for that layer from the training portion of the entire OntoNotes v5.0 release.

[16]doc/propbank/english-propbank.pdf

[17]http://cemantix.org/ontonotes.html

Layer	English Verb	English Noun	Chinese All	Arabic Verb	Arabic Noun
Sense Inventories	2702	2194	763	150	111
Frames	5672	1335	20134	2743	532

Table 7: Number of senses defined for English, Chinese and Arabic in the OntoNotes v5.0 corpus.

Parse Trees Predicted parse trees for English were produced using the Charniak parser[18] (Charniak and Johnson, 2005). Some additional tag types used in the OntoNotes trees were added to the parser's tagset, including the NML tag that has recently been added to capture internal NP structure, and the rules used to determine head words were extended correspondingly. Chinese and Arabic parses were generated using the Berkeley parser (Petrov and Klein, 2007). In the case of Arabic, the parsing community uses a mapping from rich Arabic part of speech tags, to Penn-style part of speech tags. We used the mapping that is included with the Arabic treebank.

The predicted parses for the training portion of the data were generated using 10-fold (5-fold for Arabic) cross-validation. The development and test parses were generated using a model trained on the entire training portion. We used OntoNotes v5.0 training data for training the Chinese and Arabic parser models, but the OntoNotes v4.0 subset of OntoNotes v5.0 data was used for training the English model. We decided to do the latter to be able to better compare the scores to the CoNLL-2011 evaluation given that parser is a central component to a coreference system, and the fact that OntoNotes v5.0 adds a small fraction of gold parses on top of those provided by OntoNotes v4.0. Table 6 shows the performance of the re-trained parsers on the CoNLL-2012 test set. We did not get a chance to re-train the re-ranker available for English, and since the stock re-ranker crashes when run on n-best parses containing NMLs, because it has not seen that tag in training, we could not make use of it. In addition to the parser scores and part of speech accuracy, we have also added a column for the accuracy for the NPs because they are particularly relevant to the coreference task.

[18]http://bllip.cs.brown.edu/download/reranking-parserAug06.tar.gz

[19]There was an error in processing the test set, therefore the performance on the test set was slightly lower than the correct one reported in the table. The performance of the sense tagging the offical test set is 77.6 (R), 71.5 (P) and 74.4 (F).

		All Sentences						Sentence length < 40			
		N	POS	NP	R	P	F	N	R	P	F
English	Broadcast Conversation [BC]	2,194	95.93	90.05	84.30	84.46	84.38	2,124	85.83	85.97	85.90
	Broadcast News [BN]	1,344	96.50	91.11	84.19	84.28	84.24	1,278	85.93	86.04	85.98
	Magazine [MZ]	780	95.14	91.63	87.11	87.46	87.28	736	87.71	88.04	87.87
	Newswire [NW]	2,273	96.95	90.14	87.05	87.45	87.25	2,082	88.95	89.27	89.11
	Telephone Conversation [TC	1,366	93.52	88.96	79.73	80.83	80.28	1,359	79.88	80.98	80.43
	Weblogs and Newsgroups [WB]	1,658	94.67	89.16	83.32	83.20	83.26	1,566	85.14	85.07	85.11
	Pivot Text [PT] (New Testament)	1,217	96.87	95.39	92.48	93.66	93.07	1,217	92.48	93.66	93.07
	Overall	9,615	96.03	90.78	85.25	85.43	85.34	9145	86.86	87.02	86.94
Chinese	Broadcast Conversation [BC]	885	94.79	86.32	79.35	80.17	79.76	824	80.92	81.86	81.38
	Broadcast News [BN]	929	93.85	86.00	80.13	83.49	81.78	756	81.82	84.65	83.21
	Magazine [MZ]	451	97.06	92.40	83.85	88.48	86.10	326	85.64	89.80	87.67
	Newswire [NW]	481	94.07	79.70	77.28	82.26	79.69	406	79.06	83.84	81.38
	Telephone Conversation [TC]	968	92.22	80.15	69.19	71.90	70.52	942	69.59	72.24	70.89
	Weblogs and Newsgroups [WB]	758	92.37	85.60	78.92	82.57	80.70	725	79.30	83.10	81.16
	Overall	4,472	94.12	85.74	78.93	82.23	80.55	3,979	79.80	82.79	81.27
Arabic	Newswire [NW]	1,003	94.12	80.70	75.67	74.71	75.19	766	77.44	74.99	76.19

Table 6: Parser performance on the CoNLL-2012 test set.

		Accuracy		
		R	P	F
English	Broadcast Conversation [BC]	81.3	81.2	81.2
	Broadcast News [BN]	81.5	82.0	81.7
	Magazine [MZ]	78.8	79.1	79.0
	Newswire [NW]	85.7	85.7	85.7
	Weblogs and Newsgroups [WB]	77.6	77.5	77.5
	Overall	82.5	82.5	82.5
Chinese	Broadcast Conversation [BC]	-	-	80.5
	Broadcast News [BN]	-	-	85.4
	Magazine [MZ]	-	-	82.4
	Newswire [NW]	-	-	89.1
	Overall	-	-	84.3
Arabic	Newswire [NW][19]	75.2	75.9	75.6

Table 8: Word sense performance over both verbs and nouns in the CoNLL-2012 test set.

Word Sense This year we used the IMS (It Makes Sense) (Zhong and Ng, 2010) word sense tagger.[20] Word sense information, unlike syntactic parse information is not central to approaches taken by current coreference systems and so we decided to use a better word sense tagger to get a good state of the art accuracy estimate, at the cost of a completely fair (but, still close enough) comparison with English CoNLL-2011 results. This will also allow potential future uses to benefit from it. IMS was trained on all the word sense data that is present in the training portion of the OntoNotes corpus using cross-validated predictions on the input layers similar to the proposition tagger. During testing, for English and Arabic, IMS must first uses the automatic POS information to identify the nouns and verbs in the test data, and then assign senses to the automatically identified nouns and verbs. In case of Arabic, IMS uses gold lemmas. Since automatic POS tagging is not perfect, IMS does not always output a sense to all word tokens that need to be sense tagged due to wrongly predicted POS tags. As such, recall is not the same as precision on the English and Arabic test data. Recall that in Chinese, the word senses are defined against *lemmas* and are independent of the part of speech. Since we provide gold word segmentation, IMS attempts to sense tag all correctly segmented Chinese words, so recall and precision are same and so is F_1. Table 7 gives the number of lemmas covered by the word sense inventory in the English, Chinese and Arabic portion of OntoNotes.

Table 8 shows the performance of this classifier aggregated over *both the verbs and nouns* in the CoNLL-2012 test set. For English, genres PT and TC, and for Chinese genres TC and WB, no gold standard senses were available, and so their accuracies could not be computed.

[20]We offer special thanks to Hwee Tou Ng and his student Zhi Zhong for training IMS models and providing output for the development and test sets.

Propositions We used ASSERT[21] (Pradhan et al., 2005) to predict the propositional structure for English. Similar to the parser model for English, the same proposition model that was used in the CoNLL-2011 shared task — trained on all the training portion of the OntoNotes v4.0 data using cross-validated predicted parses — was used to generate the propositions for the development and test sets for this evaluation. We took a two stage approach to tagging where The NULL arguments are first filtered out, and the remaining NON-NULL arguments are classified into one of the argument types. The argument identification module used an ensemble of ten classifiers — each trained on a tenth of the training data and combined using unweighted voting. This should still give a close to state-of-the-art performance given that the argument identification performance tends to start to be asymptotic around 10K training instances (Pradhan et al., 2005). The Chinese propositional structure was predicted with the Chinese semantic role labeler described in (Xue, 2008), retrained on all the training portion of the OntoNotes v5.0 data. No propositional structures were provided for Arabic due to resource constraints. Table 9 shows the detailed performance numbers. The CoNLL-2005 scorer was used to compute the scores. At first glance, the performance on the English newswire genre is much lower than what has been reported for WSJ Section 23. This could be attributed to several factors: i) the fact that we had to compromise on the training method, ii) the newswire in OntoNotes not only contains WSJ data, but also Xinhua news, iii) The WSJ training and test portions in OntoNotes are a subset of the standard ones that have been used to report performance earlier; iv) the PropBank guidelines were significantly revised during the OntoNotes project in order to synchronize well with the Treebank, and finally v) it includes propositions for *be* verbs missing from the original PropBank. It looks like the newly added Pivot Text data (comprising of the New Testament) shows very good performance. This is not surprising given a similar trend in it parsing performance.

[21] http://cemantix.org/assert.html

Framesets	Lemmas
1	2,722
2	321
>2	181

Table 10: Frameset polysemy across lemmas.

In addition to automatically predicting the arguments, we also trained a classifier to tag PropBank frameset IDs for the English data. Table 7 lists the number of framesets available across the three languages[22] An overwhelming number of them are monosemous, but the more frequent verbs tend to be polysemous. Table 10 gives the distribution of number of framesets per lemma in the PropBank layer of the English OntoNotes v5.0 data.

During automatic processing of the data, we tagged all the tokens that were tagged with a part of speech VBx. This means that there would be cases where the wrong token would be tagged with propositions.

Named Entities BBN's IdentiFinder™system was used to predict the named entities. For the CoNLL-2011 shared task we did not get a chance to re-train Identifinder, and used the stock model which did not have the same set of named entities as in the OntoNotes corpus, so we decided to

[22] The number of lemmas for English in Table 10 do not add up to this number because not all of them have examples in the training data, where the total number of instantiated senses amounts to 4229.

		Frameset Accuracy	Total Sentences	Total Propositions	% Perfect Propositions	Argument ID + Class P	R	F
English	Broadcast Conversation [BC]	92	2,037	5,021	52.18	82.55	64.84	72.63
	Broadcast News [BN]	91	1,252	3,310	53.66	81.64	64.46	72.04
	Magazine [MZ]	89	780	2,373	47.16	79.98	61.66	69.64
	Newswire [NW]	93	1,898	4,758	39.72	80.53	62.68	70.49
	Telephone Conversation [TC]	90	1,366	1,725	45.28	79.60	63.41	70.59
	Weblogs and Newsgroups [WB]	92	929	2,174	39.19	81.01	60.65	69.37
	Pivot Corpus [PT]	92	1,217	2,853	50.54	86.40	72.61	78.91
	Overall	91	9,479	24,668	44.69	81.47	61.56	70.13
Chinese	Broadcast Conversation [BC]	-	885	2,323	31.34	53.92	68.60	60.38
	Broadcast News [BN]	-	929	4,419	35.44	64.34	66.05	65.18
	Magazine [MZ]	-	451	2,620	31.68	65.04	65.40	65.22
	Newswire [NW]	-	481	2,210	27.33	69.28	55.74	61.78
	Telephone Conversation [TC]	-	968	1,622	32.74	48.70	59.12	53.41
	Weblogs and Newsgroups [WB]	-	758	1,761	35.21	62.35	68.87	65.45
	Overall	-	4,472	14,955	32.62	61.26	64.48	62.83

Table 9: Performance on the propositions and framesets in the CoNLL-2012 test set.

		All Genre	BC	BN	MZ	NW	TC	WB
		F	F	F	F	F	F	F
English	Cardinal	68.76	58.52	75.34	72.57	83.62	32.26	57.14
	Date	78.60	73.46	80.61	71.60	84.12	63.89	65.48
	Event	44.63	30.77	50.00	36.36	50.00	0.00	66.67
	Facility	47.29	64.20	43.14	40.00	54.17	0.00	28.57
	GPE	89.77	89.40	93.83	92.87	92.56	81.19	91.36
	Language	47.06	-	75.00	50.00	33.33	22.22	66.67
	Law	48.00	0.00	100.00	0.00	50.98	0.00	100.00
	Location	59.00	54.55	61.36	54.84	67.10	-	44.44
	Money	75.45	33.33	63.64	77.78	79.12	92.31	58.18
	NORP	88.58	94.55	93.92	94.87	90.70	78.05	85.15
	Ordinal	71.39	74.16	80.49	79.07	74.34	84.21	55.17
	Organization	76.00	60.90	78.57	69.97	84.76	48.98	51.08
	Percent	89.11	100.00	83.33	75.00	91.41	83.33	72.73
	Person	78.75	93.35	94.36	87.47	85.80	73.39	76.49
	Product	52.76	0.00	77.65	0.00	42.55	0.00	0.00
	Quantity	50.00	17.14	66.67	62.86	81.82	0.00	30.77
	Time	60.65	66.13	67.33	66.67	64.29	27.03	55.56
	Work of Art	34.03	42.42	35.62	28.57	54.24	0.00	8.70
	Overall	77.95	77.02	84.95	80.33	84.73	62.17	69.47

Table 11: Named Entity performance on the English subset of the CoNLL-2012 test set.

update the model for this round by retraining it on the English portion of the OntoNotes v5.0 corpus. Given the various constraints, we could not re-train it on the Chinese and Arabic data, Table 11 shows the overall performance of the tagger on the CoNLL-2012 English test set, as well as the performance broken down by individual name types.

Other Layers As noted earlier, systems were allowed to make use of gender and number predictions for NPs using the table from Bergsma and Lin (Bergsma and Lin, 2006), and the speaker metadata for broadcast conversations, telephone conversations and author or poster metadata for weblogs and newsgroups.

4.4.3 Data Format

In order to organize the multiple, rich layers of annotation, the OntoNotes project has created a database representation for the raw annotation layers along with a Python API to manipulate them (Pradhan et al., 2007a). In the OntoNotes distribution the data is organized as one file per layer, per document. The API requires a certain hierarchical structure with various annotation layers represented by file extensions for the documents at the leaves, and language, genre, source and section within a particular source forming the intermediate directories — `data/<language>/annotations/<genre>/<source>/<section>/<document>.<layer>`. It comes with various ways of querying and manipulating the data and allows convenient access to the information inside the sense inventory and PropBank frame files instead of having to interpret the raw `.xml`. However, maintaining format consistency with earlier CoNLL tasks was deemed convenient for sites that already had tools configured to deal with that format. Therefore, in order to distribute the data so that one could make the best of both worlds, we created a new file extension — `.conll` which logically served as another layer in addition to the `.parse`, `.prop`, `.sense`, `.name` and `.coref` layers which house the respective annotations. Each `.conll` file contained a merged representation of all the OntoNotes layers in the CoNLL-style tabular format with one line per token, and with multiple columns for each token specifying the input annotation layers relevant to that token, with the final column specifying the target coreference layer. Because we are not authorized to distribute the underlying text, and many of the layers contain inline annotation, we had to provide a skeletal form (`.skel`) of the `.conll` file which is essentially the `.conll` file, but with the column that contains the words, anonymized. We provided an assembly script that participants could use to create a `.conll` file taking as input the `.skel` file and the top-level directory of the OntoNotes distribution that they had separately downloaded from the LDC[23]. Once the `.conll` file is created, it can be used to create the individual layers such as `.parse`, `.name`, and `.coref` that have inline annotation, with the provided scripts. We provide the layers that have standoff annotation (mostly with respect to the tokens in the treebank) like the `.prop` and `.sense` along with the `.skel` file.

In the CoNLL-2011 task, there were a few issues, where some teams used the test data accidentally during training. To prevent it from happening again

[23]OntoNotes is deeply grateful to the Linguistic Data Consortium for making the source data freely available to the task participants.

Column	Type	Description
1	Document ID	This is a variation on the document filename
2	Part number	Some files are divided into multiple parts numbered as 000, 001, 002, ... etc.
3	Word number	This is the word index in the sentence
4	Word	The word itself
5	Part of Speech	Part of Speech of the word
6	Parse bit	This is the bracketed structure broken before the first open parenthesis in the parse, and the word/part-of-speech leaf replaced with a *. The full parse can be created by substituting the asterisk with the `([pos] [word])` string (or leaf) and concatenating the items in the rows of that column.
7	Lemma	The predicate/sense lemma is mentioned for the rows for which we have semantic role or word sense information. All other rows are marked with a –
8	Predicate Frameset ID	This is the PropBank frameset ID of the predicate in Column 7.
9	Word sense	This is the word sense of the word in Column 4.
10	Speaker/Author	This is the speaker or author name where available. Mostly in Broadcast Conversation and Weblog data.
11	Named Entities	These columns identifies the spans representing various named entities.
12:N	Predicate Arguments	There is one column each of predicate argument structure information for the predicate mentioned in Column 7.
N	Coreference	Coreference chain information encoded in a parenthesis structure.

Table 12: Format of the `.conll` file used in the shared task.

```
#begin document (nw/wsj/07/wsj_0771); part 000
...
...
nw/wsj/07/wsj_0771 0  0          ``   ``  (TOP(S(S*          -  -  -  -           *           *      (ARG1*            *            *      -
nw/wsj/07/wsj_0771 0  1  Vandenberg  NNP         (NP*          -  -  -  -   (PERSON)     (ARG1*           *            *            * (8|(0)
nw/wsj/07/wsj_0771 0  2         and   CC            *          -  -  -  -           *           *           *            *            *      -
nw/wsj/07/wsj_0771 0  3     Rayburn  NNP           *)          -  -  -  -   (PERSON)          *)           *            *            *(23)|8)
nw/wsj/07/wsj_0771 0  4         are  VBP         (VP*         be 01  1  -           *        (V*)           *            *            *      -
nw/wsj/07/wsj_0771 0  5      heroes  NNS     (NP(NP*)          -  -  -  -           *      (ARG2*           *            *            *      -
nw/wsj/07/wsj_0771 0  6          of   IN         (PP*          -  -  -  -           *           *           *            *            *      -
nw/wsj/07/wsj_0771 0  7        mine   NN      (NP*))))         -  -  5  -           *          *)           *            *            *   (15)
nw/wsj/07/wsj_0771 0  8           ,    ,            *          -  -  -  -           *           *           *            *            *      -
nw/wsj/07/wsj_0771 0  9          ''   ''           *)          -  -  -  -           *           *          *)            *            *      -
nw/wsj/07/wsj_0771 0 10         Mr.  NNP         (NP*          -  -  -  -           *           *      (ARG0*       (ARG0*            *    (15
nw/wsj/07/wsj_0771 0 11       Boren  NNP           *)          -  -  -  -   (PERSON)           *          *)           *)            *    15)
nw/wsj/07/wsj_0771 0 12        says  VBZ         (VP*        say 01  1  -           *           *        (V*)            *            *      -
nw/wsj/07/wsj_0771 0 13           ,    ,            *          -  -  -  -           *           *           *            *            *      -
nw/wsj/07/wsj_0771 0 14   referring  VBG      (S(VP*      refer 01  2  -           *           * (ARGM-ADV*          (V*)            *      -
nw/wsj/07/wsj_0771 0 15          as   RB       (ADVP*          -  -  -  -           *           *           *  (ARGM-DIS*            *      -
nw/wsj/07/wsj_0771 0 16        well   RB           *)          -  -  -  -           *           *           *           *)            *      -
nw/wsj/07/wsj_0771 0 17          to   IN         (PP*          -  -  -  -           *           *           *       (ARG1*            *      -
nw/wsj/07/wsj_0771 0 18         Sam  NNP      (NP(NP*          -  -  -  -    (PERSON*           *           *            *            *    (23
nw/wsj/07/wsj_0771 0 19     Rayburn  NNP           *)          -  -  -  -          *)           *           *            *            *      -
nw/wsj/07/wsj_0771 0 20           ,    ,            *          -  -  -  -           *           *           *            *            *      -
nw/wsj/07/wsj_0771 0 21         the   DT      (NP(NP*          -  -  -  -           *           *           *            *       (ARG0*      -
nw/wsj/07/wsj_0771 0 22  Democratic   JJ            *          -  -  -  -      (NORP)           *           *            *            *      -
nw/wsj/07/wsj_0771 0 23       House  NNP            *          -  -  -  -       (ORG)           *           *            *            *      -
nw/wsj/07/wsj_0771 0 24     speaker   NN           *)          -  -  -  -           *           *           *            *           *)      -
nw/wsj/07/wsj_0771 0 25         who   WP (SBAR(WHNP*)          -  -  -  -           *           *           *            *   (R-ARG0*)      -
nw/wsj/07/wsj_0771 0 26  cooperated  VBD      (S(VP*  cooperate 01  1  -           *           *           *            *         (V*)      -
nw/wsj/07/wsj_0771 0 27        with   IN         (PP*          -  -  -  -           *           *           *            *       (ARG1*      -
nw/wsj/07/wsj_0771 0 28   President  NNP         (NP*          -  -  -  -           *           *           *            *            *      -
nw/wsj/07/wsj_0771 0 29  Eisenhower  NNP *)))))))))))          -  -  -  -    (PERSON)           *          *)           *)           *)    23)
nw/wsj/07/wsj_0771 0 30           .    .          *))          -  -  -  -           *           *           *            *            *      -

nw/wsj/07/wsj_0771 0  0          ``   ``      (TOP(S*          -  -  -  -           *           *           *      -
nw/wsj/07/wsj_0771 0  1        They  PRP        (NP*)          -  -  -  -           *     (ARG0*)           *    (8)
nw/wsj/07/wsj_0771 0  2     allowed  VBD         (VP*      allow 01  1  -           *        (V*)           *      -
nw/wsj/07/wsj_0771 0  3        this   DT      (S(NP*          -  -  -  -           *      (ARG1*      (ARG1*     (6
nw/wsj/07/wsj_0771 0  4     country   NN           *)          -  -  3  -           *           *          *)     6)
nw/wsj/07/wsj_0771 0  5          to   TO         (VP*          -  -  -  -           *           *           *      -
nw/wsj/07/wsj_0771 0  6          be   VB         (VP*         be 01  1  -           *           *        (V*)   (16)
nw/wsj/07/wsj_0771 0  7    credible   JJ  (ADJP*)))))          -  -  -  -           *          *)     (ARG2*)      -
nw/wsj/07/wsj_0771 0  8           .    .          *))          -  -  -  -           *           *           *      -
#end document
```

Figure 3: Sample portion of the `.conll` file.

this year, we were advised by the steering committee to distribute the data in two installments. One for training and development and the other for testing. The test data released from LDC did not contain the coreference layer. Therefore, this year unlike previous CoNLL tasks, the test data contained some *truly unseen documents*. This made it easier to spot potential training errors such as ones that occurred in the CoNLL-2011 task. Table 12 describes the data provided in each of the column of the `.conll` format. Figure 3 shows a sample from a `.conll` file.

4.5 Evaluation

This section describes the evaluation criteria used for the shared task. Unlike propositions, word sense and named entities, where it is simply a matter of counting the correct answers, or for parsing, where there is an established metric, evaluating the accuracy of coreference continues to be contentious. Various alternative metrics have been proposed, as mentioned below, which weight different features of a proposed coreference pattern differently. The choice is not clear in part because the value of a particular set of coreference predictions is integrally tied to the consuming application. A further issue in defining a coreference metric concerns the granularity of the mentions, and how closely the predicted mentions are required to match those in the gold standard for a coreference prediction to be counted as correct. Our evaluation criterion was in part driven by the OntoNotes data structures. OntoNotes coreference makes the distinction between identity coreference and appositive coreference, treating the latter separately. Thus we evaluated systems only on the identity coreference task, which links all categories of entities and events together into equivalent classes. The situation with mentions for OntoNotes is also different than it was for MUC or ACE. OntoNotes data does not explicitly identify the minimum extents of an entity mention, but it does include hand-tagged syntactic parses. Thus for the official evaluation, we decided to use the *exact spans* of mentions for determining correctness. The NP boundaries for the test data were pre-extracted from the hand-tagged Treebank for annotation, and events triggered by verb phrases were tagged using the verbs themselves. This choice means that scores for the CoNLL-2012 coreference task are likely to be lower than for coreference evaluations based on MUC, or ACE data, where an approximate match is often allowed based on the specified head of the mentions.

4.5.1 Metrics

As noted above, the choice of an evaluation metric for coreference has been a tricky issue and there does not appear to be any silver bullet that addresses all the concerns. Three metrics have been commonly used for evaluating coreference performance over an unrestricted set of entity types: i) The **link** based MUC metric (Vilain et al., 1995), ii) The **mention** based B-CUBED metric (Bagga and Baldwin, 1998) and iii) The **entity** based CEAF (Constrained Entity Aligned F-measure) metric (Luo, 2005). Very recently BLANC (BiLateral Assessment of Noun-Phrase Coreference) measure (Recasens and Hovy, 2011) has been proposed as well. Each metric tries to address the shortcomings or biases of the earlier metrics. Given a set of key entities $\mathcal{K}$, and a set of response entities $\mathcal{R}$, with each entity comprising one or more mentions, each metric generates its variation of a precision and recall measure. The MUC measure is the oldest and most widely used. It focuses on the **links** (or, pairs of mentions) in the data.[24] The number of common links between entities in $\mathcal{K}$ and $\mathcal{R}$ divided by the number of links in $\mathcal{K}$ represents the recall, whereas, precision is the number of common links between entities in $\mathcal{K}$ and $\mathcal{R}$ divided by the number of links in $\mathcal{R}$. This metric prefers systems that have more mentions per entity — a system that creates a single entity of all the mentions will get a 100% recall without significant degradation in its precision. And, it ignores recall for singleton entities, or entities with only one mention. The B-CUBED metric tries to addresses MUC's shortcomings, by focusing on the **mentions** and computes recall and precision scores for each mention. If K is the key entity containing mention M, and R is the response entity containing mention M, then recall for the mention M is computed as $\frac{|K \cap R|}{|K|}$ and precision for the same is is computed as $\frac{|K \cap R|}{|R|}$. Overall recall and precision are the average of the individual mention scores. CEAF aligns every response entity with at most *one* key entity by finding the best one-to-one mapping between the entities using an entity similarity metric. This is a maximum bipartite matching problem and can be solved by the Kuhn-Munkres algorithm. This is thus a **entity** based measure. Depending on the similarity, there are two variations — *entity* based CEAF — CEAF_e and a *mention* based CEAF — CEAF_m. Recall is the total similarity divided by the number of mentions in $\mathcal{K}$, and precision is the total similarity divided by the number of mentions in $\mathcal{R}$. Finally, BLANC uses a variation on the Rand index (Rand, 1971) suitable for evaluating coreference. There are a few other measures — one being the ACE value, but since this is specific to a restricted set of entities (ACE types), we did not consider it.

4.5.2 Official Evaluation Metric

In order to determine the best performing system in the shared task, we needed to associate a single

[24]The MUC corpora did not tag single mention entities.

number with each system. This could have been one of the metrics above, or some combination of more than one of them. The choice was not simple, and after having consulted various researchers in the field, we came to a conclusion that each metric had its pros and cons and there is no silver bullet. Therefore we settled on the MELA metric proposed by Denis and Baldridge (2009), which takes a weighted average of three metrics: MUC, B-CUBED, and CEAF. The rationale for the combination is that each of the three metrics represents a different, important dimension. The MUC measure is based on *links*. The B-CUBED is based on *mentions*, and the CEAF is based on *entities*. We decided to use the entity based CEAF_e instead of mention based CEAF_m. For a given end application, a weighted average of the three might be optimal, but since we don't have a particular end task in mind, we decided to use the unweighted mean of the three metrics as the score on which the winning system was judged. This still leaves us with a score for each language. We wanted to encourage researchers to run their systems on all three languages. Therefore, we decided to compute the final *official* score that would determine the winning submission as the average of the MELA metric across all the three languages. We decided to give a MELA score of zero to every language that a particular group did not run its system on.

4.5.3 Scoring Metrics Implementation

We used the same core scorer implementation[25] that was used for the SEMEVAL-2010 task, and which implemented all the different metrics. There were a couple of modifications done to this scorer since then.

1. *Only exact matches were considered correct.* Previously, for SEMEVAL-2010 non-exact matches were judged partially correct with a 0.5 score if the heads were the same and the mention extent did not exceed the gold mention.
2. The modifications suggested by Cai and Strube (2010) have been incorporated in the scorer.

Since there are differences in the version used for CoNLL and the one available on the download site, and it is possible that the latter would be revised in the future, we have archived the version of the scorer on the CoNLL-2012 task webpage.[26]

5 Participants

A total of 41 different groups demonstrated interest in the shared task by registering on the task webpage. Of these, 16 groups from 6 countries submitted system outputs on the test set during the evaluation week. 15 groups participated in at least one language in the closed task, and only one group participated solely in the open track. One participant (*yang*) did not submit a final task paper. Tables 13 and 14 list the distribution of the participants by country and the participation by language and task type.

Country	Participants
Brazil	1
China	8
Germany	3
Italy	1
Switzerland	1
USA	2

Table 13: Participation by country.

	Closed	Open	Combined
English	15	1	16
Chinese	13	3	14
Arabic	7	1	8

Table 14: Participation across languages and tracks.

6 Approaches

Tables 15 and 16 summarize the approaches taken by the participating systems along some important dimensions. While referring to the participating systems, as a convention, we will use the last name of the contact person from the participating team. It is almost always the last name of the first author of the system papers, or the first name in case of conflicting last names (*xinxin*). The only exception is *chunyang* which is the first name of the second author for that system. For space and readability purposes, while referring to the systems in the paper we will refer to the system by the primary contact name in italics instead of using explicit citations.

Most of the systems divided the problem into the typical two phases — first identifying the potential mentions in the text, and then linking the mentions to form coreference chains, or entities. Many systems used rule-based approaches for mention detection, though one, *yang* did use trained models, and *li* used a hybrid approach by adding mentions from a trained model to the ones identified using rules. All systems ran a post processing stage, after linking potential mentions together, to delete the remaining unlinked mentions. It was common for the systems to represent the markables (mentions) internally in

[25] http://www.lsi.upc.edu/~esapena/downloads/index.php?id=3
[26] http://conll.bbn.com/download/scorer.v4.tar.gz

[27] The participant did not submit a final paper, so this information is based on an email correspondence.

Participant	Track	Languages	Syntax	Learning Framework	Markable Identification	Verb	Feature Selection	# Features	Train
fernandes	C	A, C, E	P	Latent Structure Perceptron	All noun phrases, pronouns and name entities	×	Latent feature induction and feature templates	196 templates (E); 197 (C) and 223 (A)	T + D
björkelund	C	A, C, E	P	LIBLINEAR for linking, and Maximum Entropy (Mallet) for anaphoricity	NP, PRP and PRP$ in all languages; PN and NR in Chinese; all NE in English. Classifier to exclude non-referential *pronouns* in English (with a probability of 0.95).	×	Greedy forward selection (semi-automatic)	28 feature templates (C) and 34 (E)[a]	T + D
chen	C, O	A, C, E	P	Hybrid — Sieve approach followed by language-specific heuristic pruning and language-independent learning based pruning; Genre specific models	NP, PRP and PRP$ and selected NE in English. NP and QP in Chinese. Exclude Chinese interrogative pronouns *what* and *where*. NP and selected NE in Arabic. Learning to prune non-referential mentions	×	Backward elimination	–	T
stamborg	C	A, C, E	D	Logistic Regression (LIBLINEAR)	NP, PRP and PRP$ in all languages; PN in Chinese; all NE in English. Exclude pleonastic *it* in English. Prune smaller mentions with same head.	×	Forward + Backward starting from CoNLL-2011 feature set for English and Soon feature set for Chinese and Arabic	18–37	T + D
martschat	C	A, C	D	Directed multigraph representation where the weights are learned over the training data (on top of BART (Versley et al., 2008))	Eight different mention types for English, and adjectival use for nations and a few NEs are filtered as well as embedded mentions and pleonastic pronouns. Four mention types in Chinese. Copulas are also handled appropriately.	×	×	In the form of negative and positive relations	20% of T (E); 15% of T (C)
chang	C	E, C	P	Latent Structure Learning	All noun phrases, pronouns and name entities	×	×	Chang, et al., 2011	T + D
uryupina	C	A, C, E	P	modification of BART using multi-objective optimization. Domain specific classifiers for *nw* and *bc* genre.	Standard rules for English and Classifier to identify markable NPs in Chinese and Arabic.	×	×	∼45	T + D
zhekova	C	A, C, E	P	Memory based learning (TiMBL)	NP, PRP and PRP$ in English, and all NP in Chinese and Arabic. Singleton classifier.	×	×	33	T + D
li	C	A, C, E	P	MaxEnt	All phrase types that are mentions in training are considered as mentions and a classifier is trained to identify potential mentions.	√	×	11 feature groups	T + D
yuan	C, O	E, C	P	C4.5 and deterministic rules	All noun phrases, pronouns and name entities	×	×	–	T + D
xu	C	E, C	P	Decision tree classifier and deterministic rules	All noun phrases, pronouns and selected named entities selected and overlapping mentions are considered when they are second-level NPs inside an NP, for example coordinating NPs	×	×	51 (E) and 61 (C)	T
chunyang	C	E, C	P	Rule-based (adaptation of Lee et al. 2011's sieve structure)	Chinese NP and pronouns using part of speech PN and names using part of speech NR excluding measure words and certain names	×	×	–	–
yang[27]	C	E	P	Structural SVM	Mention detection classifier	×	Same feature set, but per classifier	40	T (2011)
xinxin	C	E, C	P	MaxEnt	NP, PRP and PRP$ in English and Chinese	×	Greedy forward backward	71	T + D
shou	C	E	P	Modified version of Lee et al., 2011 sieve system					
xiong	O	A, C, E	P	Lee et al., 2011 system					

Table 15: Participating system profiles — Part I. In the Task column, C/O represents whether the system participated in the *closed*, *open* or both tracks. In the Syntax column, a P represents that the systems used a phrase structure grammar representation of syntax, whereas a D represents that they used a dependency representation. In the Train column T represents training data and D represents development data.

[a]Communication with Anders Björkelund.

Participant	Positive Training Examples	Negative Training Examples	Decoding
fernandes	Identify likely mentions with an aim to generate high recall using the sieve method proposed in (Lee et al., 2011). Create directed arcs between mention pairs using a set of rules		A constrained latent predictor finds the maximum scoring document tree among possible candidates
björkelund	Closest Antecedent (Soon, 2001)	Negative examples in between anaphor and closest antecedent (Soon, 2001)	Stacked resolvers — i) Best first, ii) Pronoun closest first — closest first for pronouns and best first for other mentions and iii) cluster-mention; disallow transitive nesting; proper noun mentions processed first, followed by other nouns and pronouns
chen	Rule-based sieve approach followed by heuristic and learning based pruning		
stamborg	Closest Antecedent (Soon, 2001)	Negative examples in between anaphor and closest antecedent (Soon, 2001)	Chinese and Arabic — Closest-first clustering for pronouns and Best-first clustering otherwise. English — closest-first for pronouns and averaged best-first clustering otherwise.
martschat	Weights are trained on part of the training data		Greedy clustering for English; Spectral clustering followed by greedy clustering for Chinese to reduce number of candidate antecedents.
chang	Closest Antecedent (Soon, 2001)	All preceding mentions in a union of of *gold* and *predicted* mentions. Mentions where the first is pronoun and other not are not considered	Best link strategy; separate classifiers for pronominal and non-pronominal mentions for English. Single classifier for Chinese.
uryupina	Closest Antecedent (Soon, 2001)	Negative examples in between anaphor and closest antecedent (Soon, 2001)	mention pair model without ranking as in Soon 2001
zhekova	Closest Antecedent (Soon, 2001)	Negative examples in between anaphor and closest antecedent (Soon, 2001)	All definite phrases used to create a pair for each anaphor with each mention preceding it within a window of 10 (English, Chinese) or 7 (Arabic) sentences.
li		—	Best-first clustering
yuan		—	Deterministic NP-NP followed by PP-NP
xu	Window of sentences is used to determine positive and negative examples. For English a window of 5 sentences is used whereas for Chinese a window of 10 sentences is used		All-pair linking followed by pruning or correction using a set of rules for NE-NE and NP-NP mentions for sentences outside of a 5/10 sentence window in English and Chinese respectively
chunyang	Lee et al., 2011 system		
yang	Pre-cluster pair models separate for each pair NP-NP, NP-PRP and PRP-PRP		Pre-clusters, with singleton pronoun pre-clusters, and use closest-first clustering. Different link models based on the type of linking mentions — NP-PRP, PRP-PRP and NP-NP
xinxin	Closest Antecedent (Soon, 2001)	Negative examples in between anaphor and closest antecedent (Soon, 2001)	Best-first clustering method
shou	Modified version of Lee et al., 2011 coreference system		
xiong	Lee et al., 2011 system		

Table 16: Participating system profiles — Part II. This focuses on the way positive and negative examples were generated and the decoding strategy used.

terms of individual parse tree NP constituent spans. Some systems consider only mention-specific attributes while performing the clustering, but the recent trend seems to indicate a shared attribute model, where the attributes of an entity are determined collectively by heuristically merging the attribute types and values of its constituent mentions. For example, if a mention marked *singular* is clustered with another entity marked *plural*, then the collective number for the entity is assigned to be {*singular, plural*}. Various types of trained models were used for predicting coreference. For a learning-based system, generation of positive and negative examples is very important. The participating systems used a range of sentence windows surrounding the anaphor in generating these examples. In the systems that used trained models, many systems used the approach described in Soon et al. (2001) for selecting the positive and negative training examples, while others used some of the alternative approaches that have been introduced in the literature more recently. Following on the success of rule-based linking model in the CoNLL-2011 shared task, many systems used a completely rule-based linking model, or used it as a initializing, or intermediate step in a learning based system. A hybrid approach seems to be a central theme of many high scoring systems. Also, taking cue from last year's systems, almost all systems trained pleonastic *it* classifiers, and used speaker-based constraints/features for the conversation genre. Many systems used the predicted Arabic parts of speech that were mapped-down to Penn-style parts of speech, but *stamborg* used some heuristics to convert them back to the complex part of speech type, using more frequent mapping, to get better performance for Arabic. The *fernandes* system uses feature templates defined on mention pairs. *björkelund* mentions that disallowing transitive closures gave performance improvement of 0.6 and 0.4 respectively for English and Chinese/Arabic. *björkelund* also mentions seeing a considerable increase in performance after adding features that correspond to the Shortest Edit Script (Myers, 1986) between surface forms and unvocalised Buckwalter forms, respectively. These could be better at capturing the differences in gender and number signaled by certain morphemes than hand-crafted rules. *chen* built upon the sieve architecture proposed in Raghunathan et al. (2010) and added one more sieve — head match — for Chinese and modified two sieves. Some participants tried to incorporate peculiarities of the corpus in their systems. For example, *martschat* excluded adjectival nation names. Unlike English, and especially in absence of an external resource, it is hard to make a gender distinction in Arabic and Chinese. *martschat* used the information that 先生(sir) and 女士(lady) often suggest gender information. *bo* and *martschat* used plurality markers 们 to identify plurals. For example, 同学 (student) is singular and 同学们 (students) is plural. *bo* also uses a heuristic that if the word 和 (and) appears in the middle of a mention M, and the two parts separated by 和 are sub-mentions of M, then mention M is considered to be plural. Other words which have the similar meaning of 和, such as 同, 与 and 跟, are also considered. *uryupina* used the rich part of speech tags to classify pronouns into subtype, person number and gender. Chinese and Arabic do not have definite noun phrase markers like *the* in English. In contrast to English there is no strict enforcement of using definite noun phrases when referring to an antecedent in Chinese. Both 这次演说 (the talk) and 演说 (talk) can corefer with the antecedent 克林顿在河内大选的演说 (Clinton's talk during Hanoi election). This makes it very difficult to distinguish generic expressions from referential ones. *martschat* checks whether the phrase starts with a definite/demonstrative indicator (e.g., 这(this) or 那(that)) in order to identify demonstrative and definite noun phrases. For Arabic, *uryupina* considers as definite all mentions with definite head nouns (prefixed with "Al") and all the idafa constructs with a definite modifier. *chang* uses training data to identify inappropriate mention boundaries. They perform a relaxed matching between predicted mentions and gold mentions ignoring punctuation marks and mentions that start with one of the following: *adverb*, *verb*, *determiner*, and *cardinal number*. In another extreme, *xiong* translated Chinese and Arabic to English, and ran an English system and projected mentions back to the source languages. Unfortunately, it did not work quite well by itself. One issue that they faced was that many instances of pronouns did not have a corresponding mention in the source language (since we do not consider mentions formed by dropped subjects/objects). Nevertheless, using this in addition to performing coreference resolution in these languages could be useful. Similar to last year, most participants appear not to have focused much on eventive coreference, those coreference chains that build off verbs in the data. This usually means that nominal mentions that should have linked to the eventive verb were instead linked in with some other entity, or remained unlinked. Participants may have chosen not to focus on events because they pose unique challenges while making up only a small portion of the data (Roughly 90% of mentions in the data are NPs and pronouns). Many of the trained systems were also able to improve their performance by using feature selection, the details varied depending on the example selection strategy and the classifier used.

7 Results

In this section we will take a look at the performance overview of various systems and then look at the performance for each language in various settings separately. For the official test, beyond the raw source text, coreference systems were provided only with the predictions for the other annotation layers (parses, semantic roles, word senses, and named entities). A high-level summary of the results for the systems on the primary evaluation for both *open* and *closed* tracks is shown in Table 17. The scores under the columns for each language are the average of MUC, BCUBED and CEAF_e for that language. The column **Official Score** is the average of those per-language averages, but only for the **closed** track. If a participant did not participate in all three languages, then they got a score of zero for the languages that were not attempted. The systems are sorted in descending order of this final **Official Score**. The last two columns indicate whether the systems used only the training or both training and development for the final submissions. Most top performing systems used both training and development data for training the final system. Note that all the results reported here still used the same, *predicted* information for all input layers.

It can be seen that *fernandes* got the highest combined score (58.69) across all three languages and metrics. While scores for each individual language are lower than the figures cited for other corpora, it is as expected, given that the task here includes predicting the underlying mentions and mention boundaries, the insistence on exact match, and given that the relatively easier *appositive coreference* cases are not included in this measure. The combined score across all languages is purely for ranking purposes, and does not really tell much about each individual language. Owing to the ordering based on official score, not all the best performing systems for a particular language are in sequential order. Therefore, for easier reading, the scores of the top ranking system are in bold red, and the top four systems are underlined in the table.

Looking at the the English performance, we can see that *fernandes* gets the best average across the three selected metrics (MUC, BCUBED and CEAF_e). The next best system is *martschat* (61.31) followed very closely by *björkelund* (61.24) and then *chang* (60.18). The performance differences between the better-scoring systems were not large, with only about three points separating the top four systems, and only six out of a total of sixteen systems getting a score lower than 58 points which was the highest performing score in CoNLL-2011.[28]

In case of Chinese, it is seen that *chen* performs the best with a score of 62.24. This is then followed by *yuan* (60.69), and then *björkelund* (59.97) and *xu* (59.22). It is interesting to note that the scores for the top performing systems for both English and Chinese are very close. For all we know, this is just a coincidence. Also, for both English and Chinese, the top performing system is almost 2 points higher than the second best system.

On the Arabic language front, once again, *fernandes* has the highest score of 54.22, followed closely by *björkelund* (53.55) and then *uryupina* (50.41)

Since the majority of mentions in all the three languages are noun phrases or pronouns, the accuracy with which these are predicted in the parse trees should directly bear on the coreference scores. Since pronouns are a closed class and single words, the main focus falls on the accuracy of the noun phrases. By no means is the accuracy of noun phrases the only factor determining the overall coreference accuracy, but it cannot be ignored either. It can be observed that the coreference scores for the three languages are in the same trend as the noun phrase accuracies for those languages as seen in Table 6. Recall that in case of both Chinese and Arabic, there are roughly 11% instances of dropped pronouns that were not considered as part of the evaluation. The performance for Chinee and Arabic would decrease somewhat if these were considered in the set of gold mentions (and entities).

Tables 18 and 19 show similar information for the two supplementary tasks — one given *gold mention boundaries* (GB) and one given correct, *gold mentions* (GM). We have however, kept the same relative ordering of the system participants as in Table 17 for ease of reading. Looking at Table 18 carefully, we can see that for English and Arabic the relative ranking of the systems remain almost the same, except for a few outliers: *chang* performs the best given *gold mentions* — by almost 7 points over the next best performing system. In the case of Chinese, *chen* performs almost 6 points better than the official performance given *gold boundaries*, and another 9 points given *gold mentions* and almost 8 points better than the next best system using *gold mentions*. We will look at more details in the following sections.

As mentioned earlier in Section 4.2 we conducted some supplementary evaluations. These can be categorized by a combination of two parameters. One of which applies to both training and test set, and one can only apply to the test set. The two parameters are: i) Syntax and ii) Mention Quality. Syntax can take two values: i) *predicted* (PS), or ii) *gold* (GS), and can be applicable during either training or test; and, the mention quality can be of three values: i) No boundaries (NB), ii) Gold mention boundaries

[28]More precise comparison later in Section 8.

Participant	Open			Closed			Official	Final model	
	English	Chinese	Arabic	English	Chinese	Arabic	Score	Train	Dev
fernandes				63.37	58.49	54.22	58.69	√	√
björkelund				61.24	59.97	53.55	58.25	√	√
chen		63.53		59.69	62.24	47.13	56.35	√	×
stamborg				59.36	56.85	49.43	55.21	√	√
uryupina				56.12	53.87	50.41	53.47	√	√
zhekova				48.70	44.53	40.57	44.60	√	√
li				45.85	46.27	33.53	41.88	√	√
yuan		61.02		58.68	60.69		39.79	√	√
xu				57.49	59.22		38.90	√	×
martschat				61.31	53.15		38.15	√	×
chunyang				59.24	51.83		37.02	–	–
yang				55.29			18.43	√	×
chang				60.18	45.71		35.30	√	×
xinxin				48.77	51.76		33.51	√	√
shou				58.25			19.42	√	×
xiong	59.23	44.35	44.37				0.00	√	√

Table 17: Performance on primary **open** and **closed** tracks using all predicted information.

Participant	Open			Closed			Suppl.	Final model	
	English	Chinese	Arabic	English	Chinese	Arabic	Score	Train	Dev
fernandes				63.16	61.48	53.90	59.51	√	√
björkelund				60.75	62.76	53.50	59.00	√	√
chen		70.00		60.33	68.55	47.27	58.72	√	×
stamborg				57.35	54.30	49.59	53.75	√	√
zhekova				49.30	44.93	40.24	44.82	√	√
li				43.04	43.28	31.46	39.26	√	√
yuan				59.50	64.42		41.31	√	√
xu				56.47	64.08		40.18	√	×
chang				60.89			20.30	√	√

Table 18: Performance on supplementary **open** and **closed** tracks using all predicted information, given **gold mention boundaries**.

Participant	Open			Closed			Suppl.	Final model	
	English	Chinese	Arabic	English	Chinese	Arabic	Score	Train	Dev
fernandes				69.35	66.36	63.49	66.40	√	√
björkelund				68.20	69.92	59.14	65.75	√	√
chen		78.98		70.46	77.77	52.26	66.83	√	×
stamborg				68.66	66.97	53.35	62.99	√	√
zhekova				59.06	51.44	55.72	55.41	√	√
li				51.40	59.93	40.62	50.65	√	√
yuan				69.88	76.05		48.64	√	√
xu				63.46	69.79		44.42	√	×
chang				77.22			25.74	√	√

Table 19: Performance on supplementary **open** and **closed** tracks using all predicted information, given **gold mentions**.

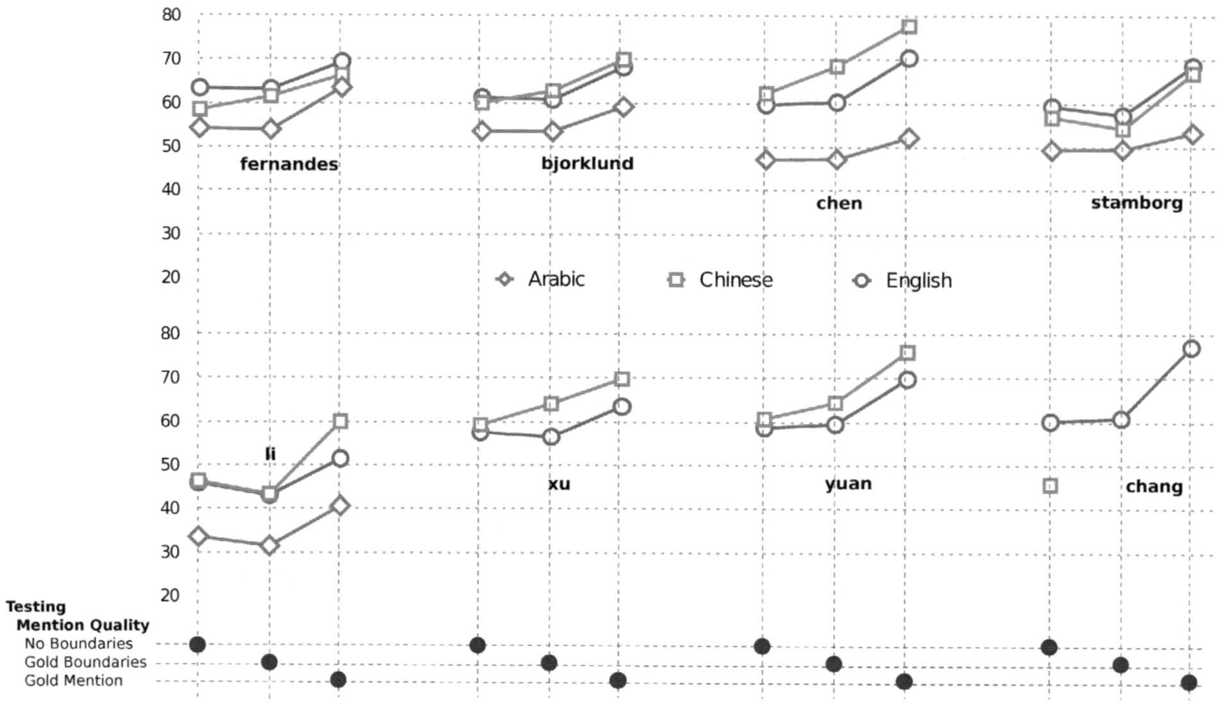

Figure 4: Performance for eight participating systems for the three languages, across the three mention qualities.

(GB) and iii) Gold mentions (GM), and can only be applicable during testing (since this information is not optional during training, as is the case with using gold or predicted syntax). There are a total of twelve combinations that we can form of using these parameters. Out of these, we thought six were particularly interesting. This is the product of the three cases of mention quality — NB, GB and GM, and two cases of syntax – GS and PS used during testing.

Figure 4 shows a performance plot for eight participating systems that attempted both the supplementary tasks — GB and GM in addition to the main NB for at least one of the three languages. These are all in the *closed* setting. At the bottom of the plot you can see dots that indicate what test condition to which a particular point refers. In most cases, for the hardest task — NB — the English and Chinese performances track quite close to each other. When provided with gold mention boundaries (GB), systems, *chen*, *xu* and *yuan* do significantly better in Chinese. There is almost no positive effect on the English performance across the board. In fact, performance of the *stamborg* and *li* systems drops noticeably. There is also a drop in performance for the *björkelund* system, but the difference is probably not significant. Finally, when provided with *gold mentions*, the performance of all systems increases across all languages, with *chang* showing the highest gain for English, and *chen* showing the highest gain for Chinese.

Figure 5 is a box and whiskers plot of the performance for all the systems for each language and variations — NB, GB, and GM. The circle in the center indicates the mean of the performances. The horizontal line in between the box indicates the median, and the bottom and top of the boxes indicate the first and third quartiles respectively, with the whiskers indicating the highest and lowest performance on that task. It can be easily seen that the English systems have the least divergence, with the divergence large for the GM case probably owing to *chang*. This is somewhat expected as this is the second year for the English task, and so it does show a more mature and stable performance. On the other hand, both Chinese and Arabic plots show much more divergence, with the Chinese and Arabic GB case showing the highest divergence. Also, except for Chinese GM condition, there is some skewness in the score distribution one way or the other.

Some participants ran their systems on six of the twelve possible combinations for all three languages. Figure 6 shows a plot for these tree participants — *fernandes*, *björkelund*, and *chen*. As in Figure 4, the dots at the bottom help identify which particular combination of parameters the point on the plot represents. In addition to the three test conditions related to mention quality, we now also have two more test conditions relating to the syntax.

We can see that the *fernandes* and *björkelund*, system performance tracks very close to each other. In other words, using gold standard parses during testing does not show much benefit in those cases. In case of *chen*, however, using gold parses shows a significant jump in scores for the NB condition. It seems that somehow, *chen* makes much better use of the gold parses. In fact, the performance is very close to the one with the GB condition. It is not clear what this system is doing differently that makes this possible. Adding more information, i.e., the GM condition, improves the performance by almost the same delta as going from NB to GB.

Finally, Figure 7 shows the plot for one system — *björkelund* — that was ran on ten of the twelve different settings. As usual the dots at the bottom help identify the conditions for a point on the plot. Now, there is a condition related to the quality of syntax during training as well. For some reasons, using *gold* syntax hurts performance — though slightly — in the NB and GB settings. Chinese does show some improvement when *gold* parse is used for training, only when *gold mentions* are available during testing.

One point to note is that we cannot compare these results to the ones obtained in the SEMEVAL-2010 coreference task which used a small portion of OntoNotes data because it was only using nominal entities, and had heuristically added singleton mentions[29].

[29] The documentation that comes with the SEMEVAL data package from LDC (LDC2011T01) states: "Only nominal mentions and identical (IDENT) types were taken from the OntoNotes coreference annotation, thus excluding coreference relations with verbs and appositives. Since OntoNotes is only annotated with multi-mention entities, singleton referential elements were identified heuristically: all NPs and possessive determiners were annotated as singletons excluding those functioning as appositives or as pre-modifiers but for NPs in the possessive case. In coordinated NPs, single constituents as well as the entire NPs were considered to be mentions. There is no reliable heuristic to automatically detect English expletive pronouns, thus they were (although inaccurately) also annotated as singletons."

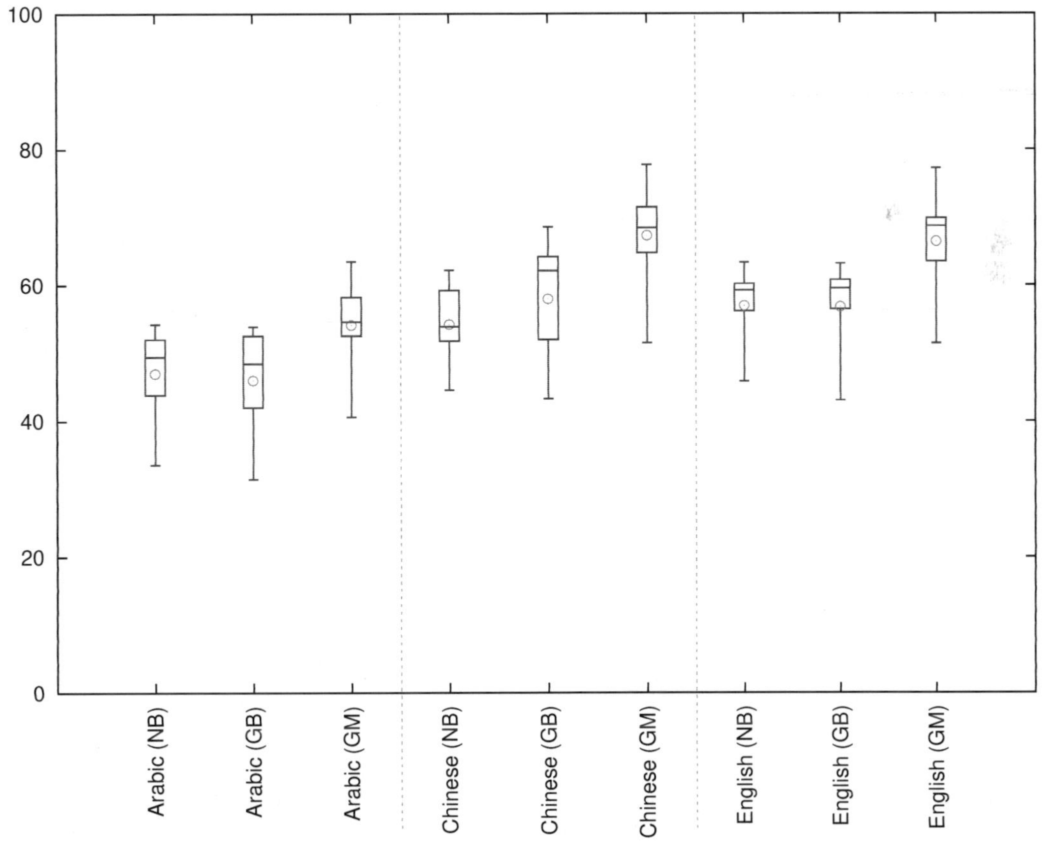

Figure 5: A box and whiskers plot of the performance for the three languages across the three mention qualities.

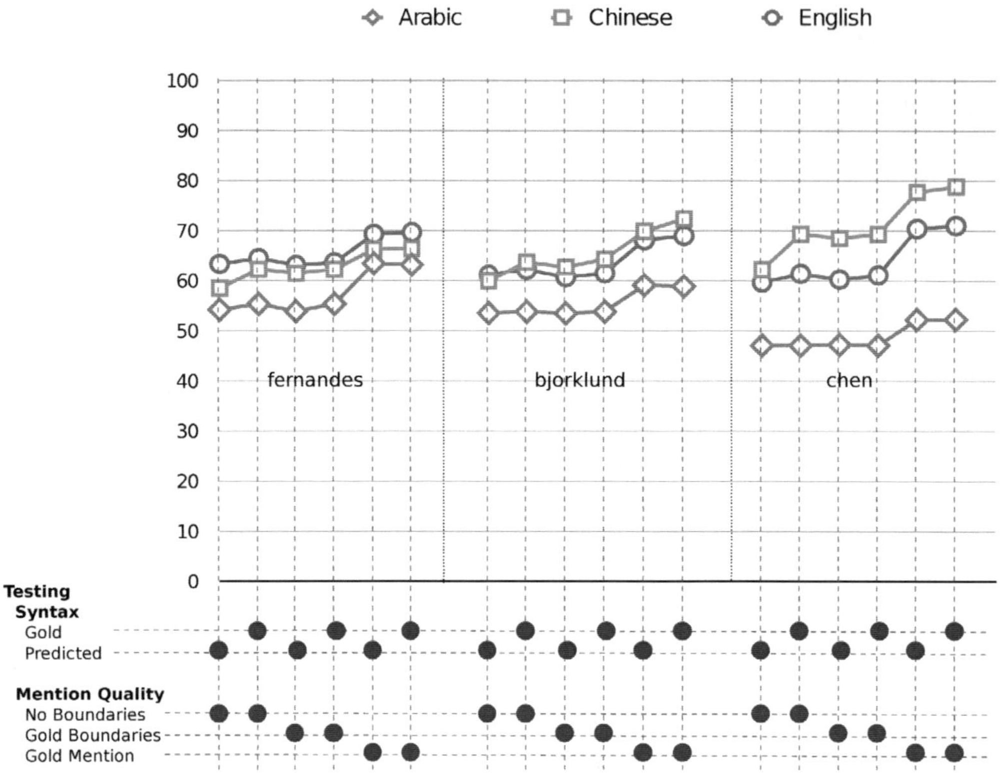

Figure 6: Performance of *fernandes*, *björkelund* and *chen* over six different settings.

In the following sections we will look at the results for the three languages, in various settings in more detail. It might help to describe the format of the tables first. Given that our choice of the official metric was somewhat arbitrary, it is also useful to look at the individual metrics. The tables are similar in structure to Table 20. Each table provides results across multiple dimensions. For completeness, the tables include the raw precision and recall scores from which the F-scores were derived. Each table shows the scores for a particular system for the task of *mention detection* and *coreference resolution* separately. The tables also include two additional scores (BLANC and CEAF_m) that did not factor into the official score. Useful further analysis may be possible based on these results beyond the preliminary results presented here. As you recall, OntoNotes does not contain any *singleton* mentions. Owing to this peculiar nature of the data, the mention detection scores cannot be interpreted independently of the coreference resolution scores. In this scenario, a mention is effectively an anaphoric mention that has at least one other mention coreferent with it in the document. Most systems removed singletons from the response as a post-processing step, so not only will they not get credit for the singleton entities that they incorrectly removed from the data, but they will be penalized for the ones that they accidentally linked with another mention. What this number does indicate is the ceiling on recall that a system would have got in absence of being penalized for making mistakes in coreference resolution. The tables are sub-divided into several logical horizontal sections separated by two horizontal lines. There can be a total of 12 sections, each categorized by a combination of two parse quality features GS and PS for each training and test set and three variations on the mention qualities — NB, GB, and GM, as described earlier. Just like we used the dots below the graphs earlier to indicate the parameters that were chosen for a particular point on the plot, we use small black squares in the tables after the participant name, to indicate the conditions chosen for the results on that particular row. Since there are many rows to each table, in order to facilitate finding which number we are referring to, we have added a ID column which uses letters **e**, **c**, and **a** to refer to the three languages — English, Chinese and Arabic. This is followed by a decimal number, in which the number before the decimal identifies the logical block within the table

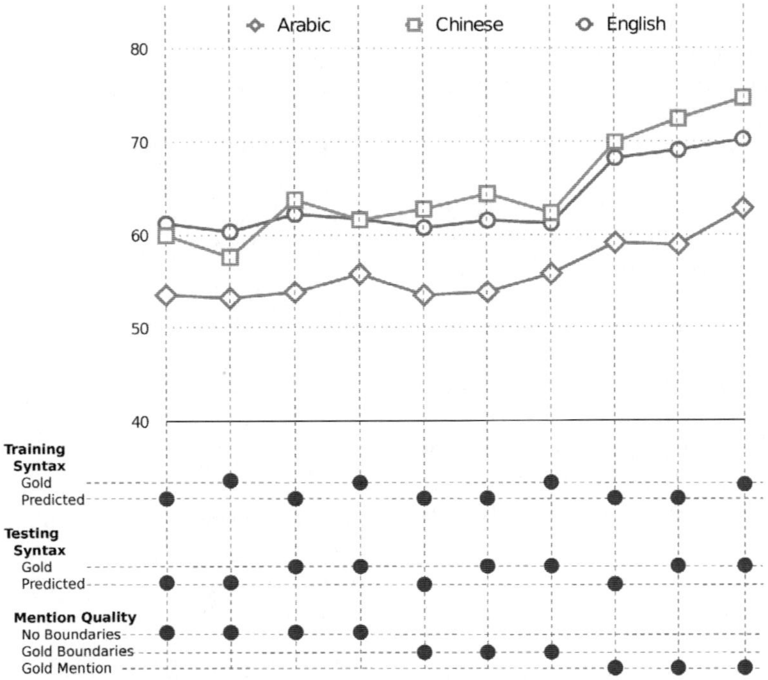

Figure 7: Performance of *björkelund* over ten different settings.

that share the same experiment parameters, and the one after the decimal indicates the index of a particular system in that block. Systems are sorted by the official score within each block. All the systems with NB setting are listed first, followed by GB, followed by GM. One participant (*björkelund*) ran more variations than we had originally planned, but since it falls under the general permutation and combination of the settings that we were considering, it makes sense to list those results here as well.

7.1 English *Closed*

Table 20 shows the performance for the English language in greater detail.

Official Setting Recall is quite important in the mention detection stage because the full coreference system has no way to recover if the mention detection stage misses a potentially anaphoric mention. The linking stage indirectly impacts the final mention detection accuracy. After a complete pass through the system some correct mentions could remain unlinked with any other mentions and would be deleted thereby lowering recall. Most systems tend to get a close balance between recall and precision for the mention detection task. A few systems had a considerable gap between the final mention detection recall and precision (*fernandes, xu, yang, li* and *xinxin*). It is not clear why this might be the case. One commonality between the ones that had a much higher precision than recall was that they used machine learned classifiers for mention detection. This could be possible because any classifier that is trained will not normally contain singleton mentions (as none have been annotated in the data) unless one explicitly adds them to the set of training examples (which is not mentioned in any of the respective system papers). A hybrid rule-based and machine learned model (*fernandes*) performed the best. Apart from some local differences, the ranking for all the systems is roughly the same irrespective of which metric is chosen. The $CEAF_e$ measure seems to penalize systems more harshly than the other measures. If the $CEAF_e$ measure does indicate the accuracy of entities in the response, this suggests that *fernandes* is doing better on getting coherent entities than any other system.

Gold Mention Boundaries In this case, all possible mention boundaries are provided to the system. This is very similar to what annotators see when they annotate the documents. One difficulty with this supplementary evaluation is that these boundaries alone provide only very partial information. For the roughly 10 to 20% of mentions that the automatic parser did not correctly identify, while the systems knew the correct boundaries, they had no structural syntactic or semantic information, and they also had to further approximate the already heuristic head word identification. This incomplete data complicates the systems' task and also complicates interpretation of the results. While most systems did slightly better here in terms of raw scores, the performance was not much different from the official task, indicating that mention boundary errors resulting from problems in parsing do not contribute significantly to the final output.[30]

Gold Mentions Another supplementary condition that we explored was if the systems were supplied with the manually-annotated spans for *all* and *only* those mentions that did participate in the gold standard coreference chains. This supplies significantly more information than the previous case, where exact spans were supplied for all NPs, since the gold mentions will also include verb headwords that are linked to event NPs, and will not include singleton mentions, which do not end up as part of any chain. The latter constraint makes this test seem artificial, since it directly reveals part of what the systems are designed to determine, but it still has some value in quantifying the impact that mention detection and anaphoricity determination has on the overall task and what the results are if they are perfectly known. The results show that performance does go up significantly, indicating that it is markedly easier for the systems to generate better entities given *gold mentions*. Although, ideally, one would expect a perfect mention detection score, it is the case that many of the systems did not get a 100% recall. This could possibly be owing to unlinked singletons that were removed in post-processing. *chang* along with *fernandes* are the only systems that got a perfect 100% recall. The reason is most likely because they had a hard constraint to link all mentions with at least one other mention. *chang* (77.22 [e7.00]) stands out in that it has a 7 point lead on the next best system in this category. This indicates that the linking algorithm for this system is significantly superior than the other systems — especially since the performance of the only other system that gets 100% mention score (*fernandes*) is much lower (69.35 [e7.03])

Gold Test Parses Looking at Table 20 it can be seen that there is a slight increase (~1 point) in performance across all the systems when gold parses across all settings — NB, GB, and GM. In the case of *björkelund* for the NB setting, the overall performance improves by a percent when using gold test parse during testing (61.24 [e0.02] vs 62.23 [e1.02]), but strangely if gold parses are used during training as well, the performance is slightly lower (61.71 [e3.00]), although this difference is probably not statistically significant.

[30]It would be interesting to measure the overlap between the entity clusters for these two cases, to see whether there was any substantial difference in the mention chains, besides the expected differences in boundaries for individual mentions.

7.2 Chinese *Closed*

Table 21 shows the performance for the Chinese language in greater detail.

7.2.1 Official Setting

In this case, it turns out that *chen* does about 2 points better than the next best system across all the metrics. We know that this system had some more Chinese-specific improvements. It is strange that *fernandes* has a much lower mention recall with a much higher precision as compared to *chen*. As far as the system descriptions go, both systems seem to have used the same set of mentions — except for *chen* including QP phrases and not considering interrogative pronouns. One thing we found about *chen* was that they dealt with nested NPs differently in case of the NW genre to achieve some performance improvement. This unfortunately seems to be addressing a quirk in the Chinese newswire data owing to a possible data inconsistency in the release.

7.2.2 Gold Mention Boundaries

Unlike English, just the addition of *gold mention boundaries* improves the performance of almost all systems significantly. The delta improvement for *fernandes* turns out to be small, but it does gain on the mention recall as compared to the NB case. It is not clear why this might be the case. One explanation could be that the parser performance for constituents that represent mentions — primarily NP might be significantly worse than that for English. The mention recall of all the systems is boosted by roughly 10%.

7.2.3 Gold Mentions

Providing *gold mention* information further significantly boosts all systems. More so is the case with *chen* [e8.00] which gains another 9 points over the *gold mention boundary* condition in spite of the fact that they don't have a perfect recall. On the other hand, *fernandes* gets a perfect mention recall and precision, but ends up getting a 11 point lower performance [c8.05] than *chen*. Another thing to note is that for the CEAF_e metric, the incremental drop in performance from the best to the next best and so on, is substantial, with a difference of 17 points between *chen* and *fernandes*. It does seem that the *chen* and *yuan* algorithm for linking is much better than the others.

7.2.4 Gold Test Parses

When provided with *gold parses* for the test set, there is a substantial increase in performance for the NB condition – numerically more so than in case of English. The degree of improvement decreases for the GB and GM conditions.

ID	Participant	Train		Test					MENTION DETECTION			COREFERENCE RESOLUTION															Official
		Syntax		Syntax		Mention Qlty.						MUC			BCUBED			CEAF$_m$			CEAF$_e$			BLANC			$\frac{F_1+F_2+F_3}{3}$
		A	G	A	G	NB	GB	GM	R	P	F	R	P	F_1	R	P	F_2	R	P	F	R	P	F_3	R	P	F	
e0.00	fernandes	■		■		■			72.75	83.45	77.73	65.83	75.91	70.51	65.79	77.69	71.24	61.94	61.94	61.94	55.00	43.17	48.37	77.35	78.07	77.70	63.37
e0.01	martschat	■		■		■			74.23	76.10	75.15	65.21	68.83	66.97	66.50	74.69	70.36	59.61	59.61	59.61	48.64	44.72	46.60	73.29	78.94	75.73	61.31
e0.02	björkelund	■		■		■			73.75	77.09	75.38	65.23	70.10	67.58	65.90	75.24	70.26	59.20	59.20	59.20	48.60	43.42	45.87	73.47	78.81	75.80	61.24
e0.03	chang	■		■		■			72.48	76.25	74.32	64.77	68.06	66.38	67.04	71.81	69.34	58.28	58.28	58.28	46.64	43.11	44.81	75.24	74.73	74.98	60.18
e0.04	chen	■		■		■			75.08	72.60	73.82	63.47	63.96	63.71	66.57	71.52	68.96	58.13	58.13	58.13	46.68	46.15	46.41	71.30	79.15	74.48	59.69
e0.05	stamborg	■		■		■			75.51	72.39	73.92	66.26	63.98	65.10	69.09	69.54	69.31	56.76	56.76	56.76	42.53	44.89	43.68	74.03	77.28	75.52	59.36
e0.06	chunyang	■		■		■			75.23	72.24	73.71	64.08	63.57	63.82	66.45	70.71	68.51	57.24	57.24	57.24	45.13	45.67	45.40	71.12	77.92	73.95	59.24
e0.07	yuan	■		■		■			73.19	71.88	72.53	62.08	63.02	62.55	66.23	70.45	68.27	57.28	57.28	57.28	45.74	44.74	45.23	72.05	76.86	74.16	58.68
e0.08	shou	■		■		■			75.35	72.08	73.68	63.46	62.39	62.92	65.31	68.90	67.05	55.68	55.68	55.68	44.20	45.35	44.77	69.43	75.08	71.81	58.25
e0.09	xu	■		■		■			62.64	84.55	71.96	59.11	75.18	66.18	62.28	73.29	67.34	53.19	53.19	53.19	48.29	32.64	38.95	75.16	68.37	70.95	57.49
e0.10	uryupina	■		■		■			71.82	69.96	70.88	61.00	60.78	60.89	63.59	68.48	65.95	52.44	52.44	52.44	41.42	41.64	41.53	67.40	72.83	69.65	56.12
e0.11	yang	■		■		■			64.28	73.99	68.79	55.29	65.20	59.84	60.38	72.74	65.99	51.90	51.90	51.90	45.20	35.95	40.05	68.69	71.66	70.03	55.29
e0.12	xinxin	■		■		■			73.93	54.55	62.78	55.48	42.72	48.27	66.93	56.67	61.37	44.83	44.83	44.83	31.68	43.55	36.68	64.77	66.14	65.42	48.77
e0.13	zhekova	■		■		■			65.78	68.49	67.11	54.28	52.79	53.52	62.26	54.90	58.35	43.54	43.54	43.54	33.52	34.96	34.22	67.23	58.77	60.63	48.70
e0.14	li	■		■		■			45.78	86.72	59.93	39.12	72.57	50.84	43.03	80.06	55.98	41.97	41.97	41.97	49.44	22.30	30.74	64.01	66.86	65.24	45.85
e1.00	fernandes	■			■	■			74.76	84.81	79.47	67.73	77.25	72.18	66.42	78.01	71.75	63.05	63.05	63.05	56.16	44.51	49.66	76.89	78.60	77.71	64.53
e1.01	martschat	■			■	■			76.87	77.33	77.10	67.90	70.37	69.11	67.83	75.34	71.39	60.92	60.92	60.92	49.38	46.61	47.96	74.07	79.77	76.54	62.82
e1.02	björkelund	■			■	■			75.53	77.86	76.68	67.00	71.17	69.02	66.56	75.71	70.84	59.90	59.90	59.90	49.22	44.68	46.84	73.42	80.19	76.27	62.23
e1.03	chen	■			■	■			77.13	75.15	76.13	66.30	66.99	66.65	67.73	72.77	70.16	59.70	59.70	59.70	47.99	47.21	47.60	72.63	80.08	75.70	61.47
e1.04	zhekova	■			■	■			66.05	69.62	67.79	54.45	53.59	54.02	61.66	55.62	58.48	43.71	43.71	43.71	33.82	34.65	34.23	66.84	59.27	61.20	48.91
e2.00	björkelund		■	■		■			76.23	72.64	74.39	66.50	65.22	65.85	68.45	71.01	69.71	58.35	58.35	58.35	44.85	46.21	45.52	74.36	77.29	75.72	60.36
e3.00	björkelund		■		■	■			78.68	73.83	76.18	68.96	66.73	67.83	69.70	71.47	70.58	59.55	59.55	59.55	45.55	47.97	46.73	74.98	77.92	76.35	61.71
e4.00	fernandes	■		■			■		71.91	85.29	78.03	64.92	77.53	70.67	64.25	78.95	70.85	61.59	61.59	61.59	56.48	41.69	47.97	76.28	77.87	77.05	63.16
e4.01	chang	■		■			■		72.01	79.83	75.72	64.58	71.36	67.80	66.07	73.87	69.75	58.51	58.51	58.51	49.14	41.71	45.12	75.92	73.95	74.88	60.89
e4.02	björkelund	■		■			■		71.95	78.97	75.30	63.44	71.63	67.29	63.95	76.59	69.70	58.48	58.48	58.48	50.00	41.35	45.27	73.05	78.99	75.59	60.75
e4.03	chen	■		■			■		74.78	75.70	75.24	63.26	66.78	64.97	65.38	73.56	69.23	58.57	58.57	58.57	48.81	44.92	46.79	71.85	80.22	75.20	60.33
e4.04	yuan	■		■			■		75.73	70.84	73.20	64.50	62.79	63.64	68.53	69.99	69.25	57.90	57.90	57.90	44.73	46.53	45.61	72.86	76.93	74.69	59.50
e4.05	stamborg	■		■			■		76.46	67.30	71.59	66.16	58.80	62.26	71.21	64.98	67.95	55.20	55.20	55.20	38.46	45.83	41.83	76.19	73.58	74.80	57.35
e4.06	xu	■		■			■		66.31	75.82	70.74	62.15	67.13	64.55	67.53	66.97	67.25	52.02	52.02	52.02	40.04	35.45	37.60	77.29	67.42	70.74	56.47
e4.07	zhekova	■		■			■		66.45	70.91	68.61	54.96	54.67	54.82	61.85	55.60	58.56	43.96	43.96	43.96	34.38	34.67	34.53	68.49	59.51	61.52	49.30
e4.08	li	■		■			■		60.00	44.47	51.08	44.17	33.66	38.21	66.37	53.93	59.51	39.30	39.30	39.30	27.53	36.51	31.39	63.26	60.00	61.33	43.04
e5.00	fernandes	■			■		■		72.69	86.11	78.83	65.65	78.26	71.40	64.36	79.09	70.97	62.00	62.00	62.00	57.36	42.23	48.65	75.89	78.28	77.02	63.67
e5.01	björkelund	■			■		■		73.24	79.25	76.13	64.75	72.29	68.31	64.62	77.01	70.27	59.20	59.20	59.20	50.45	42.36	46.05	73.22	80.28	76.17	61.54
e5.02	chen	■			■		■		75.59	76.58	76.08	64.67	68.07	66.33	66.09	74.02	69.83	59.38	59.38	59.38	49.36	45.55	47.38	72.09	80.41	75.43	61.18
e5.03	stamborg	■			■		■		77.17	67.14	71.81	66.88	58.82	62.59	71.55	64.97	68.10	55.30	55.30	55.30	38.28	46.34	41.93	76.16	73.62	74.81	57.54
e5.04	zhekova	■			■		■		65.82	71.72	68.65	54.68	55.51	55.09	61.22	56.59	58.82	43.90	43.90	43.90	34.85	34.04	34.44	68.10	59.76	61.79	49.45
e6.00	björkelund		■		■		■		76.26	75.47	75.86	66.55	68.00	67.27	67.60	73.05	70.22	59.04	59.04	59.04	46.99	45.42	46.19	74.60	78.38	76.32	61.23
e7.00	chang	■		■				■	100.00	100.00	100.00	83.16	88.48	85.74	75.36	79.69	77.46	73.76	73.76	73.76	75.38	62.71	68.46	81.23	78.99	80.05	77.22
e7.01	chen	■		■				■	80.82	100.00	89.39	72.29	89.40	79.94	64.60	85.92	73.75	68.35	68.35	68.35	76.25	46.40	57.69	75.41	84.80	79.12	70.46
e7.02	yuan	■		■				■	80.03	100.00	88.91	72.22	89.16	79.80	64.75	84.68	73.39	67.76	67.76	67.76	74.49	45.46	56.46	75.60	83.10	78.69	69.88
e7.03	fernandes	■		■				■	100.00	100.00	100.00	70.69	91.21	79.65	65.46	85.61	74.19	67.64	67.64	67.64	74.71	42.55	54.22	79.41	80.17	79.78	69.35
e7.04	stamborg	■		■				■	78.17	100.00	87.74	71.22	88.12	78.77	64.75	83.16	72.81	66.74	66.74	66.74	71.94	43.74	54.41	78.68	81.47	79.99	68.66
e7.05	björkelund	■		■				■	75.69	100.00	86.16	69.51	90.71	78.70	62.37	87.03	72.67	66.32	66.32	66.32	74.14	41.52	53.23	76.49	82.90	79.22	68.20
e7.06	xu	■		■				■	67.09	100.00	80.30	64.81	89.94	75.34	62.88	80.57	70.63	59.13	59.13	59.13	65.28	33.67	44.42	78.60	72.37	74.87	63.46
e7.07	zhekova	■		■				■	78.55	100.00	87.98	68.38	78.11	72.92	63.04	58.60	60.74	50.35	50.35	50.35	52.64	37.10	43.53	69.87	61.19	62.74	59.06
e7.08	li	■		■				■	57.18	99.99	72.75	48.04	81.51	60.45	44.13	81.21	57.18	47.82	47.82	47.82	61.82	25.98	36.58	65.26	69.93	67.12	51.40
e8.00	chen	■			■			■	81.46	100.00	89.78	73.22	89.69	80.62	65.32	85.87	74.20	68.87	68.87	68.87	76.43	47.26	58.40	75.66	84.84	79.31	71.07
e8.01	fernandes	■			■			■	100.00	100.00	100.00	71.18	91.24	79.97	65.81	85.51	74.38	67.83	67.83	67.83	74.93	43.09	54.72	79.65	80.31	79.97	69.69
e8.02	stamborg	■			■			■	78.83	100.00	88.16	71.96	88.40	79.33	65.31	83.28	73.21	67.26	67.26	67.26	72.29	44.48	55.07	78.92	81.59	80.17	69.20
e8.03	björkelund	■			■			■	76.94	100.00	86.97	70.66	91.15	79.60	62.90	87.56	73.21	66.90	66.90	66.90	74.88	42.65	54.35	76.42	84.43	79.71	69.05
e8.04	zhekova	■			■			■	78.73	100.00	88.10	68.54	78.10	73.01	63.14	58.63	60.80	50.61	50.61	50.61	52.84	37.44	43.83	70.28	61.55	63.23	59.21
e9.00	björkelund		■		■			■	79.55	100.00	88.61	72.59	90.04	80.38	64.94	85.72	73.89	68.14	68.14	68.14	74.77	45.27	56.40	78.23	83.31	80.48	70.22

Table 20: Performance of systems in the *primary* and *supplementary* evaluations for the *closed track* for English.

ID	Participant	Train		Test					MENTION DETECTION			COREFERENCE RESOLUTION															Official
		Syntax		Syntax		Mention Qlty.						MUC			BCUBED			CEAF$_m$			CEAF$_e$			BLANC			
		A	G	A	G	NB	GB	GM	R	P	F	R	P	F$_1$	R	P	F$_2$	R	P	F	R	P	F$_3$	R	P	F	$\frac{F_1+F_2+F_3}{3}$
c0.00	chen	■		■		■			71.12	72.16	71.64	59.92	64.69	62.21	69.73	77.81	73.55	62.18	62.18	62.18	53.43	48.73	50.97	72.79	84.53	77.34	62.24
c0.01	yuan	■		■		■			72.75	64.09	68.15	62.36	58.42	60.33	73.12	72.67	72.90	59.59	59.59	59.59	47.10	50.70	48.83	73.72	78.22	75.76	60.69
c0.02	björkelund	■		■		■			69.45	63.54	66.37	58.72	58.49	58.61	71.23	75.07	73.10	59.01	59.01	59.01	48.09	48.29	48.19	72.25	81.61	76.07	59.97
c0.03	xu	■		■		■			64.33	66.10	65.20	55.02	61.47	58.07	68.39	76.38	72.16	57.46	57.46	57.46	50.40	44.81	47.44	71.64	74.57	73.00	59.22
c0.04	fernandes	■		■		■			57.24	78.28	66.13	52.69	70.58	60.34	62.99	80.57	70.70	57.73	57.73	57.73	53.75	37.88	44.44	75.06	79.59	77.11	58.49
c0.05	stamborg	■		■		■			57.65	71.93	64.01	52.56	64.13	57.77	64.43	77.55	70.38	55.57	55.57	55.57	47.90	38.04	42.41	72.74	77.84	75.00	56.85
c0.06	uryupina	■		■		■			50.98	70.09	59.03	45.62	63.13	52.97	59.17	80.78	68.31	52.40	52.40	52.40	48.47	34.52	40.32	68.72	80.76	73.11	53.87
c0.07	martschat	■		■		■			48.49	74.02	58.60	42.71	67.80	52.41	55.37	85.24	67.13	51.30	51.30	51.30	51.81	32.46	39.92	63.96	82.81	69.18	53.15
c0.08	chunyang	■		■		■			61.11	62.12	61.61	50.02	49.64	49.83	65.81	65.50	65.66	49.88	49.88	49.88	39.84	40.17	40.00	67.12	65.83	66.45	51.83
c0.09	xinxin	■		■		■			55.68	56.09	55.89	47.64	48.55	48.09	66.16	70.60	68.31	49.92	49.92	49.92	39.26	38.53	38.89	69.48	73.91	71.44	51.76
c0.10	li	■		■		■			36.60	87.01	51.53	32.48	71.44	44.65	45.51	86.06	59.54	45.70	45.70	45.70	55.11	25.24	34.62	64.99	76.63	68.92	46.27
c0.11	chang	■		■		■			39.43	59.97	47.58	30.85	49.22	37.93	53.02	78.31	63.23	44.89	44.89	44.89	44.92	29.99	35.97	59.82	71.24	63.16	45.71
c0.12	zhekova	■		■		■			35.12	72.52	47.32	31.19	57.97	40.56	49.49	77.65	60.45	41.86	41.86	41.86	45.92	25.24	32.58	64.29	61.64	62.79	44.53
c1.00	chen	■			■	■			83.22	79.25	81.19	72.14	72.77	72.46	75.32	80.20	77.68	68.67	68.67	68.67	58.37	57.64	58.00	76.48	87.07	80.80	69.38
c1.01	yuan	■			■	■			83.69	70.33	76.43	73.73	65.50	69.38	77.97	74.37	76.13	64.77	64.77	64.77	49.99	58.38	53.86	77.12	79.84	78.41	66.46
c1.02	xu	■			■	■			75.02	73.07	74.03	65.95	69.28	67.58	73.28	77.65	75.40	62.53	62.53	62.53	53.90	50.72	52.26	76.50	75.17	75.81	65.08
c1.03	björkelund	■			■	■			77.77	68.03	72.57	66.76	63.36	65.01	74.21	75.84	75.02	62.17	62.17	62.17	49.74	52.92	51.28	74.38	82.36	77.77	63.77
c1.04	fernandes	■			■	■			63.83	81.73	71.68	59.35	74.49	66.07	66.31	81.43	73.10	61.19	61.19	61.19	55.97	41.50	47.66	78.11	81.28	79.60	62.28
c1.05	stamborg	■			■	■			63.07	75.21	68.61	58.32	67.95	62.76	67.47	78.54	72.58	58.98	58.98	58.98	49.80	41.15	45.06	76.29	80.09	78.05	60.13
c1.06	uryupina	■			■	■			56.61	71.38	63.14	50.74	64.53	56.81	61.78	80.11	69.76	54.59	54.59	54.59	48.94	37.49	42.45	70.37	80.87	74.42	56.34
c1.07	martschat	■			■	■			52.94	77.17	62.80	47.30	72.19	57.15	57.31	86.69	69.00	53.92	53.92	53.92	54.11	34.40	42.06	65.39	84.86	70.95	56.07
c1.08	chunyang	■			■	■			67.52	65.33	66.41	56.11	52.81	54.41	68.27	64.49	66.33	51.92	51.92	51.92	40.39	43.47	41.88	69.16	65.03	66.80	54.21
c1.09	xinxin	■			■	■			62.59	58.21	60.32	53.49	50.44	51.92	68.70	69.78	69.24	51.95	51.95	51.95	39.65	42.18	40.87	71.40	74.66	72.90	54.01
c1.10	yang	■			■	■			58.66	56.52	57.57	48.74	49.49	49.11	65.61	72.91	69.07	49.61	49.61	49.61	40.11	39.52	39.81	64.51	73.91	67.95	52.66
c1.11	li	■			■	■			40.34	89.74	55.66	34.85	73.77	47.33	46.00	86.06	59.95	46.79	46.79	46.79	56.58	25.77	35.42	66.01	77.39	69.96	47.57
c1.12	chang	■			■	■			43.28	62.16	51.03	33.36	50.29	40.11	53.96	77.60	63.65	45.94	45.94	45.94	45.06	31.10	36.80	60.40	71.57	63.79	46.85
c1.13	zhekova	■			■	■			37.84	74.84	50.27	33.95	60.29	43.44	50.95	77.28	61.41	43.34	43.34	43.34	46.68	26.13	33.50	65.98	62.15	63.73	46.12
c2.00	björkelund		■	■		■			74.86	55.07	63.46	61.06	48.92	54.32	76.08	67.35	71.45	57.39	57.39	57.39	42.39	53.10	47.15	73.42	77.96	75.48	57.64
c3.00	björkelund		■		■	■			85.29	59.87	70.36	70.92	54.07	61.36	79.51	67.83	73.21	60.80	60.80	60.80	43.61	59.31	50.26	76.26	78.94	77.53	61.61
c4.00	chen	■		■			■		81.99	78.97	80.45	70.76	72.12	71.43	74.37	79.91	77.04	67.87	67.87	67.87	57.95	56.41	57.17	75.95	86.75	80.32	68.55
c4.01	yuan	■		■			■		82.89	66.86	74.02	72.12	61.59	66.44	77.96	72.30	75.02	62.96	62.96	62.96	47.17	57.47	51.81	75.77	78.48	77.05	64.42
c4.02	xu	■		■			■		73.21	72.68	72.94	63.54	68.73	66.03	71.36	78.70	74.85	61.57	61.57	61.57	53.90	49.07	51.37	72.90	77.06	74.80	64.08
c4.03	björkelund	■		■			■		71.88	70.18	71.02	61.69	65.54	63.56	70.42	79.14	74.52	61.32	61.32	61.32	52.03	48.51	50.20	72.44	85.49	77.40	62.76
c4.04	fernandes	■		■			■		64.21	79.18	70.91	58.76	71.46	64.49	66.62	79.88	72.65	60.40	60.40	60.40	54.09	42.02	47.29	77.69	80.96	79.22	61.48
c4.05	stamborg	■		■			■		71.21	55.28	62.24	61.13	47.20	53.27	75.47	63.09	68.73	52.82	52.82	52.82	35.81	47.71	40.91	74.53	71.12	72.69	54.30
c4.06	zhekova	■		■			■		36.97	73.98	49.30	32.09	58.30	41.39	49.43	77.38	60.32	42.09	42.09	42.09	46.35	25.71	33.07	63.41	61.47	62.34	44.93
c4.07	li	■		■			■		68.22	41.88	51.90	52.56	30.62	38.70	76.15	48.52	59.27	41.06	41.06	41.06	25.14	43.51	31.86	67.82	58.70	61.47	43.28
c5.00	chen	■			■		■		83.22	79.25	81.19	72.14	72.77	72.46	75.32	80.20	77.68	68.67	68.67	68.67	58.37	57.64	58.00	76.48	87.07	80.80	69.38
c5.01	yuan	■			■		■		83.75	67.46	74.72	73.25	62.49	67.44	78.46	72.68	75.46	63.52	63.52	63.52	47.54	58.13	52.30	76.10	78.79	77.37	65.07
c5.02	björkelund	■			■		■		76.53	70.28	73.27	65.46	65.87	65.66	72.79	78.38	75.49	62.91	62.91	62.91	52.21	51.82	52.01	73.70	85.52	78.36	64.39
c5.03	fernandes	■			■		■		63.83	81.73	71.68	59.35	74.49	66.07	66.31	81.43	73.10	61.19	61.19	61.19	55.97	41.50	47.66	78.11	81.28	79.60	62.28
c5.04	stamborg	■			■		■		71.36	55.32	62.32	61.17	47.27	53.33	75.64	63.41	68.99	53.26	53.26	53.26	36.11	48.05	41.23	75.75	72.53	74.02	54.52
c5.05	zhekova	■			■		■		37.89	74.79	50.30	33.93	60.19	43.39	50.87	77.27	61.35	43.29	43.29	43.29	46.62	26.13	33.49	65.91	62.31	63.81	46.08
c5.06	li	■			■		■		74.10	40.23	52.14	56.15	28.50	37.81	79.00	43.67	56.25	39.32	39.32	39.32	22.49	45.72	30.15	68.12	57.08	59.83	41.40
c6.00	björkelund		■		■		■		84.09	61.19	70.83	69.85	55.71	61.98	78.57	69.93	74.00	61.52	61.52	61.52	45.23	58.43	50.99	75.38	81.33	78.02	62.32
c7.00	björkelund		■		■			■	81.07	100.00	89.55	72.72	92.28	81.34	69.47	91.38	78.93	72.24	72.24	72.24	81.32	52.45	63.77	77.30	89.40	82.09	74.68
c8.00	chen	■		■				■	84.72	100.00	91.73	76.60	92.41	83.77	72.95	91.43	81.15	75.83	75.83	75.83	83.56	57.86	68.38	79.21	91.38	84.09	77.77
c8.01	yuan	■		■				■	81.72	99.79	89.85	74.77	92.74	82.79	70.91	91.21	79.79	73.67	73.67	73.67	81.98	54.65	65.58	77.48	88.14	81.81	76.05
c8.02	björkelund	■		■				■	71.63	100.00	83.47	65.36	93.23	76.85	64.44	93.51	76.30	68.30	68.30	68.30	78.59	44.24	56.61	75.77	91.56	81.56	69.92
c8.03	xu	■		■				■	71.51	100.00	83.38	65.63	94.07	77.32	65.05	91.23	75.95	66.22	66.22	66.22	78.13	43.77	56.11	73.98	79.71	76.48	69.79
c8.04	stamborg	■		■				■	68.97	100.00	81.63	63.52	88.23	73.86	63.54	88.12	73.84	65.60	65.60	65.60	72.56	42.01	53.21	76.96	83.70	79.89	66.97
c8.05	fernandes	■		■				■	100.00	100.00	100.00	61.64	90.81	73.43	63.55	89.43	74.30	65.10	65.10	65.10	72.78	39.68	51.36	80.21	83.39	81.71	66.36
c8.06	li	■		■				■	63.59	99.95	77.73	55.28	82.28	66.13	55.95	82.99	66.84	57.50	57.50	57.50	66.76	36.06	46.83	70.53	77.67	73.47	59.93
c8.07	zhekova	■		■				■	47.53	100.00	64.43	42.02	79.57	55.00	50.22	80.81	61.94	46.88	46.88	46.88	60.27	27.08	37.37	68.60	63.62	65.58	51.44
c9.00	chen	■			■			■	85.92	100.00	92.42	77.88	92.85	84.71	74.02	91.67	81.91	76.76	76.76	76.76	84.33	59.45	69.74	79.63	91.55	84.45	78.79
c9.01	yuan	■			■			■	82.58	99.80	90.38	75.69	93.06	83.48	71.62	91.39	80.30	74.23	74.23	74.23	82.40	55.60	66.40	77.77	88.30	82.06	76.73
c9.02	björkelund	■			■			■	75.93	100.00	86.32	68.94	93.76	79.46	66.88	93.48	77.97	70.30	70.30	70.30	80.53	47.73	59.93	76.06	91.11	81.66	72.45
c9.03	stamborg	■			■			■	69.08	100.00	81.71	63.52	88.24	73.87	63.56	88.56	74.00	65.89	65.89	65.89	72.93	42.22	53.48	77.43	85.65	80.91	67.12
c9.04	fernandes	■			■			■	100.00	100.00	100.00	61.70	91.45	73.69	63.57	89.76	74.43	65.06	65.06	65.06	72.84	39.49	51.21	80.08	83.21	81.55	66.44
c9.05	li	■			■			■	68.68	100.00	81.43	58.88	81.04	68.20	58.37	80.25	67.59	58.74	58.74	58.74	66.44	38.85	49.03	71.31	76.92	73.72	61.61
c9.06	zhekova	■			■			■	48.82	100.00	65.61	44.12	80.89	57.10	51.79	80.53	63.04	47.84	47.84	47.84	60.37	27.69	37.96	70.49	64.06	66.45	52.70

Table 21: Performance of systems in the *primary* and *supplementary* evaluations for the *closed track* for Chinese.

ID	Participant	Train Syntax A	Train Syntax G	Test Syntax A	Test Syntax G	Test Mention Qlty. NB	Test Mention Qlty. GB	Test Mention Qlty. GM	MENTION DETECTION R	MENTION DETECTION P	MENTION DETECTION F	MUC R	MUC P	MUC F_1	BCUBED R	BCUBED P	BCUBED F_2	CEAF$_m$ R	CEAF$_m$ P	CEAF$_m$ F	CEAF$_e$ R	CEAF$_e$ P	CEAF$_e$ F_3	BLANC R	BLANC P	BLANC F	Official $\frac{F_1+F_2+F_3}{3}$
a0.00	fernandes	■		■		■			62.72	67.00	64.79	43.63	49.69	46.46	62.70	72.19	67.11	55.59	55.59	55.59	52.49	46.09	49.08	63.98	71.91	66.97	54.22
a0.01	björkelund	■		■		■			56.78	64.86	60.55	43.90	52.51	47.82	62.89	75.32	68.54	53.42	53.42	53.42	48.45	40.80	44.30	66.45	74.61	69.63	53.55
a0.02	uryupina	■		■		■			56.47	54.35	55.39	41.33	41.66	41.49	65.77	69.23	67.46	50.82	50.82	50.82	42.43	42.13	42.28	65.58	70.56	67.69	50.41
a0.03	stamborg	■		■		■			56.10	63.28	59.47	39.11	43.49	41.18	61.57	67.95	64.61	50.16	50.16	50.16	44.86	40.36	42.49	66.80	66.94	66.87	49.43
a0.04	chen	■		■		■			56.16	63.95	59.80	38.13	39.96	39.02	60.59	62.51	61.53	47.49	47.49	47.49	41.89	39.84	40.84	66.45	61.84	63.69	47.13
a0.05	zhekova	■		■		■			27.54	80.34	41.02	19.64	62.13	29.85	41.91	90.72	57.33	42.74	42.74	42.74	56.79	24.81	34.53	57.10	79.19	60.65	40.57
a0.06	li	■		■		■			18.17	80.43	29.65	10.77	55.60	18.05	36.17	93.34	52.14	37.03	37.03	37.03	55.45	20.95	30.41	52.91	73.93	54.12	33.53
a1.00	fernandes	■			■	■			65.03	68.71	66.82	46.38	51.78	48.93	63.53	72.37	67.66	56.49	56.49	56.49	52.57	46.88	49.56	64.84	72.97	67.94	55.38
a1.01	björkelund	■			■	■			58.33	64.60	61.30	45.14	52.15	48.39	63.73	74.45	68.68	53.52	53.52	53.52	47.78	41.53	44.44	66.81	73.83	69.65	53.84
a1.12	chen	■			■	■			56.41	63.41	59.70	38.22	39.57	38.89	60.91	62.06	61.48	47.73	47.73	47.73	41.80	40.27	41.02	66.70	61.86	63.78	47.13
a1.13	zhekova	■			■	■			28.00	82.21	41.78	15.47	45.92	23.15	39.22	84.86	53.65	39.52	39.52	39.52	55.10	24.22	33.65	54.13	61.78	55.63	36.82
a2.00	björkelund		■	■		■			61.88	62.52	62.20	46.11	47.66	46.87	65.83	69.74	67.73	53.77	53.77	53.77	45.82	44.33	45.06	67.69	70.71	69.06	53.22
a3.00	björkelund		■		■	■			67.07	62.44	64.67	51.57	49.76	50.65	69.53	69.88	69.71	56.21	56.21	56.21	46.26	47.98	47.11	71.09	72.67	71.85	55.82
a4.00	fernandes	■		■			■		65.34	64.82	65.08	45.18	47.39	46.26	64.56	69.44	66.91	54.88	54.88	54.88	49.73	47.39	48.53	64.28	70.09	66.64	53.90
a4.01	björkelund	■		■			■		57.77	63.74	60.61	44.78	51.47	47.90	63.75	74.27	68.61	53.18	53.18	53.18	47.16	41.24	44.00	66.94	73.43	69.61	53.50
a4.02	stamborg	■		■			■		57.43	64.62	60.81	40.22	44.17	42.10	61.45	67.24	64.22	49.92	49.92	49.92	44.60	40.50	42.46	66.79	66.08	66.42	49.59
a4.03	chen	■		■			■		57.21	62.55	59.76	38.66	39.24	38.95	61.52	61.77	61.65	47.84	47.84	47.84	41.55	40.90	41.22	66.78	61.94	63.87	47.27
a4.04	zhekova	■		■			■		27.48	75.53	40.29	18.75	56.47	28.16	42.67	89.25	57.74	42.57	42.57	42.57	55.53	25.36	34.82	56.61	76.35	59.86	40.24
a4.05	li	■		■			■		52.95	20.71	29.78	20.62	7.78	11.30	79.37	41.21	54.25	33.68	33.68	33.68	21.73	42.87	28.84	54.04	51.10	51.46	31.46
a5.00	fernandes	■			■		■		65.03	68.71	66.82	46.38	51.78	48.93	63.53	72.37	67.66	56.49	56.49	56.49	52.57	46.88	49.56	64.84	72.97	67.94	55.38
a5.01	björkelund	■			■		■		58.29	64.63	61.30	45.14	52.20	48.41	63.71	74.50	68.68	53.52	53.52	53.52	47.80	41.51	44.44	66.81	73.84	69.65	53.84
a5.02	stamborg	■			■		■		57.68	64.18	60.76	40.53	43.98	42.18	61.70	66.75	64.13	49.55	49.55	49.55	44.01	40.47	42.16	65.23	64.89	65.06	49.49
a5.03	chen	■			■		■		56.41	63.45	59.72	38.22	39.59	38.89	60.90	62.07	61.48	47.73	47.73	47.73	41.81	40.26	41.02	66.70	61.86	63.78	47.13
a5.04	zhekova	■			■		■		28.06	82.39	41.87	15.56	46.18	23.28	39.23	84.95	53.67	39.52	39.52	39.52	55.10	24.20	33.63	54.15	61.95	55.66	36.86
a6.00	björkelund		■		■				67.04	62.47	64.67	51.57	49.80	50.67	69.52	69.92	69.72	56.21	56.21	56.21	46.27	47.95	47.10	71.10	72.70	71.86	55.83
a7.00	fernandes	■		■				■	100.00	100.00	100.00	57.25	76.48	65.48	60.27	79.81	68.68	62.56	62.56	62.56	72.61	46.00	56.32	69.03	74.87	71.49	63.49
a7.01	björkelund	■		■				■	61.85	100.00	76.43	49.57	78.62	60.81	55.55	85.35	67.29	59.50	59.50	59.50	70.28	37.99	49.32	70.69	80.85	74.61	59.14
a7.02	zhekova	■		■				■	57.95	100.00	73.38	42.48	80.36	55.58	50.87	89.69	64.92	55.42	55.42	55.42	71.96	34.52	46.66	61.36	82.00	66.12	55.72
a7.03	stamborg	■		■				■	56.13	100.00	71.90	41.99	69.78	52.43	50.45	81.30	62.26	54.00	54.00	54.00	66.16	34.52	45.37	67.37	73.46	69.87	53.35
a7.04	chen	■		■				■	58.29	100.00	73.65	41.72	63.23	50.28	50.00	75.25	60.08	53.16	53.16	53.16	64.60	36.24	46.43	67.15	66.65	66.90	52.26
a7.05	li	■		■				■	35.67	100.00	52.58	22.43	64.62	33.31	38.67	88.07	53.74	42.25	42.25	42.25	60.95	24.36	34.81	55.64	68.52	57.96	40.62
a8.00	fernandes	■			■			■	100.00	100.00	100.00	56.89	76.27	65.17	60.07	80.02	68.62	62.62	62.62	62.62	72.24	45.58	55.90	69.35	75.51	71.93	63.23
a8.01	björkelund	■			■			■	61.05	100.00	75.81	49.17	78.31	60.41	55.51	85.40	67.28	59.41	59.41	59.41	70.01	37.71	49.02	70.97	80.92	74.84	58.90
a8.02	zhekova	■			■			■	65.68	100.00	79.29	45.58	73.27	56.20	52.27	82.35	63.95	55.11	55.11	55.11	70.17	37.54	48.91	59.94	72.07	63.28	56.35
a8.03	stamborg	■			■			■	56.72	100.00	72.38	42.88	70.42	53.30	51.17	80.83	62.67	54.12	54.12	54.12	66.21	34.85	45.66	67.10	72.32	69.29	53.88
a8.04	chen	■			■			■	58.26	100.00	73.63	41.81	63.28	50.36	50.10	75.19	60.13	53.19	53.19	53.19	64.59	36.27	46.46	67.19	66.52	66.85	52.32
a9.00	björkelund		■		■			■	68.50	100.00	81.30	55.21	78.84	64.94	59.85	83.75	69.81	63.12	63.12	63.12	72.24	42.75	53.71	73.35	80.61	76.41	62.82

Table 22: Performance of systems in the *primary* and *supplementary* evaluations for the *closed track* for Arabic.

7.3 Arabic *Closed*

Table 22 shows the performance for the Arabic language in greater detail.

7.3.1 Official Setting

Unlike English and Chinese, none of the system was particularly tuned for Arabic. This gives us an unique opportunity to test the performance variation of a mostly statistical, roughly language independent mechanism. Although, there could possibly be a significant bias that Arabic language brings to the mix. The overall performance for Arabic seems to be about ten points below both English and Chinese. On the mention detection front, most of the systems have a balanced precision and recall, and the drop in performance seems quite steady. *björkelund* has a slight edge on *fernandes* on the MUC, BCUBED and BLANC metrics, but *fernandes* has a much larger lead on both the CEAF metrics, putting it on the top in the official score. We haven't reported the development set numbers here, but another thing to note especially for Arabic is that performance on Arabic test set is significantly better than on the development set as pointed out by *björkelund*. This is probably because of the smaller size of the training set and therefore a higher relative increment over training set. The size of the training set (which is roughly about a third of either Engish or Chinese) also could itself be a factor that explains the lower performance, and that Arabic performance might gain from more data. *chen* did not use development data for the final models. Using that could have increased their score.

7.3.2 Gold Mention Boundaries

The system performance given gold boundaries followed more of the trend in English than Chinese. There was not much improvement over the primary NB evaluation. Interestingly, *chen* uses *gold boundaries* for Chinese so well, but does not get any performance improvement. This might indicate that the technique that helped that system in Chinese does not generalize well across languages.

7.3.3 Gold Mentions

Performance given *gold mentions* seems to be about ten points higher than in the NB case. *björkelund* does well on BLANC metric than *fernandes* even after getting a big hit in recall for mention detection. In absence of *chang*, it seems like *fernandes* is the only one that explicitly adds a constraint for the GM case and gets a perfect mention detection score. All other systems loose significantly on recall.

7.3.4 Gold Test Parses

Finally, providing gold parses during testing does not have much of an impact on the scores.

7.4 All Languages *Open*

Tables 24, 25 and 26, give the performance for the systems that participated in the open track. Not many systems participated in this track, so there is not a lot to observe. One thing to note is that *chen* modified precise constructs sieve to add named entity information in the open track sieve which gave them a point improvement in performance. With *gold mentions* and *gold syntax* during testing the *chen* system performance almost approaches an F-score of 80 (79.79)

7.5 Headword-based and Genre specific scores

Since last year's task showed that there was only some very local difference in ranking between systems scored using the strict boundaries versus the ones using headword based scoring, we did not compute the headword based evaluation.

Owing to space constraints, we cannot present a detailed analysis of the variation across genre. However, since genre variation is important to note, we present the performance of the highest performing system across all the three languages and genres in Table 23. For each language there are three logical performance blocks: i) The *official*, predicted version, with no provided boundaries is the first block; ii) The *supplementary* version with *gold mention boundaries* is the second block; and iii) The third block shows the performance for the *supplementary* version given *gold mentions*.

Looking at the Engish performance on the *official, closed* track, there seems to be a cluster of genre – BC, BN, NW and WB – where the performance is very close to a score of 60. Whereas, genres TC, MZ and PT are increasingly better. Surprisingly, a simplistic look at the individual metrics does indicate a similar trend, except for the CEAF$_e$ score for the TC and WB being somewhat reversed. It so happens that these the two genres — MZ and PT – are professional human translations from a foreign language. As seen earlier, there is not a huge shift in performance when the systems are provided with *gold mention boundaries*. However, when provided with *gold mentions* there is a big improvement in performance across the board. Especially so with MZ genre for which the improvement is more than double (9.5 points) over the improvement in PT genre (3.5 points) with the most notable improvement (of 5 points) in the CEAF$_e$ metric, which also is another indication that this metric does a good job of rewarding correct anaphoric mentions.

Looking at the Chinese performance, we see that the NW genre does particularly worse than all others on the *official, closed* track. The BC genre does somewhat worse than WB, MZ, and TC all of which seem to be around the same ballpark, with BN leading the pack. Again, provided *gold mention bound-*

Genre	Train Syntax		Test Syntax		Test Mention Qlty.			MD	COREFERENCE RESOLUTION MUC	BCUBED	$CEAF_m$	$CEAF_e$	BLANC	Official
	A	G	A	G	NB	GB	GM	F	F_1	F_2	F	F_3	F	$\frac{F_1+F_2+F_3}{3}$
ENGLISH														
Pivot Text [PT]	■		■		■			89.13	82.49	72.66	68.92	54.47	79.20	69.87
Magazine [MZ]	■		■		■			77.70	69.57	77.29	68.88	57.07	81.84	67.98
Telephone Conversation [TC]	■		■		■			79.95	76.75	72.31	62.06	43.22	79.24	64.09
Weblogs and Newsgroups [WB]	■		■		■			78.21	71.66	68.61	59.42	45.24	76.42	61.84
Broadcast News [BN]	■		■		■			74.60	65.15	70.60	60.90	49.52	74.45	61.76
Brodcast Conversation [BC]	■		■		■			75.67	67.54	69.14	57.70	44.99	76.74	60.56
Newswire [NW]	■		■		■			71.24	62.67	71.01	60.61	47.73	75.40	60.47
Pivot Text [PT]	■		■			■		89.50	82.74	72.65	68.98	54.28	79.42	69.89
Magazine [MZ]	■		■			■		77.27	68.68	76.53	67.51	55.63	79.72	66.95
Telephone Conversation [TC]	■		■			■		81.95	78.18	72.53	63.33	44.32	77.99	65.01
Weblogs and Newsgroups [WB]	■		■			■		79.08	72.62	68.94	60.09	45.74	76.46	62.43
Broadcast News [BN]	■		■			■		75.10	65.56	69.98	60.47	49.14	74.10	61.56
Brodcast Conversation [BC]	■		■			■		75.96	67.64	68.51	57.14	44.85	74.81	60.33
Newswire [NW]	■		■			■		70.44	61.63	70.04	59.44	46.57	73.51	59.41
Magazine [MZ]	■		■				■	100.00	82.87	83.10	78.02	66.93	87.00	77.63
Pivot Text [PT]	■		■				■	100.00	86.20	74.30	71.67	59.43	80.12	73.31
Telephone Conversation [TC]	■		■				■	100.00	84.74	75.18	66.29	49.68	77.37	69.87
Weblogs and Newsgroups [WB]	■		■				■	100.00	82.38	71.43	66.08	53.28	77.96	69.03
Newswire [NW]	■		■				■	100.00	74.00	74.41	67.39	53.28	81.03	67.23
Broadcast News [BN]	■		■				■	100.00	74.51	73.31	65.71	52.96	79.15	66.93
Brodcast Conversation [BC]	■		■				■	100.00	77.52	71.49	63.73	50.54	79.59	66.52
CHINESE														
Broadcast News [BN]	■		■		■			78.02	71.71	78.80	68.93	55.87	83.85	68.79
Weblogs and Newsgroups [WB]	■		■		■			79.29	71.30	71.05	60.68	46.81	80.94	63.05
Magazine [MZ]	■		■		■			75.34	70.26	72.32	62.63	46.42	81.34	63.00
Telephone Conversation [TC]	■		■		■			79.79	72.58	71.14	61.16	43.78	76.82	62.50
Brodcast Conversation [BC]	■		■		■			73.80	64.22	67.68	55.38	42.89	72.98	58.26
Newswire [NW]	■		■		■			52.38	49.74	67.97	54.82	43.79	75.63	53.83
Broadcast News [BN]	■		■			■		78.02	71.71	78.80	68.93	55.87	83.85	68.79
Weblogs and Newsgroups [WB]	■		■			■		79.29	71.30	71.05	60.68	46.81	80.94	63.05
Magazine [MZ]	■		■			■		75.34	70.26	72.32	62.63	46.42	81.34	63.00
Telephone Conversation [TC]	■		■			■		79.79	72.58	71.14	61.16	43.78	76.82	62.50
Brodcast Conversation [BC]	■		■			■		73.80	64.22	67.68	55.38	42.89	72.98	58.26
Newswire [NW]	■		■			■		52.38	49.74	67.97	54.82	43.79	75.63	53.83
Broadcast News [BN]	■		■				■	100.00	81.03	81.34	75.07	62.99	86.18	75.12
Telephone Conversation [TC]	■		■				■	100.00	87.31	77.80	71.01	59.44	78.78	74.85
Weblogs and Newsgroups [WB]	■		■				■	100.00	80.36	72.46	64.49	51.93	81.10	68.25
Magazine [MZ]	■		■				■	100.00	75.18	73.12	65.90	48.81	84.17	65.70
Brodcast Conversation [BC]	■		■				■	100.00	76.42	70.01	61.75	49.81	74.14	65.41
Newswire [NW]	■		■				■	100.00	51.42	67.83	55.29	43.81	76.53	54.35
ARABIC														
Newswire [NW]	■		■		■			64.79	46.46	67.11	55.59	49.08	66.97	54.22
Newswire [NW]	■		■			■		65.08	46.26	66.91	54.88	48.53	66.64	53.90
Newswire [NW]	■		■				■	100.00	65.48	68.68	62.56	56.32	71.49	63.49

Table 23: Per genre performance for *fernandes* on the *closed*, *official* and *supplementary* evaluations.

aries there is very little or no change in performance. And, when given the *gold mentions* the performance again shoots up by a significant margin. Here again, we see that the delta improvement in one particular genre TC – is much higher (12 points) than in BN (6 points), and once again the most improvement among all the metrics happens to be for the $CEAF_e$. Extremely surprising is the fact that the NW genre shows the lowest improvement among all genre. In fact, the performance drops for the BCUBED metric. This might have something to do with the fact that Chinese NW genre gets the lowest ITA among all other (see Table 1), but then the better scoring TC genre which has the second lowest ITA does considerably better (leading by roughly 10 points in the *official* setting, and 20 points in the *gold mentions* settings with respect to the TC genre). It could also be possible that this has something to do with the fact (and pointed out earlier when discussing *chen*'s results) that there is some overlapping mentions that were mistakenly included in the release.

As for Arabic, since there was only one NW genre, there is nothing more to be analyzed. We plan to report more detailed tables and analysis on the task webpage.

8 Comparison with CoNLL-2011

Table 27 shows the performance of the systems on CoNLL-2011 test subset which included only the English portion of OntoNotes v4.0. For the English subset, the size of training data in CoNLL-2011 was roughly 76% of CoNLL-2012 training data (1M vs 1.3M words respectively). Although the models used to generate this table were trained on the CoNLL-2012 English data and therefore on about 200K more words, it is still a small fraction of the total training data. In the past, coreference scores have shown to asymptote after a small fraction of the total training data. Therefore, the 5% absolute gap between the best performing systems of last year can be attributed to algorithmic improvement, and possibly better rules. Given that a 200K data addition to a 1M word corpus is unlikely to help identify novel rules, and given that *björkelund* reported adding (about 160K) development data (to the training portion) to train the final model had very little improvement in performance over using just the training data by itself, the possibility that the gain is from algorithmic improvements seems even more plausible.

It is interesting to note that although the winning

Participant	Train Syntax		Test Syntax		Test Mention Qlty.			MENTION DETECTION			COREFERENCE RESOLUTION MUC			BCUBED			CEAF$_m$			CEAF$_e$			BLANC			Official
	A	G	A	G	NB	GB	GM	R	P	F	R	P	F$_1$	R	P	F$_2$	R	P	F	R	P	F$_3$	R	P	F	$\frac{F_1+F_2+F_3}{3}$
xiong	■		■		■			75.22	72.23	73.69	64.08	63.57	63.82	66.47	70.69	68.52	57.23	57.23	57.23	45.09	45.64	45.36	71.12	77.90	73.94	59.23
xiong	■			■	■			77.85	73.44	75.58	67.03	65.27	66.14	68.03	71.14	69.55	58.58	58.58	58.58	45.60	47.53	46.54	72.03	78.58	74.78	60.74

Table 24: Performance of systems in the *primary* and *supplementary* evaluations for the *open* track for English.

Participant	Train Syntax		Test Syntax		Test Mention Qlty.			MENTION DETECTION			COREFERENCE RESOLUTION MUC			BCUBED			CEAF$_m$			CEAF$_e$			BLANC			Official
	A	G	A	G	NB	GB	GM	R	P	F	R	P	F$_1$	R	P	F$_2$	R	P	F	R	P	F$_3$	R	P	F	$\frac{F_1+F_2+F_3}{3}$
chen	■		■		■			71.45	73.45	72.44	62.48	67.08	64.70	71.21	78.35	74.61	63.48	63.48	63.48	53.64	49.10	51.27	75.15	84.29	78.94	63.53
yuan	■		■		■			73.71	63.97	68.49	63.67	58.48	60.96	74.04	72.16	73.09	60.05	60.05	60.05	46.75	51.52	49.02	74.32	77.99	76.02	61.02
xiong	■		■		■			39.47	67.55	49.82	30.00	51.20	37.83	49.37	77.45	60.30	42.71	42.71	42.71	46.10	28.12	34.93	57.98	67.08	60.59	44.35
chen	■			■	■			83.50	80.44	81.95	74.77	74.93	74.85	77.14	80.80	78.93	70.13	70.13	70.13	58.64	58.46	58.55	78.87	86.63	82.24	70.78
yuan	■			■	■			83.92	69.85	76.24	74.24	65.11	69.37	78.61	73.74	76.10	64.84	64.84	64.84	49.41	58.70	53.66	77.60	79.45	78.49	66.38
xiong	■			■	■			42.78	71.10	53.42	32.57	53.89	40.60	49.50	77.38	60.37	43.66	43.66	43.66	47.04	28.83	35.75	58.24	67.37	60.90	45.57
chen	■		■			■		82.39	80.11	81.24	73.50	74.28	73.88	76.30	80.49	78.34	69.40	69.40	69.40	58.22	57.32	57.77	78.44	86.39	81.88	70.00
chen	■			■		■		83.50	80.44	81.95	74.77	74.93	74.85	77.14	80.80	78.93	70.13	70.13	70.13	58.64	58.46	58.55	78.87	86.63	82.24	70.78
chen	■		■				■	84.80	100.00	91.77	78.12	93.19	84.99	75.04	91.59	82.50	77.50	77.50	77.50	84.03	59.17	69.44	81.46	90.73	85.41	78.98
chen	■			■			■	85.71	100.00	92.31	79.07	93.59	85.72	75.83	91.94	83.11	78.26	78.26	78.26	84.77	60.42	70.55	81.71	91.00	85.67	79.79

Table 25: Performance of systems in the *primary* and *supplementary* evaluations for the *open* track for Chinese.

Participant	Train Syntax		Test Syntax		Test Mention Qlty.			MENTION DETECTION			COREFERENCE RESOLUTION MUC			BCUBED			CEAF$_m$			CEAF$_e$			BLANC			Official
	A	G	A	G	NB	GB	GM	R	P	F	R	P	F$_1$	R	P	F$_2$	R	P	F	R	P	F$_3$	R	P	F	$\frac{F_1+F_2+F_3}{3}$
xiong	■		■		■			55.08	52.75	53.89	28.20	28.43	28.31	60.89	62.81	61.83	47.31	47.31	47.31	43.12	42.82	42.97	57.05	60.75	58.46	44.37
xiong	■			■	■			57.55	52.98	55.17	30.99	30.10	30.54	62.16	62.55	62.36	47.73	47.73	47.73	42.48	43.59	43.03	57.78	61.39	59.20	45.31

Table 26: Performance of systems in the *primary* and *supplementary* evaluations for the *open* track for Arabic.

Participant	Train Syntax		Test Syntax		Test Mention Qlty.			MENTION DETECTION			COREFERENCE RESOLUTION MUC			BCUBED			CEAF$_m$			CEAF$_e$			BLANC			Official
	A	G	A	G	NB	GB	GM	R	P	F	R	P	F$_1$	R	P	F$_2$	R	P	F	R	P	F$_3$	R	P	F	$\frac{F_1+F_2+F_3}{3}$
2011 best	■		■		■			75.07	66.81	70.70	61.76	57.53	59.57	68.40	68.23	68.31	56.37	56.37	56.37	43.41	47.75	45.48	70.63	76.21	73.02	57.79
fernandes	■		■		■			70.12	81.27	75.28	62.74	73.46	67.68	65.03	78.05	70.95	60.61	60.61	60.61	54.18	42.50	47.63	75.31	78.53	76.80	62.09
martschat	■		■		■			71.96	73.57	72.76	62.80	66.23	64.47	67.09	74.50	70.60	58.84	58.84	58.84	48.05	44.55	46.23	73.17	78.04	75.32	60.43
björkelund	■		■		■			70.99	74.91	72.90	62.25	67.72	64.87	65.66	75.32	70.16	57.99	57.99	57.99	48.12	42.67	45.23	72.81	77.64	74.94	60.09
chang	■		■		■			69.94	73.36	71.61	62.51	65.54	63.99	67.76	71.97	69.80	57.49	57.49	57.49	45.86	42.82	44.29	75.35	74.13	74.72	59.36
chen	■		■		■			73.13	69.56	71.30	60.84	60.70	60.77	67.34	71.37	69.30	57.47	57.47	57.47	45.98	46.13	46.05	70.89	78.69	74.06	58.71
stamborg	■		■		■			72.83	69.78	71.27	63.47	61.16	62.29	69.10	69.19	69.14	55.37	55.37	55.37	41.89	44.13	42.98	72.86	75.67	74.16	58.14
chunyang	■		■		■			73.14	69.31	71.17	61.78	60.57	61.17	67.43	70.31	68.84	56.62	56.62	56.62	44.48	45.70	45.08	71.31	76.91	73.72	58.36
yuan	■		■		■			70.44	68.87	69.64	58.99	60.09	59.53	66.66	71.38	68.94	56.95	56.95	56.95	45.48	44.38	44.92	72.20	78.69	74.95	57.80
shou	■		■		■			73.26	69.16	71.15	61.02	59.24	60.12	66.14	68.34	67.22	54.88	54.88	54.88	43.52	45.35	44.42	69.00	73.39	70.92	57.25
xu	■		■		■			58.90	82.61	68.77	55.14	73.28	62.93	60.50	75.93	67.35	52.81	52.81	52.81	48.71	32.17	38.75	72.80	70.05	71.30	56.34
uryupina	■		■		■			69.64	66.80	68.19	58.92	57.72	58.31	65.05	68.26	66.62	52.25	52.25	52.25	40.71	41.83	41.26	68.07	72.25	69.89	55.40
yang	■		■		■			61.51	70.97	65.90	52.15	61.88	56.60	60.37	73.02	66.09	51.07	51.07	51.07	44.69	35.98	39.87	66.20	71.27	68.29	54.19
xinxin	■		■		■			71.16	50.98	59.40	52.88	39.37	45.13	68.73	56.16	61.81	44.68	44.68	44.68	31.27	43.50	36.38	65.71	64.79	65.23	47.77
zhekova	■		■		■			63.16	65.73	64.42	50.64	49.51	50.07	61.71	56.53	59.01	43.40	43.40	43.40	34.01	35.09	34.54	65.49	58.37	60.21	47.87
li	■		■		■			43.39	84.81	57.40	36.45	70.53	48.06	43.11	81.37	56.36	41.88	41.88	41.88	49.52	22.69	31.12	62.31	67.02	64.12	45.18

Table 27: Performance of all the systems on the CoNLL-2011 portion (English) of the CoNLL-2012 test set.

system in the CoNLL-2011 task was a completely rule-based one, modified version of the same system used by *shou* and *xiong* ranked close to 10. This does indicate that a hybrid approach has some advantage over a purely rule-based system. Improvement seems to be mostly owing to higher precision in mention detection, MUC, BCUBED, and higher recall in CEAF_e

9 Conclusions

In this paper we described the anaphoric coreference information and other layers of annotation in the OntoNotes corpus, over three languages — English, Chinese and Arabic — and presented the results from an evaluation on learning such unrestricted entities and events in text. The following represents our conclusions on reviewing the results:

- Most top performing systems used a hybrid-approach combining rule-based strategies with machine learning. Rule-based approach does seem to bring a system to a close-to-best performance region. The most significant advantage of the rule-based approach seems to be that it captures most confident links before considering less confident ones. Discourse information when present is quite helpful to disambiguate pronominal mentions. Using information from appositives and copular constructions seems beneficial to bridge across various lexicalized mentions. It is not clear how much more can be gained using further strategies. The features for coreference prediction are certainly more complex than for many other language processing tasks, which makes it more challenging to generate effective feature combinations.
- Most top performing systems did significant feature engineering – expecially a heavy use of lexicalized features, which was possible given the size of the corpus, and performed feature selection.
- It might be possible that the Chinese accuracy with gold boundaries and mentions is better because the distribution of mentions across the various genres is different, and if there are more mentions in better scoring genres, then the performance would improve overall.
- Gold parse during testing does seem to help quite a bit. Gold boundaries are not of much significance for English and Arabic, but seem to be very useful for Chinese. The reason probably has some roots in the parser performance gap for Chinese.
- It does seem that collecting information about an entity by merging information across the various attributes of the mentions that comprise it can be useful, though not all systems that attempted this achieved a benefit, and has to be done carefully.
- It is noteworthy that systems did not seem to attempt the kind of joint inference that could make use of the full potential of various layers available in OntoNotes, but this could well have been owing to the limited time available for the shared task.
- We had expected to see more attention paid to event coreference, which is a novel feature in this data, but again, given the time constraints and given that events represent only a small portion of the total, it is not surprising that most systems chose not to focus on it.
- Scoring coreference seems to remain a significant challenge. There does not seem to be an objective way to establish one metric in preference to another in the absence of a specific application. On the other hand, the system rankings do not seem terribly sensitive to the particular metric chosen. It is interesting that the CEAF_e metric — which tries to capture the goodness of the entities in the output — seem much lower than the other metric, though it is not clear whether that means that our systems are doing a poor job of creating coherent entities or whether that metric is just especially harsh.

Acknowledgments

We gratefully acknowledge the support of the Defense Advanced Research Projects Agency (DARPA/IPTO) under the GALE program, DARPA/CMO Contract No. HR0011-06-C-0022. We would like to thank all the participants. Without their hard work, patience and perseverance this evaluation would not have been a success. We would also like to thank the Linguistic Data Consortium for making the OntoNotes v5.0 corpus freely and timely available in training/development/test sets to the participants. Emili Sapena, who graciously allowed the use of his scorer implementation. Hwee Tou Ng and his student Zhi Zhong for training the word sense models and providing outputs for the training/development and test sets. Slav Petrov and Dan Klein for letting us use their parser. Additionally, we are indebted to Slav for his help in retraining the parser for Arabic. Alessandro Moschitti and Olga Uryupina have been partially funded by the European Community's Seventh Framework Programme (FP7/2007-2013) under the grant number 288024 (LIMOSINE).

References

Olga Babko-Malaya, Ann Bies, Ann Taylor, Szuting Yi, Martha Palmer, Mitch Marcus, Seth Kulick, and Libin Shen. 2006. Issues in synchronizing the English treebank and propbank. In *Workshop on Frontiers in Linguistically Annotated Corpora 2006*, July.

Amit Bagga and Breck Baldwin. 1998. Algorithms for Scoring Coreference Chains. In *The First International Conference on Language Resources and Evaluation Workshop on Linguistics Coreference*, pages 563–566.

Elizabeth Baran and Nianwen Xue. 2011. Singular or Plural? Exploiting Parallel Corpora for Chinese Number Prediction. In *Proceedings of Machine Translation Summit XIII*.

Shane Bergsma and Dekang Lin. 2006. Bootstrapping path-based pronoun resolution. In *Proceedings of the 21st International Conference on Computational Linguistics and 44th Annual Meeting of the Association for Computational Linguistics*, pages 33–40, Sydney, Australia, July.

Jie Cai and Michael Strube. 2010. Evaluation metrics for end-to-end coreference resolution systems. In *Proceedings of the 11th Annual Meeting of the Special Interest Group on Discourse and Dialogue*, SIGDIAL '10, pages 28–36.

Jie Cai, Eva Mujdricza-Maydt, and Michael Strube. 2011a. Unrestricted coreference resolution via global hypergraph partitioning. In *Proceedings of the Fifteenth Conference on Computational Natural Language Learning: Shared Task*, pages 56–60, Portland, Oregon, USA, June. Association for Computational Linguistics.

Shu Cai, David Chiang, and Yoav Goldberg. 2011b. Language-independent parsing with empty elements. In *Proceedings of the 49th Annual Meeting of the Association for Computational Linguistics: Human Language Technologies*, pages 212–216, Portland, Oregon, USA, June. Association for Computational Linguistics.

Wendy W Chapman, Prakash M Nadkarni, Lynette Hirschman, Leonard W D'Avolio, Guergana K Savova, and Ozlem Uzuner. 2011. Overcoming barriers to NLP for clinical text: the role of shared tasks and the need for additional creative solutions. *Journal of American Medical Informatics Association*, 18(5), September.

Eugene Charniak and Mark Johnson. 2001. Edit detection and parsing for transcribed speech. In *Proceedings of the Second Meeting of North American Chapter of the Association of Computational Linguistics*, June.

Eugene Charniak and Mark Johnson. 2005. Coarse-to-fine n-best parsing and maxent discriminative reranking. In *Proceedings of the 43rd Annual Meeting of the Association for Computational Linguistics (ACL)*, Ann Arbor, MI, June.

Nancy Chinchor and Beth Sundheim. 2003. Message understanding conference (MUC) 6. In *LDC2003T13*.

Nancy Chinchor. 2001. Message understanding conference (MUC) 7. In *LDC2001T02*.

Aron Culotta, Michael Wick, Robert Hall, and Andrew McCallum. 2007. First-order probabilistic models for coreference resolution. In *HLT/NAACL*, pages 81–88.

Pascal Denis and Jason Baldridge. 2007. Joint determination of anaphoricity and coreference resolution using integer programming. In *Proceedings of HLT/NAACL*.

Pascal Denis and Jason Baldridge. 2009. Global joint models for coreference resolution and named entity classification. *Procesamiento del Lenguaje Natural*, (42):87–96.

George Doddington, Alexis Mitchell, Mark Przybocki, Lance Ramshaw, Stephanie Strassel, and Ralph Weischedel. 2004. The automatic content extraction (ACE) program-tasks, data, and evaluation. In *Proceedings of LREC*.

Charles Fillmore, Christopher Johnson, and Miriam R. L. Petruck. 2003. Background to FrameNet. *International Journal of Lexicography*, 16(3).

Ryan Gabbard. 2010. *Null Element Restoration*. Ph.D. thesis, University of Pennsylvania.

Aria Haghighi and Dan Klein. 2010. Coreference resolution in a modular, entity-centered model. In *Human Language Technologies: The 2010 Annual Conference of the North American Chapter of the Association for Computational Linguistics*, pages 385–393, Los Angeles, California, June.

Jan Hajič, Massimiliano Ciaramita, Richard Johansson, Daisuke Kawahara, Maria Antònia Martí, Lluís Màrquez, Adam Meyers, Joakim Nivre, Sebastian Padó, Jan Štěpánek, Pavel Straňák, Mihai Surdeanu, Nianwen Xue, and Yi Zhang. 2009. The CoNLL-2009 shared task: Syntactic and semantic dependencies in multiple languages. In *Proceedings of the Thirteenth Conference on Computational Natural Language Learning (CoNLL 2009): Shared Task*, pages 1–18, Boulder, Colorado, June.

Sanda M. Harabagiu, Razvan C. Bunescu, and Steven J. Maiorano. 2001. Text and knowledge mining for coreference resolution. In *NAACL*.

Lynette Hirschman and Nancy Chinchor. 1997. Coreference task definition (v3.0, 13 jul 97). In *Proceedings of the Seventh Message Understanding Conference*.

Lynette Hirschman, Patricia Robinson, John Burger, and Marc Vilain. 1998. Automating coreference: The role of annotated training data. In *Proceedings of AAAI Spring Symposium on Applying Machine Learning to Discourse Processing*.

Eduard Hovy, Mitchell Marcus, Martha Palmer, Lance Ramshaw, and Ralph Weischedel. 2006. OntoNotes: The 90% solution. In *Proceedings of HLT/NAACL*, pages 57–60, New York City, USA, June. Association for Computational Linguistics.

Karin Kipper, Anna Korhonen, Neville Ryant, and Martha Palmer. 2000. A large-scale classification of english verbs. *Language Resources and Evaluation*, 42(1):21 – 40.

Heeyoung Lee, Yves Peirsman, Angel Chang, Nathanael Chambers, Mihai Surdeanu, and Dan Jurafsky. 2011. Stanford's multi-pass sieve coreference resolution system at the conll-2011 shared task. In *Proceedings of the Fifteenth Conference on Computational Natural Language Learning: Shared Task*, pages 28–34, Portland, Oregon, USA, June. Association for Computational Linguistics.

Xiaoqiang Luo. 2005. On coreference resolution performance metrics. In *Proceedings of Human Language Technology Conference and Conference on Empirical Methods in Natural Language Processing*, pages 25–32, Vancouver, British Columbia, Canada, October.

Mohamed Maamouri and Ann Bies. 2004. Developing an arabic treebank: Methods, guidelines, procedures, and tools. In Ali Farghaly and Karine Megerdoomian, editors, *COLING 2004 Computational Approaches to Arabic Script-based Languages*, pages 2–9, Geneva, Switzerland, August 28th. COLING.

Mitchell P. Marcus, Beatrice Santorini, and Mary Ann Marcinkiewicz. 1993. Building a large annotated corpus of English: The Penn treebank. *Computational Linguistics*, 19(2):313–330, June.

Andrew McCallum and Ben Wellner. 2004. Conditional models of identity uncertainty with application to noun coreference. In *Advances in Neural Information Processing Systems (NIPS)*.

Joseph McCarthy and Wendy Lehnert. 1995. Using decision trees for coreference resolution. In *Proceedings of the Fourteenth International Conference on Artificial Intelligence*, pages 1050–1055.

Thomas S. Morton. 2000. Coreference for nlp applications. In *Proceedings of the 38th Annual Meeting of the Association for Computational Linguistics*, October.

Eugene W. Myers. 1986. An O(ND) difference algorithm and its variations. *Algorithmica*, 1(2):251—-266.

Vincent Ng. 2007. Shallow semantics for coreference resolution. In *Proceedings of the IJCAI*.

Vincent Ng. 2010. Supervised noun phrase coreference research: The first fifteen years. In *Proceedings of the 48th Annual Meeting of the Association for Computational Linguistics*, pages 1396–1411, Uppsala, Sweden, July.

David S. Pallett. 2002. The role of the National Institute of Standards and Technology in DARPA's Broadcast News continuous speech recognition research program. *Speech Communication*, 37(1-2), May.

Martha Palmer, Daniel Gildea, and Paul Kingsbury. 2005. The Proposition Bank: An annotated corpus of semantic roles. *Computational Linguistics*, 31(1):71–106.

Martha Palmer, Hoa Trang Dang, and Christiane Fellbaum. 2007. Making fine-grained and coarse-grained sense distinctions, both manually and automatically.

Martha Palmer, Olga Babko-Malaya, Ann Bies, Mona Diab, Mohammed Maamouri, Aous Mansouri, and Wajdi Zaghouani. 2008. A pilot arabic propbank. In *Proceedings of the International Conference on Language Resources and Evaluation (LREC)*, Marrakech, Morocco, May 28-30.

Rebecca Passonneau. 2004. Computing reliability for coreference annotation. In *Proceedings of LREC*.

Slav Petrov and Dan Klein. 2007. Improved Inferencing for Unlexicalized Parsing. In *Proc of HLT-NAACL*.

Massimo Poesio and Ron Artstein. 2005. The reliability of anaphoric annotation, reconsidered: Taking ambiguity into account. In *Proceedings of the Workshop on Frontiers in Corpus Annotations II: Pie in the Sky*.

Massimo Poesio. 2004. The mate/gnome scheme for anaphoric annotation, revisited. In *Proceedings of SIGDIAL*.

Simone Paolo Ponzetto and Massimo Poesio. 2009. State-of-the-art nlp approaches to coreference resolution: Theory and practical recipes. In *Tutorial Abstracts of ACL-IJCNLP 2009*, page 6, Suntec, Singapore, August.

Simone Paolo Ponzetto and Michael Strube. 2005. Semantic role labeling for coreference resolution. In *Companion Volume of the Proceedings of the 11th Meeting of the European Chapter of the Association for Computational Linguistics*, pages 143–146, Trento, Italy, April.

Simone Paolo Ponzetto and Michael Strube. 2006. Exploiting semantic role labeling, WordNet and Wikipedia for coreference resolution. In *Proceedings of the HLT/NAACL*, pages 192–199, New York City, N.Y., June.

Sameer Pradhan, Kadri Hacioglu, Valerie Krugler, Wayne Ward, James Martin, and Dan Jurafsky. 2005. Support vector learning for semantic argument classification. *Machine Learning Journal*, 60(1):11–39.

Sameer Pradhan, Eduard Hovy, Mitchell Marcus, Martha Palmer, Lance Ramshaw, and Ralph Weischedel. 2007a. OntoNotes: A Unified Relational Semantic Representation. *International Journal of Semantic Computing*, 1(4):405–419.

Sameer Pradhan, Lance Ramshaw, Ralph Weischedel, Jessica MacBride, and Linnea Micciulla. 2007b. Unrestricted Coreference: Indentifying Entities and Events in OntoNotes. In *in Proceedings of the IEEE International Conference on Semantic Computing (ICSC)*, September 17-19.

Karthik Raghunathan, Heeyoung Lee, Sudarshan Rangarajan, Nate Chambers, Mihai Surdeanu, Dan Jurafsky, and Christopher Manning. 2010. A multi-pass sieve for coreference resolution. In *Proceedings of the 2010 Conference on Empirical Methods in Natural Language Processing*, pages 492–501, Cambridge, MA, October. Association for Computational Linguistics.

Altaf Rahman and Vincent Ng. 2009. Supervised models for coreference resolution. In *Proceedings of the 2009 Conference on Empirical Methods in Natural Language Processing*, pages 968–977, Singapore, August. Association for Computational Linguistics.

William M. Rand. 1971. Objective criteria for the evaluation of clustering methods. *Journal of the American Statistical Association*, 66(336).

Marta Recasens and Eduard Hovy. 2011. Blanc: Implementing the rand index for coreference evaluation. *Natural Language Engineering*.

Marta Recasens, Lluís Màrquez, Emili Sapena, M. Antònia Martí, Mariona Taulé, Véronique Hoste, Massimo Poesio, and Yannick Versley. 2010. Semeval-2010 task 1: Coreference resolution in multiple languages. In *Proceedings of the 5th International Workshop on Semantic Evaluation*, pages 1–8, Uppsala, Sweden, July.

Wee Meng Soon, Hwee Tou Ng, and Daniel Chung Yong Lim. 2001. A machine learning approach to coreference resolution of noun phrase. *Computational Linguistics*, 27(4):521–544.

Veselin Stoyanov, Nathan Gilbert, Claire Cardie, and Ellen Riloff. 2009. Conundrums in noun phrase coreference resolution: Making sense of the state-of-the-art. In *Proceedings of the Joint Conference of the 47th Annual Meeting of the ACL and the 4th International Joint Conference on Natural Language Processing of the AFNLP*, pages 656–664, Suntec, Singapore, August. Association for Computational Linguistics.

Mihai Surdeanu, Richard Johansson, Adam Meyers, Lluís Màrquez, and Joakim Nivre. 2008. The CoNLL 2008 shared task on joint parsing of syntactic and semantic dependencies. In *CoNLL 2008: Proceedings of the Twelfth Conference on Computational Natural Language Learning*, pages 159–177, Manchester, England, August.

Ozlem Uzuner, Andreea Bodnari, Shuying Shen, Tyler Forbush, John Pestian, and Brett R South. 2012. Evaluating the state of the art in coreference resolution for electronic medical records. *Journal of American Medical Informatics Association*, 19(5), September.

Yannick Versley, Simone Paolo Ponzetto, Massimo Poesio, Vladimir Eidelman, Alan Jern, Jason Smith, Xiaofeng Yang, and Alessandro Moschitti. 2008. BART: A modular toolkit for coreference resolution. In *Proceedings of the 6th International Conference on Language Resources and Evaluation*, Marrakech, Morocco, May.

Yannick Versley. 2007. Antecedent selection techniques for high-recall coreference resolution. In *Proceedings of the 2007 Joint Conference on Empirical Methods in Natural Language Processing and Computational Natural Language Learning (EMNLP-CoNLL)*.

Marc Vilain, John Burger, John Aberdeen, Dennis Connolly, and Lynette Hirschman. 1995. A model theoretic coreference scoring scheme. In *Proceedings of the Sixth Message Undersatnding Conference (MUC-6)*, pages 45–52.

Ralph Weischedel and Ada Brunstein. 2005. BBN pronoun coreference and entity type corpus LDC catalog no.: LDC2005T33. BBN Technologies.

Ralph Weischedel, Eduard Hovy, Mitchell Marcus, Martha Palmer, Robert Belvin, Sameer Pradhan, Lance Ramshaw, and Nianwen Xue. 2011. OntoNotes: A large training corpus for enhanced processing. In Joseph Olive, Caitlin Christianson, and John McCary, editors, *Handbook of Natural Language Processing and Machine Translation: DARPA Global Autonomous Language Exploitation*. Springer.

Nianwen Xue and Martha Palmer. 2009. Adding semantic roles to the Chinese Treebank. *Natural Language Engineering*, 15(1):143–172.

Nianwen Xue, Fei Xia, Fu dong Chiou, and Martha Palmer. 2005. The Penn Chinese TreeBank: Phrase Structure Annotation of a Large Corpus. *Natural Language Engineering*, 11(2):207–238.

Nianwen Xue. 2008. Labeling Chinese Predicates with Semantic Roles. *Computational Linguistics*, 34(2):225–255.

Yaqin Yang and Nianwen Xue. 2010. Chasing the ghost: recovering empty categories in the chinese treebank. In *Proceedings of Proceedings of the 23rd International Conference on Computational Linguistics (COLING)*, Beijing, China.

Wajdi Zaghouani, Mona Diab, Aous Mansouri, Sameer Pradhan, and Martha Palmer. 2010. The revised arabic propbank. In *Proceedings of the Fourth Linguistic Annotation Workshop*, pages 222–226, Uppsala, Sweden, July.

Zhi Zhong and Hwee Tou Ng. 2010. It makes sense: A wide-coverage word sense disambiguation system for free text. In *Proceedings of the ACL 2010 System Demonstrations*, pages 78–83, Uppsala, Sweden.

Latent Structure Perceptron with Feature Induction for Unrestricted Coreference Resolution

Eraldo Rezende Fernandes
Departamento de Informática
PUC-Rio
Rio de Janeiro, Brazil
efernandes@inf.puc-rio.br

Cícero Nogueira dos Santos
Brazilian Research Lab
IBM Research
Rio de Janeiro, Brazil
cicerons@br.ibm.com

Ruy Luiz Milidiú
Departamento de Informática
PUC-Rio
Rio de Janeiro, Brazil
milidiu@inf.puc-rio.br

Abstract

We describe a machine learning system based on large margin structure perceptron for unrestricted coreference resolution that introduces two key modeling techniques: latent coreference trees and entropy guided feature induction. The proposed latent tree modeling turns the learning problem computationally feasible. Additionally, using an automatic feature induction method, we are able to efficiently build nonlinear models and, hence, achieve high performances with a linear learning algorithm. Our system is evaluated on the CoNLL-2012 Shared Task *closed* track, which comprises three languages: Arabic, Chinese and English. We apply the same system to all languages, except for minor adaptations on some language dependent features, like static lists of pronouns. Our system achieves an official score of 58.69, the best one among all the competitors.

1 Introduction

The CoNLL-2012 Shared Task (Pradhan et al., 2012) is dedicated to the modeling of coreference resolution for multiple languages. The participants are provided with corpora for three languages: Arabic, Chinese and English. These corpora are provided by the OntoNotes project and, besides accurate anaphoric coreference information, contain various annotation layers such as part-of-speech (POS) tagging, syntax parsing, named entities (NE) and semantic role labeling (SRL). The shared task consists in the automatic identification of coreferring mentions of entities and events, given predicted information on other OntoNotes layers.

We propose a machine learning system for coreference resolution that is based on the large margin structure perceptron algorithm (Collins, 2002; Fernandes and Milidiú, 2012). Our system learns a predictor that takes as input a set of candidate mentions in a document and directly outputs the clusters of coreferring mentions. This predictor comprises an optimization problem whose objective is a function of the clustering features. To embed classic cluster metrics in this objective function is practically infeasible since most of such metrics lead to NP-hard optimization problems. Thus, we introduce *coreference trees* in order to represent a cluster by a directed tree over its mentions. In that way, the prediction problem optimizes over trees instead of clusters, which makes our approach computationally feasible. Since coreference trees are not given in the training data, we assume that these structures are *latent* and use the latent structure perceptron (Fernandes and Brefeld, 2011; Yu and Joachims, 2009) as the learning algorithm.

To provide high predicting power features to our model, we use *entropy guided feature induction* (Fernandes and Milidiú, 2012). By using this technique, we automatically generate several feature templates that capture coreference specific local context knowledge. Furthermore, this feature induction technique extends the structure perceptron framework by providing an efficient general method to build strong nonlinear classifiers.

Our system is evaluated on the CoNLL-2012 Shared Task *closed* track and achieves the scores

54.22, 58.49 and 63.37 on Arabic, Chinese and English test sets, respectively. The official score – the mean over the three languages – is 58.69, which is the best score achieved in the shared task.

The remainder of this paper is organized as follows. In Section 2, we present our machine learning modeling for the unrestricted coreference resolution task. In Section 3, we present the corpus preprocessing steps. The experimental findings are depicted in Section 4 and, in Section 5, we present our final remarks.

2 Task Modeling

Coreference resolution consists in identifying mention clusters in a document. We split this task into two subtasks: mention detection and mention clustering. For the first subtask, we apply the strategy proposed in (dos Santos and Carvalho, 2011). The second subtask requires a complex output. Hence, we use a structure learning approach that has been successfully applied to many similar structure finding NLP tasks (Collins, 2002; Tsochantaridis et al., 2005; McDonald et al., 2006; Fernandes and Brefeld, 2011; Fernandes and Milidiú, 2012).

2.1 Mention Detection

For each text document, we generate a list of candidate mentions using the strategy of (dos Santos and Carvalho, 2011). The basic idea is to use all noun phrases, and, additionally, pronouns and named entities, even if they are inside larger noun phrases. We do not include verbs as mentions.

2.2 Mention Clustering

In the mention clustering subtask, a *training* instance $(\boldsymbol{x}, \boldsymbol{y})$ consists of a set of mentions $\boldsymbol{x}$ from a document and the correct coreferring clusters $\boldsymbol{y}$. The structure perceptron algorithm learns a predictor from a given training set $\mathcal{D} = \{(\boldsymbol{x}, \boldsymbol{y})\}$ of correct input-output pairs. More specifically, it learns the weight vector $\boldsymbol{w}$ of the parameterized predictor given by

$$F(\boldsymbol{x}) = \arg \max_{y' \in \mathcal{Y}(\boldsymbol{x})} s(\boldsymbol{y}'; \boldsymbol{w}),$$

where $\mathcal{Y}(\boldsymbol{x})$ is the set of clusterings over mentions $\boldsymbol{x}$ and s is a $\boldsymbol{w}$-parameterized scoring function over clusterings.

We use the *large margin* structure perceptron (Fernandes and Milidiú, 2012) that, during training, embeds a loss function in the prediction problem. Hence, it uses a loss-augmented predictor given by

$$F^{\ell}(\boldsymbol{x}) = \arg \max_{y' \in \mathcal{Y}(\boldsymbol{x})} s(\boldsymbol{y}'; \boldsymbol{w}) + \ell(\boldsymbol{y}, \boldsymbol{y}'),$$

where ℓ is a non-negative loss function that measures how a candidate clustering $\boldsymbol{y}'$ differs from the ground truth $\boldsymbol{y}$. The training algorithm makes intense use of the predictor, hence the prediction problem must be efficiently solved. Letting s be a classic clustering metric is infeasible, since most of such metrics lead to NP-hard optimization problems.

2.2.1 Coreference Trees

In order to reduce the complexity of the prediction problem, we introduce *coreference trees* to represent clusters of coreferring mentions. A coreference tree is a directed tree whose nodes are the coreferring mentions and arcs represent *some* coreference relation between mentions. In Figure 1, we present a document with seven highlighted mentions comprising two clusters. One plausible coreference tree for the cluster $\{a_1,a_2,a_3,a_4\}$ is presented in Figure 2.

North Korea$_{a_1}$ opened **its**$_{a_2}$ doors to the U.S. today, welcoming **Secretary of State Madeleine Albright**$_{b_1}$. **She**$_{b_2}$ says **her**$_{b_3}$ visit is a good start. The U.S. remains concerned about **North Korea's**$_{a_3}$ missile development program and **its**$_{a_4}$ exports of missiles to Iran.

Figure 1: Exemplary document with seven highlighted mentions comprising two clusters: $\{a_1,a_2,a_3,a_4\}$ and $\{b_1,b_2,b_3\}$. The letter in the mention subscript indicates its cluster and the number uniquely identifies the mention within the cluster.

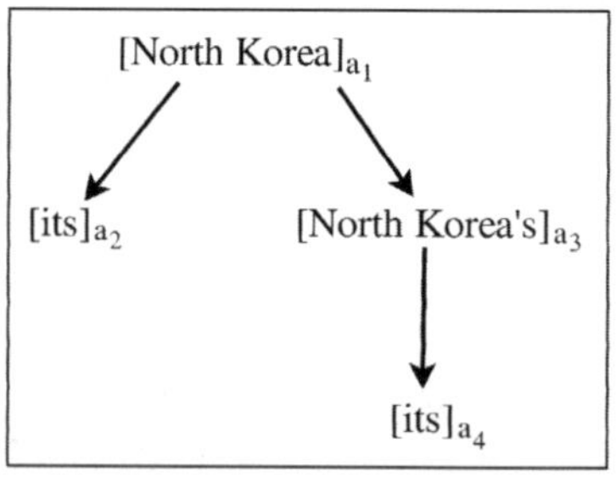

Figure 2: Coreference tree for the cluster a in Figure 1.

We are not concerned about the semantics underlying coreference trees, since they are just auxiliary structures for the clustering task. However, we argue that this concept is linguistically plausible, since there is a dependency relation between coreferring mentions. Observing the aforementioned example, one may agree that mention a_3 (North Korea's) is indeed more likely to be associated with mention a_1 (North Korea) than with mention a_2 (its), even considering that a_2 is closer than a_1 in the text.

For a given document, we have a forest of coreference trees, one tree for each coreferring cluster. However, for the sake of simplicity, we link the root node of every coreference tree to an *artificial* root node, obtaining the *document tree*. In Figure 3, we depict a document tree for the text in Figure 1.

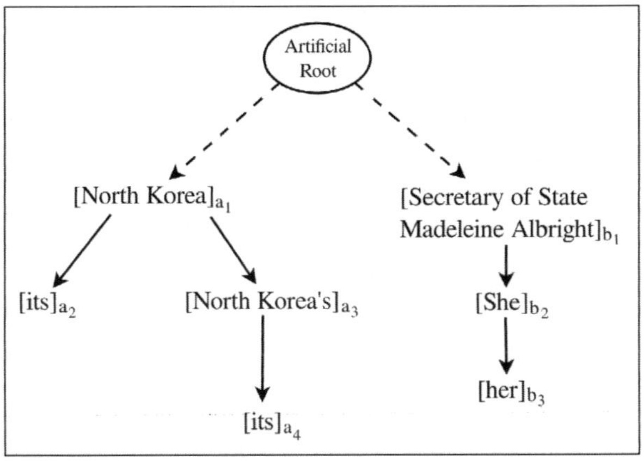

Figure 3: Document tree with two coreference trees for the text in Figure 1. Dashed lines indicate artificial arcs.

2.2.2 Latent Structure Learning

Coreference trees are not given in the training data. Thus, we assume that these structures are *latent* and make use of the latent structure perceptron (Fernandes and Brefeld, 2011; Yu and Joachims, 2009) to train our models. We decompose the original predictor into two predictors, that is

$$F(\boldsymbol{x}) \equiv F_y(F_h(\boldsymbol{x})),$$

where the *latent predictor* $F_h(\boldsymbol{x})$ is defined as $\arg\max_{h \in \mathcal{H}(\boldsymbol{x})} \langle \boldsymbol{w}, \boldsymbol{\Phi}(\boldsymbol{x}, \boldsymbol{h}) \rangle$, $\mathcal{H}(\boldsymbol{x})$ is the set of feasible document trees for $\boldsymbol{x}$ and $\boldsymbol{\Phi}(\boldsymbol{x}, \boldsymbol{h})$ is the joint feature vector representation of mentions $\boldsymbol{x}$ and document tree $\boldsymbol{h}$. Hence, the latent predictor finds a maximum scoring rooted tree over the given mentions $\boldsymbol{x}$, where a tree score is given by a linear function over its features. $F_y(\boldsymbol{h})$ is a straightforward procedure that creates a cluster for each subtree connected to the artificial root node in the document tree $\boldsymbol{h}$.

In Figure 4, we depict the proposed latent structure perceptron algorithm for the mention clustering task. Like its univariate counterpart (Rosenblatt,

$\boldsymbol{w}_0 \leftarrow \mathbf{0}$
$t \leftarrow 0$
while no convergence
  for each $(\boldsymbol{x}, \boldsymbol{y}) \in \mathcal{D}$
    $\tilde{\boldsymbol{h}} \leftarrow \arg\max_{h \in \mathcal{H}(\boldsymbol{x}, \boldsymbol{y})} \langle \boldsymbol{w}_t, \boldsymbol{\Phi}(\boldsymbol{x}, \boldsymbol{h}) \rangle$
    $\hat{\boldsymbol{h}} \leftarrow \arg\max_{h \in \mathcal{H}(\boldsymbol{x})} \langle \boldsymbol{w}_t, \boldsymbol{\Phi}(\boldsymbol{x}, \boldsymbol{h}) \rangle + \ell_r(\boldsymbol{h}, \tilde{\boldsymbol{h}})$
    $\boldsymbol{w}_{t+1} \leftarrow \boldsymbol{w}_t + \boldsymbol{\Phi}(\boldsymbol{x}, \tilde{\boldsymbol{h}}) - \boldsymbol{\Phi}(\boldsymbol{x}, \hat{\boldsymbol{h}})$
    $t \leftarrow t + 1$
$\boldsymbol{w} \leftarrow \frac{1}{t} \sum_{i=1}^{t} \boldsymbol{w}_i$

Figure 4: Latent structure perceptron algorithm.

1957), the structure perceptron is an online algorithm that iterates through the training set. For each training instance, it performs two major steps: (i) a prediction for the given input using the current model; and (ii) a model update based on the difference between the predicted and the ground truth outputs. The latent structure perceptron performs an additional step to predict the latent ground truth $\tilde{\boldsymbol{h}}$ using a specialization of the latent predictor and the current model. This algorithm learns to predict document trees that help to solve the clustering task. Thereafter, for an unseen document $\boldsymbol{x}$, the predictor $F_h(\boldsymbol{x})$ and the learned model $\boldsymbol{w}$ are employed to produce a predicted document tree $\boldsymbol{h}$ which, in turn, is fed to $F_y(\boldsymbol{h})$ to give the predicted clusters.

Golden coreference trees are not available. However, during training, for a given input $\boldsymbol{x}$, we have the golden clustering $\boldsymbol{y}$. Thus, we predict the *constrained document tree* $\tilde{\boldsymbol{h}}$ for the training instance $(\boldsymbol{x}, \boldsymbol{y})$ using a specialization of the latent predictor – the *constrained latent predictor* – that makes use of $\boldsymbol{y}$. The constrained predictor finds the maximum scoring document tree among all rooted trees of $\boldsymbol{x}$ that follow the correct clustering $\boldsymbol{y}$, that is, rooted trees that only include arcs between mentions that are coreferent according to $\boldsymbol{y}$, plus one arc from the artificial node to each cluster. In that way, the constrained predictor optimizes over a subset $\mathcal{H}(\boldsymbol{x}, \boldsymbol{y})$ contained in $\mathcal{H}(\boldsymbol{x})$ and, moreover, it guarantees that

$F_y(\tilde{\boldsymbol{h}}) = \boldsymbol{y}$, for any $\boldsymbol{w}$. The constrained tree is used as the ground truth on each iteration. Therefore, the model update is determined by the difference between the constrained document tree and the document tree predicted by the ordinary predictor.

The loss function measures the impurity in the predicted document tree. In our modeling, we use a simple loss function that just counts how many predicted edges are not present in the constrained document tree. For the arcs from the artificial root node, we use a different loss value. We set that through the parameter r, which we call the *root loss value*.

We decompose the joint feature vector $\boldsymbol{\Phi}(\boldsymbol{x}, \boldsymbol{h})$ along tree edges, that is, pairs of candidate coreferring mentions. This approach is similar to previous structure learning modelings for dependency parsing (McDonald et al., 2005; Fernandes and Milidiú, 2012). Thus, the prediction problem reduces to a maximum branching problem, which is efficiently solved by the *Chu-Liu-Edmonds algorithm* (Chu and Liu, 1965; Edmonds, 1967). We also use the *averaged* structure perceptron as suggested by (Collins, 2002), since it provides a more robust model.

3 Data Preparation

It is necessary to perform some corpus processing steps in order to prepare training and test data. In this section, we detail the methodology we use to generate coreference arcs and the features that describe them.

3.1 Coreference Arcs Generation

The input for the prediction problem is a graph whose nodes are the mentions in a document. Ideally, we could consider the complete graph for each document, thus every mention pair would be an option for building the document tree. However, since the total number of mentions is huge and a big portion of arcs can be easily identified as incorrect, we filter the arcs and, thus, include only candidate mention pairs that are more likely to be coreferent.

We filter arcs by simply adapting the sieves method proposed in (Lee et al., 2011). However, in our filtering strategy, precision is not a concern and the application order of filters is not important. The objective here is to build a small set of candidate arcs that shows good recall.

Given a mention pair (m_i, m_j), where m_i appears before m_j in the text, we create a directed arc from m_i to m_j if at least one of the following conditions holds: (1) the number of mentions between m_i and m_j is not greater than a given parameter; (2) m_j is an alias of m_i; (3) there is a match of both mentions strings up to their head words; (4) the head word of m_i matches the head word of m_j; (5) test shallow discourse attributes match for both mentions; (6) m_j is a pronoun and m_i has the same gender, number, speaker and animacy of m_j; (7) m_j is a pronoun and m_i is a compatible pronoun or proper name.

Sieves 2 to 7 are obtained from (Lee et al., 2011). We only introduce sieve 1 to lift recall without using other strongly language-dependent sieves.

3.2 Basic Features

We use a set of 70 basic features to describe each pair of mentions (m_i, m_j). The feature set includes lexical, syntactic, semantic, and positional information. Our feature set is very similar to the one used by (dos Santos and Carvalho, 2011). However, here we do not use the semantic features derived from WordNet. In the following, we briefly describe some of these basic features.

Lexical: *head word* of $m_{i/j}$; *String matching* of (head word of) m_i and m_j (y/n); *Both are pronouns* and their strings match (y/n); *Previous/Next two words* of $m_{i/j}$; *Length* of $m_{i/j}$; *Edit distance* of head words; $m_{i/j}$ is a definitive NP (y/n); $m_{i/j}$ is a demonstrative NP (y/n); *Both are proper names* and their strings match (y/n).

Syntactic: *POS tag* of the $m_{i/j}$ head word; *Previous/Next two POS tags* of $m_{i/j}$; m_i and m_j are *both pronouns / proper names* (y/n); *Previous/Next predicate* of $m_{i/j}$; *Compatible pronouns*, which checks whether two pronouns agree in number, gender and person (y/n); *NP embedding level*; *Number of embedded NPs* in $m_{i/j}$.

Semantic: the result of a *baseline system*; *sense* of the $m_{i/j}$ head word; *Named entity* type of $m_{i/j}$; m_i and m_j have the *same named entity*; *Semantic role of* $m_{i/j}$ for the prev/next predicate; *Concatenation of semantic roles of* m_i *and* m_j for the same predicate (if they are in the same sentence); *Same speaker* (y/n); m_j is an *alias* of m_i (y/n).

Distance and Position: Distance between m_i and m_j in sentences; Distance in number of mentions;

Distance in number of person names (applies only for the cases where m_i and m_j are both pronouns or one of them is a person name); One mention is in apposition to the other (y/n).

3.3 Language Specifics

Our system can be easily adapted to different languages. In our experiments, only small changes are needed in order to train and apply the system to three different languages. The adaptations are due to: lack of input features for some languages; different POS tagsets are used in the corpora; and creation of static list of language specific pronouns.

Some input features, that are available for the English corpus, are not available in Arabic and Chinese corpora. Namely, the Arabic corpus does not contain NE, SRL and speaker features. Therefore, for this language we do not derive basic features that make use of these input features. For Chinese, we do not use features derived from NE data, since this data is not provided. Additionally, the Chinese corpus uses a different POS tagset. Hence, some few mappings are needed during the basic feature derivation stage.

The lack of input features for Arabic and Chinese also impact the sieve-based arcs generation. For Chinese, we do not use sieve 6, and, for Arabic, we only use sieves 1, 3, 4 and 7. Sieve 7 is not used for the English corpus, since it is a specialization of sieve 6. The first sieve parameter is 4 for Arabic and Chinese, and 8 for English.

In the arcs generation and basic feature derivation steps, our system makes use of static lists of language specific pronouns. In our experiments, we use the POS tagging information and the golden coreference chains to automatically extract these pronoun lists from training corpora.

3.4 Entropy Guided Feature Induction

In order to improve the predictive power of our system, we add complex features that are combinations of the basic features described in the previous section. We use feature templates to generate such complex features. However, we automatically generate templates using the entropy guided feature induction approach (Fernandes and Milidiú, 2012; Milidiú et al., 2008). These automatically generated templates capture complex contextual information and are difficult to be handcrafted by humans. Furthermore, this feature induction mechanism extends the structure perceptron framework by providing an efficient general method to build strong nonlinear predictors.

We experiment with different template sets for each language. The main difference between these sets is basically the training data used to induce them. We obtain better results when merging different template sets. For the English language, it is better to use a template set of 196 templates, which merges two different sets: (a) a set induced using training data that contains mention pairs produced by filters 2 to 6; and (b) another set induced using training data that contains mention pairs produced by all filters. For Chinese and Arabic, it is better to use template sets induced specifically for these languages merged with the template set (a) generated for the English language. The final set for the Chinese language has 197 templates, while the final set for Arabic has 223.

4 Empirical Results

We train our system on the corpora provided in the CoNLL-2012 Shared Task. There are corpora available on three languages: Arabic, Chinese and English. For each language, results are reported using three metrics: MUC, B^3 and $CEAF_e$. We also report the mean of the F-scores on these three metrics, which gives a unique score for each language. Additionally, the official score on the CoNLL-2012 shared task is reported, that is the mean of the scores obtained on the three languages.

We report our system results on development and test sets. The development results are obtained with systems trained only on the training sets. However, test set results are obtained by training on a larger dataset – the one obtained by concatenating training and development sets. During training, we use the *gold standard* input features, which produce better performing models than using the provided automatic values. That is usually the case on NLP tasks, since golden values eliminate the additional noise introduced by automatic features. On the other hand, during evaluation, we use the automatic values provided in the CoNLL shared task corpora.

In Table 1, we present our system performances on the CoNLL-2012 development sets for the three languages. Given the size of the Arabic training cor-

Language	MUC			B^3			$CEAF_e$			Mean
	R	P	F_1	R	P	F_1	R	P	F_1	
Arabic	43.00	47.87	45.30	61.41	70.38	65.59	49.42	44.19	46.66	**52.52**
Chinese	54.40	68.19	60.52	64.17	78.84	70.76	51.42	38.96	44.33	**58.54**
English	64.88	74.74	69.46	66.53	78.28	71.93	54.93	43.68	48.66	**63.35**
									Official Score	**58.14**

Table 1: Results on the development sets.

Language	MUC			B^3			$CEAF_e$			Mean
	R	P	F_1	R	P	F_1	R	P	F_1	
Arabic	34.18	58.85	43.25	50.61	82.13	62.63	57.37	33.75	42.49	**49.45**
Chinese	49.17	76.03	59.72	58.16	86.33	69.50	57.56	34.38	43.05	**57.42**
English	62.75	77.41	69.31	63.88	81.34	71.56	57.46	41.08	47.91	**62.92**
									Official Score	**56.59**

Table 2: Results on the development sets *without* root loss value.

Language	MUC			B^3			$CEAF_e$			Mean
	R	P	F_1	R	P	F_1	R	P	F_1	
Arabic	43.63	49.69	46.46	62.70	72.19	67.11	52.49	46.09	49.08	**54.22**
Chinese	52.69	70.58	60.34	62.99	80.57	70.70	53.75	37.88	44.44	**58.49**
English	65.83	75.91	70.51	65.79	77.69	71.24	55.00	43.17	48.37	**63.37**
									Official Score	**58.69**

Table 3: Official results on the test sets.

Language	Parse / Mentions	MUC			B^3			$CEAF_e$			Mean
		R	P	F_1	R	P	F_1	R	P	F_1	
Arabic	Auto / GB	45.18	47.39	46.26	64.56	69.44	66.91	49.73	47.39	48.53	**53.90**
	Auto / GM	57.25	76.48	65.48	60.27	79.81	68.68	72.61	46.00	56.32	**63.49**
	Golden / Auto	46.38	51.78	48.93	63.53	72.37	67.66	52.57	46.88	49.56	**55.38**
	Golden / GB	46.38	51.78	48.93	63.53	72.37	67.66	52.57	46.88	49.56	**55.38**
	Golden / GM	56.89	76.27	65.17	60.07	80.02	68.62	72.24	45.58	55.90	**63.23**
Chinese	Auto / GB	58.76	71.46	64.49	66.62	79.88	72.65	54.09	42.02	47.29	**61.48**
	Auto / GM	61.64	90.81	73.43	63.55	89.43	74.30	72.78	39.68	51.36	**66.36**
	Golden / Auto	59.35	74.49	66.07	66.31	81.43	73.10	55.97	41.50	47.66	**62.28**
	Golden / GB	59.35	74.49	66.07	66.31	81.43	73.10	55.97	41.50	47.66	**62.28**
	Golden / GM	61.70	91.45	73.69	63.57	89.76	74.43	72.84	39.49	51.21	**66.44**
English	Auto / GB	64.92	77.53	70.67	64.25	78.95	70.85	56.48	41.69	47.97	**63.16**
	Auto / GM	70.69	91.21	79.65	65.46	85.61	74.19	74.71	42.55	54.22	**69.35**
	Golden / Auto	67.73	77.25	72.18	66.42	78.01	71.75	56.16	44.51	49.66	**64.53**
	Golden / GB	65.65	78.26	71.40	64.36	79.09	70.97	57.36	42.23	48.65	**63.67**
	Golden / GM	71.18	91.24	79.97	65.81	85.51	74.38	74.93	43.09	54.72	**69.69**

Table 4: Supplementary results on the test sets alternating parse quality and mention candidates. Parse quality can be automatic or golden; and mention candidates can be automatically identified (Auto), golden mention boundaries (GB) or golden mentions (GM).

pus and the feature limitations for Arabic and Chinese, the performance variations among the three languages are no more than expected. One important parameter that we introduce in this work is the root loss value, a different loss function value on arcs from the artificial root node. The effect of this parameter is to diminish the creation of clusters, thus stimulating bigger clusters and adjusting the balance between precision and recall. Using the development sets for tuning, we set the value of the root loss value parameter to 6, 2 and 1.5 for Arabic, Chinese and English, respectively. In Table 2, we present our system performances on the development sets when we set this parameter to 1 for all languages, that is equivalent to not use this parameter at all. We can observe, by comparing these results with the ones in Table 1, that this parameter really causes a better balancing between precision and recall, and consequently increases the F_1 scores. Its effect is accentuated on Arabic and Chinese, since the unbalancing issue is worse on these languages.

The official results on the test sets are depicted in Table 3. For Chinese and English, these performances are virtually identical to the performances on the development sets. On the other hand, the official performance for the Arabic language is significantly higher than the development set performance. This difference is likely due to the fact that the Arabic training set is much smaller than the Chinese and English counterparts. Thus, by including the development set in the training of the final Arabic system, we significantly improve the official performance.

We report in Table 4 the *supplementary* results provided by the shared task organizers on the test sets. These additional experiments investigate two key aspects of any coreference resolution system: the parse feature and the mention candidates that are given to the clustering procedure. We alternate the parse feature between the official *automatic* parse and the *golden* parse from OntoNotes. Regarding mention candidates, we use three different strategies: automatic mentions (Auto, in Table 4), golden mention boundaries (GB) and golden mentions (GM). Automatic mentions are completely detected by our system, as described in Section 2.1. Golden mention boundaries comprise all noun phrases in the *golden* parse tree, even when the automatic parse is used as input feature. Golden mentions are all non-singleton mentions, i.e., all mentions that take part in some entity cluster. It is important to notice that golden mention information is much stronger than golden boundaries.

By observing Table 4, it is clear that the most beneficial information is golden mentions (compare the Auto/GM results in Table 4 with the results in Table 3). The mean F-score over all languages when using golden mentions is almost 8 points higher than the official score. These results are not surprising since to identify non-singleton mentions greatly reduces the final task complexity. Golden mention boundaries (Auto/GB) increase the mean F-score for Chinese by almost 3 points. Conversely, for the other two languages, the results are decreased when this information is given. This is probably due to parameter tuning, since any additional information potentially changes the learning problem and, nevertheless, we use exactly the same three models – one per language – to produce all the results on Tables 3 and 4. One can observe, for instance, that the recall/precision balance greatly varies among the different configurations in these experiments. The golden parse feature (Golden/Auto) causes big improvements on the mean F-scores for all languages, specially for Chinese.

5 Conclusion

In this paper, we describe a machine learning system based on large margin latent structure perceptron for unrestricted coreference resolution. We introduce two modeling approaches that have direct impact on the final system performance: latent coreference trees and entropy guided feature induction.

According to our experiments, latent coreference trees are powerful enough to model the complexity of coreference structures in a document, while turning the learning problem computationally feasible. Our empirical findings also show that entropy guided feature induction enables learning of effective nonlinear classifiers.

Our system is evaluated on the CoNLL-2012 Shared Task *closed* track, which consists on modeling coreference resolution for three languages: Arabic, Chinese and English. In order to cope with this multi-language task, our system needs only minor adaptations on some language dependent features.

As future work, we plan to include second order features and cluster sensitive features.

Acknowledgments

This work was partially funded by Conselho Nacional de Desenvolvimento Científico e Tecnológico (CNPq), Fundação de Amparo à Pesquisa do Estado do Rio de Janeiro and Fundação Cearense de Apoio ao Desenvolvimento Científico e Tecnológico through grants 557.128/2009-9, E-26/170028/2008 and 0011-00147.01.00/09, respectively. The first author was also supported by a CNPq doctoral fellowship and by the Instituto Federal de Educação, Ciência e Tecnologia de Goiás.

References

Y. J. Chu and T. H. Liu. 1965. On the shortest arborescence of a directed graph. *Science Sinica*, 14:1396–1400.

Michael Collins. 2002. Discriminative training methods for hidden Markov models: theory and experiments with perceptron algorithms. In *Proceedings of the ACL-02 Conference on Empirical Methods in Natural Language Processing*, pages 1–8.

Cicero Nogueira dos Santos and Davi Lopes Carvalho. 2011. Rule and tree ensembles for unrestricted coreference resolution. In *Proceedings of the Fifteenth Conference on Computational Natural Language Learning: Shared Task*, pages 51–55, Portland, Oregon, USA, June. Association for Computational Linguistics.

J. Edmonds. 1967. Optimum branchings. *Journal of Research of the National Bureau of Standards*, 71B:233–240.

Eraldo R. Fernandes and Ulf Brefeld. 2011. Learning from partially annotated sequences. In *Proceedings of the European Conference on Machine Learning and Principles and Practice of Knowledge Discovery in Databases (ECML-PKDD)*, Athens, Greece.

Eraldo R. Fernandes and Ruy L. Milidiú. 2012. Entropy-guided feature generation for structured learning of Portuguese dependency parsing. In *Proceedings of the Conference on Computational Processing of the Portuguese Language (PROPOR)*, volume 7243 of *Lecture Notes in Computer Science*, pages 146–156. Springer Berlin / Heidelberg.

Heeyoung Lee, Yves Peirsman, Angel Chang, Nathanael Chambers, Mihai Surdeanu, and Dan Jurafsky. 2011. Stanford's multi-pass sieve coreference resolution system at the CoNLL-2011 shared task. In *Proceedings of the Fifteenth Conference on Computational Natural Language Learning: Shared Task*, CoNLL Shared Task 2011, pages 28–34, Stroudsburg, PA, USA. Association for Computational Linguistics.

Ryan McDonald, Koby Crammer, and Fernando Pereira. 2005. Online large-margin training of dependency parsers. In *Proceedings of the 43rd Annual Meeting on Association for Computational Linguistics*, ACL'05, pages 91–98.

Ryan McDonald, Kevin Lerman, and Fernando Pereira. 2006. Multilingual dependency analysis with a two-stage discriminative parser. In *Proceedings of the Conference on Computational Natural Language Learning (CoNLL)*, pages 216–220.

Ruy L. Milidiú, Cícero N. dos Santos, and Julio C. Duarte. 2008. Phrase chunking using entropy guided transformation learning. In *Proceedings of ACL2008*, Columbus, Ohio.

Sameer Pradhan, Alessandro Moschitti, Nianwen Xue, Olga Uryupina, and Yuchen Zhang. 2012. CoNLL-2012 shared task: Modeling multilingual unrestricted coreference in OntoNotes. In *Proceedings of the Sixteenth Conference on Computational Natural Language Learning (CoNLL 2012)*, Jeju, Korea.

Frank Rosenblatt. 1957. The Perceptron – a perceiving and recognizing automaton. Technical report, Cornell Aeronautical Laboratory. Report 85-460-1.

I. Tsochantaridis, T. Joachims, T. Hofmann, and Y. Altun. 2005. Large margin methods for structured and interdependent output variables. *Journal of Machine Learning Research*, 6:1453–1484.

Chun-Nam Yu and Thorsten Joachims. 2009. Learning structural SVMs with latent variables. In *Proceedings of the International Conference on Machine Learning (ICML)*.

Data-driven Multilingual Coreference Resolution using Resolver Stacking

Anders Björkelund and **Richárd Farkas**
Institute for Natural Language Processing
University of Stuttgart
{anders,farkas}@ims.uni-stuttgart.de

Abstract

This paper describes our contribution to the CoNLL 2012 Shared Task.[1] We present a novel decoding algorithm for coreference resolution which is combined with a standard pair-wise coreference resolver in a stacking approach. The stacked decoders are evaluated on the three languages of the Shared Task. We obtain an official overall score of 58.25 which is the second highest in the Shared Task.

1 Introduction

In this paper we present our contribution to the CoNLL 2012 Shared Task (Pradhan et al., 2012). We follow the standard architecture where mentions are extracted in the first step, then they are clustered using a pair-wise classifier (see e.g., (Ng, 2010)). For English, the set of extracted mentions is filtered by removing non-referential occurrences of certain pronouns. Our coreference resolver at its core relies on a pair-wise classifier. To overcome the problems associated with the isolated pair-wise decisions, we devised a novel decoding algorithm which compares a mention to partially built clusters. For our Shared Task contribution we combined this algorithm with conventional pair-wise decoding algorithms in a stacking approach.

In the Shared Task evaluation, our system received an overall official score of 58.25, which is the second highest among the sixteen participants.[2]

[1] The system is available for download on `http://www.ims.uni-stuttgart.de/~anders/`

[2] The overall score is the average of MUC, B^3, and CEAFE, averaged over all three languages

2 Mention Extraction

Since all mentions are not annotated in Shared Task data, but only mentions that take part in coreference chains, training a general-purpose anaphoricity classifier is non-trivial. We thus implemented a high-recall, low-precision mention extraction module that allows the coreference resolver to see most of the possible mentions, but has to learn to sort out the non-referential mentions.

The mention extraction module relies mainly on the syntactic parse tree, but also on named entities (which were only provided for English in the predicted versions of the Shared Task data).

Since the part-of-speech tags vary a bit across the languages, so do our extraction rules: For Arabic, we extract all NP's, and all terminals with part-of-speech tags PRP and PRP$; for Chinese, we extract all NP's, and all terminals with part-of-speech tags PN and NR; for English, we extract all NP's, all terminals with part-of-speech tags PRP and PRP$, and all named entities.

Early experiments indicated that the English coreference resolver frequently makes mistakes related to non-referential instances of the pronouns *it* (often referred to as expletive or pleonastic in the literature), *we*, and *you* (generic mentions, which are not annotated according to the OntoNotes annotation guidelines). To address this issue, we developed a **referential/non-referential** mention classifier in order to identify these mentions. The classifier acts as a filter after the mention extraction module and removes clear cases of non-referential mentions.

Our basic assumption was that when these pro-

	$th = 0.5$			$th = 0.95$			
	Precision	Recall	F_1	Precision	Recall	F_1	# occurrences
it	75.41	61.92	68	86.78	38.65	53.48	10,307
we	65.93	41.61	51.02	75.41	24.20	36.64	5,323
you	79.10	74.26	76.60	88.36	51.59	65.15	11,297
Average	75.73	63.05	68.81	86.17	41.04	55.60	26,927

Table 1: Performance of the non-referential classifier used for English. Precision, recall, and F-measure are broken down by pronoun (top three rows), and the micro-average over all three (bottom row). The left side uses a probability threshold of 0.5, and the right one a threshold of 0.95. The last column denotes the number of occurrences of the corresponding token. All numbers are computed on the development set.

nouns do not participate in any coreference chain, they are examples of non-referential mentions. Based on this assumption, we extracted referential and non-referential examples from the training set and trained binary MaxEnt classifiers using the Mallet toolkit (McCallum, 2002).

Since the mentions filtered by these classifiers are permanently removed, they are never presented as potential mentions to the coreference resolver. Hence, we aim for a classifier that yields few false positives (i.e., mentions classified as non-referential although they were not). False negatives, on the other hand, may be passed on to the resolver, which, ideally, does not assign them to a cluster. The precision/recall tradeoff can easily be controlled by adjusting the threshold of the posterior probability of these classifiers, requiring a very high probability that a mention is non-referential. Preliminary experiments indicated that a threshold of 0.95 worked best when the coreference resolver was trained and evaluated on these filtered mentions.

We also found that the target pronouns should be handled separately, i.e., instead of training one single classifier we trained independent classifiers for each of the target pronouns. The individual performance of the classifiers, as well as the micro-average over all three pronouns are shown in Table 1, both using the default probability threshold of 0.5, and the higher 0.95. In the final, fine-tuned English coreference system, we found that the use of the classifiers with the higher threshold improved in all coreference metrics, and gave an increase of about 0.5 in the official CoNLL score.

The feature set used by the classifiers describes the (in-sentence) context of the pronoun. It consists of the uni-, bi-, and trigrams of word forms and POS tags in a window of ± 5; the position inside the sentence; the preceding and following verb and adjective; the distance to the following named entity; the genre of the document; and whether the mention is between quotes. For English, we additionally extended this general feature set by re-implementing the features of Boyd et al. (2005).

We investigated similar classifiers for Arabic and Chinese as well. We selected targets based on the frequency statistics of tokens being referential and non-referential on the training set and used the general feature set described above. However, these classifiers did not contribute to the more complex coreference system, hence the non-referential classifiers are included only in the English system.

3 Training Instance generation

To generate training instances for the pair-wise classifier, we employed the approach described by Soon et al. (2001). In this approach, for every extracted anaphoric mention m_j, we create a positive training instance with its closest preceding antecedent m_i: $P = \{(m_i, m_j)\}$. Negative examples are constructed by considering all the pairs of m_j and the (non-coreferent) mentions m_k between m_i and m_j: $N = \{(m_k, m_j) | i < k < j\}$. We extract the training examples on the version of the training set that uses predicted information, and restrict the mentions considered to the ones extracted by our mention extraction module. Using these training examples, we train a linear logistic regression classifier using the LIBLINEAR package (Fan et al., 2008).

To create training examples for the English classifier, which uses the non-referential classifier for pronouns, we made a 10-fold cross-annotation on the training set with this classifier. I.e., the documents were partitioned into 10 sets $D_1, D_2, ..., D_{10}$, and when extracting training examples for documents in D_p, the non-referential classifier trained on $D_p^t = \bigcup_{i \neq p} D_i$ was applied.

4 Decoding

We implemented several decoding algorithms for our resolver. The two most common decoding algorithms often found in literature are the so-called *BestFirst* (henceforth BF) and *ClosestFirst* (CF) algorithms (Ng, 2010). Both work in a similar manner and consider mentions linearly ordered as they occur in the document. They proceed left-to-right and for every mention m_j, they consider all pairs (m_i, m_j), where m_i precedes m_j, and queries the classifier whether they are coreferent or not. The main difference between the two algorithms is that the CF algorithm selects the *closest* preceding mention deemed coreferent with m_j by the classifier, while the BF algorithm selects the *most probable* preceding mention. Most probable is determined by some sort of confidence measure of how likely two mentions are to corefer according to the classifier. For both algorithms, the threshold can also be tuned separately, e.g., requiring a probability larger than a certain threshold th_{coref} in order to establish a link between two mentions. Since the logistic classifiers we use directly model a probability distribution, we simply use the posterior probability of the $coref$ class as our confidence score.

Following Björkelund and Nugues (2011) we also implemented a decoder that works differently depending on whether m_j is a pronoun or not. Specifically, for pronouns, the CF algorithm is used, otherwise the BF algorithm is used. In the remainder, we shall refer to this decoder as *PronounsClosestFirst*, or simply PCF.

4.1 Disallowing transitive nesting

A specific kind of mistake we frequently saw in our output is that two clearly disreferent nested mentions are put in the same cluster. Although nestedness can be used as a feature for the classifier, and this appeared to improve performance, two nested mentions can still be put into the same cluster because they are both classified as coreferent with a different, preceding mention. The end result is that the two nested mentions are inadvertently clustered through transitivity.

For example, consider the two occurrences of the phrase *her mother* in (1) below. The spans in the example are labeled alphabetically according to their linear order in the document.[3] Before the resolver considers the last mention d, it has already successfully placed (a, c) in the same cluster. The first pair involving d is (c, d), which is correctly classified as disreferent (here, the feature set informs the classifier that (c, d) are nested). However, the pair (a, d) is easily classified as coreferent since the head noun of a agrees in gender and number with d (and they are not nested).

A different problem is related to named entities in possessive constructions. Consider (2), where our mention extractor extracted e, because it was an NP, and f, because it was tagged as a GPE by the named entity recognizer. Again, the pair (e, f) is correctly classified as disreferent, but both e and f are likely to be classified as coreferent with preceding mentions of *Taiwan*, since our string matching feature ignores possessive markers.

(1) ... she seemed to have such a good relationship with [[her]$_b$ mother]$_a$. Like [[her]$_d$ mother]$_c$ treated her like a human being ...

(2) [[Taiwan]$_f$'s]$_e$

To circumvent this problem, we let the decoders build the clusters incrementally as they work their way through a document and disallow this type of transitive nesting. For instance, when the decoder is trying to find an antecedent for d in (1), a and c have already been clustered together, and when the pair (c, d) is classified as disreferent, the decoder is constrained to skip over other members of c's cluster as it moves backwards in the document. This modification gave an increase of about 0.6 in the CoNLL score for English, and about 0.4 for Arabic and Chinese, and we used this constraint whenever we use the above-mentioned decoders.

4.2 A Cluster-Mention Decoding Algorithm

The pair-wise classifier architecture has, justifiably, received much criticism as it makes decisions based on single pairs of mentions only. We therefore de-

[3]We impose a total order on the mentions by sorting them by starting point. For multiple mentions with the same starting point, the longer is considered to precede the shorter.

vised a decoding algorithm that has a better perspective on entire clusters.

The algorithm works by incrementally merging clusters as mentions are processed. Initially, every mention forms its own cluster. When the next mention m_j is processed, it is compared to all the preceding mentions, $M = \{m_i | i < j\}$. The score of linking m_j with m_i is defined according to:

$$score(m_i, m_j) = (\prod_{m_c \in C} P(coref|(m_c, m_j)))^{1/|C|}$$

where $P(coref|(m_i, m_j))$ is the posterior probability that m_i and m_j are coreferent according to the pair-wise classifier, and C denotes the cluster that m_i belongs to.

After considering all preceding mentions, the cluster of m_j is merged with the cluster of the mention with which it had the highest score, assuming this score is higher than a given threshold th_{coref}. Otherwise it remains in its own cluster.

The task of the $score$ function is to capture cluster-level information. When m_j is compared to a mention m_i, the score is computed as the geometric mean of the product of the probabilities of linking m_j to *all* mentions in the cluster that m_i belongs to. Also note that for two preceding mentions m_{i_1} and m_{i_2} that already belong to the same cluster, $score(m_{i_1}, m_j) = score(m_{i_2}, m_j)$. I.e., the score is the same when m_j is compared to all mentions belonging to the same cluster. Since this algorithm works by maximizing the average probability for linking a mention, we dub this algorithm *AverageMaxProb*, or AMP for short.

It should also be noted that other definitions of the cluster score function $score$ are conceivable.[4] However, initial experiments with other cluster score functions performed worse than the definition above, and time prevented us from exploring this conclusively.

Contrary to the pair-wise decoding algorithms where pair-wise decisions are made in isolation, the order in which mentions are processed make a difference to the AMP decoder. It is generally accepted that named entities are more informative and easier to resolve than common noun phrases and pronouns. To leverage this, we follow Sapena et al. (2010) who reorder mentions based on mention type. Specifically, we first process proper noun phrases, then common noun phrases, and finally pronouns. This implies that common noun phrases have to have a reasonable agreement not only with preceding proper noun phrases of a cluster, but *all* proper noun phrases in a document (where reasonable means that the geometric average of all posterior probabilities stay reasonably high). Similarly, pronouns are forced agree reasonably with all proper and common nouns phrases in a given cluster, and not only the preceding ones. Early experiments showed an increase in performance using reordering, and we consequently used reordering for all languages in the experiments.

5 Features

An advantage of the pair-wise model and of the linear classifiers we use is that they can easily accommodate very large feature spaces, while still remaining reasonably fast. We exploited this by building a large number of parametrized feature templates, that allowed us to experiment easily and quickly with different feature sets. Additionally, since our classifiers are linear, we also evaluated a large number of feature conjunctions, which proved to be crucial to gain reasonable performance.

Due to space restrictions we can not list the complete set of features used in this paper but mention briefly what type of features we used. Most of them are taken from previous work on coreference resolution (Soon et al., 2001; Luo and Zitouni, 2005; Sapena et al., 2010; Björkelund and Nugues, 2011). For a complete list of features the reader can refer to the download of the resolver, which includes the feature sets and parameters used for every language.

One set of feature templates we use is based on surface forms and part-of-speech tags of the first and last, previous and following, and head tokens of the spans that make up mentions. Another set of templates are based on the syntax trees, including both subcategorization frames as well as paths in the syntax tree. To extract head words of mentions, we used the head percolation rules of Choi and Palmer (2010) for Arabic and English, and those of Zhang

[4] In the extreme case, one could take the maximum of the link probabilities over the mentions that belong to the cluster C, in which case the algorithm collapses into the BF algorithm.

and Clark (2011) for Chinese.

While Chinese and English display no or relatively small variety in morphological inflection, Arabic has a very complex morphology. This means that Arabic suffers from greater data sparseness with respect to lexical features. This is exaggerated by the fact that the Arabic training set is considerably smaller than the Chinese and English ones. Hence, we used the lemmas and unvocalised Buckwalter forms that were provided in the Arabic dataset.

We also tried to extract number and gender information based on affixes of Arabic surface forms. These features did, however, not help much. We did however see a considerable increase in performance when we added features that correspond to the Shortest Edit Script (Myers, 1986) between surface forms and unvocalised Buckwalter forms, respectively. We believe that edit scripts are better at capturing the differences in gender and number signaled by certain morphemes than our hand-crafted rules.

Arabic	BF	PCF	AMP	Stacked
MD	58.63	58.49	58.21	60.51
MUC	45.8	45.4	43.2	46.66
B^3	66.65	66.56	66.39	66.3
CEAFE	41.52	41.58	43.1	42.57
CoNLL	51.32	51.18	50.9	51.84
Chinese	BF	PCF	AMP	Stacked
MD	67.22	67.19	66.79	67.61
MUC	59.58	59.43	57.23	59.84
B^3	72.9	72.82	72.7	73.35
CEAFE	46.99	46.98	48.25	47.7
CoNLL	59.82	59.74	59.39	60.30
English	BF	PCF	AMP	Stacked
MD	74.33	74.42	73.75	74.96
MUC	66.76	66.93	62.74	67.12
B^3	70.96	71.11	68.05	71.18
CEAFE	45.46	45.83	46.49	46.84
CoNLL	61.06	61.29	59.09	61.71

Table 2: Performance of different decoders on the development set for each language. The configuration of the Stacked systems is described in detail in Section 7.

6 Resolver Stacking

In Table 2 we present a comparison of the BF, PCF, and AMP resolvers. We omit the results of the CF decoder, since it always did worse and the corresponding numbers would not add more to the picture. The table shows F-measures of mention detection (MD), the MUC metric, the B^3 metric, and the entity-based CEAF metric. The CoNLL score, which is computed as the arithmetic mean of MUC, B^3, and CEAFE, is shown in the last row.

Comparing the AMP decoder to the pair-wise decoders, we find that it generally – i.e., with respect to the CoNLL average – performs worse though it always obtains higher scores with the CEAFE metric. When we looked at the precision and recall for mention detection, we also found that the AMP decoder suffers from lower recall, but higher precision. This led us to conclude that this decoder is more conservative in terms of clustering mentions, and builds smaller, but more consistent clusters. We could also verify this when we computed average cluster sizes on the output of the different decoders.

In order to combine the strengths of the AMP decoder and the pair-wise decoders we employed *stacking*, i.e., we feed the output of one resolver as input to a second. The second resolver is informed about the decision of the first one by introducing an additional feature that encodes the decision of the first resolver. This feature can take five values, depending on how the first resolver treated the two mentions in question: NEITHER, when none of the mentions were placed in a cluster; IONLY, when only the first (antecedent) mention was placed in a cluster; JONLY, when only the second (anaphor) mention was placed in a cluster; COREF, when both mentions were placed in the same cluster; and DISREF, when both mentions were clustered, but in different clusters.

In addition to the stacking feature, the second resolver uses the exact same feature set as the first resolver. To generate the information for the stack feature for training, we made a 10-fold cross-annotation on the training set, in the same way that we cross-annotated the non-referential classifier for English.

In early stacking experiments, we experimented with several combinations of the different decoders. We found that stacking different pair-wise decoders did not give any improvement. We believe the reason for this is that these decoders are too similar and hence can not really benefit from each other. However, when we used the AMP decoder as the first step, and a pair-wise decoder as the second, we saw an increase in performance, particularly with respect to the CEAFE metric.

7 Feature and Parameter Tuning

For every language we tuned decoder parameters and feature sets individually. The feature sets were tuned semi-automatically by evaluating the addition of a new feature template (or template conjunction) to a baseline set. Ideally, we would add feature templates to the baseline set incrementally one at a time, following a cross-validation on the training set. However, to reduce computational effort and time consumption, we resorted to doing only one or two folds out of a 4-fold cross-validation, and adding the two to three most contributing templates in every iteration to the baseline set. The feature sets were optimized to maximize the official CoNLL score using the standard BF decoder.

For the final submission we tuned the thresholds for each decoder, and the choice of pair-wise decoder to use as the second decoder for each language. Modifying the threshold of the AMP decoder gave very small differences in overall score and we kept the threshold for this decoder at 0.5. However, when we increased the probability threshold for the second resolver, we found that performance increased across all languages.

The choice of decoder for the second resolver, and the probability threshold for this, was determined by a 4-fold cross-validation on the training set. For our final submission, as well as in the column *Stacked* in Table 2, we used the following combinations: For Arabic, the threshold was set to 0.60, and the PCF decoder was used; for Chinese, the threshold was set to 0.65, and the BF decoder was used; for English, the threshold was set to 0.65, and the PCF decoder was used.

8 Official Results

The final scores of our system are presented in Table 3. The table also includes the results on the supplementary tracks: gold mention boundaries (GB), when the perfect boundaries of mentions were given; and gold mentions (GM), when only the mentions in the gold standard were given (with gold boundaries). For all three settings we used the same model, which was trained on the concatenation of the training and the development sets.

Arabic	PM	GB	GM
MD	60.55	60.61	76.43
MUC	47.82	47.90	60.81
B^3	68.54	68.61	67.29
CEAFE	44.3	44	49.32
CoNLL	53.55	53.50	59.14
Chinese	PM	GB	GM
MD	66.37	71.02	83.47
MUC	58.61	63.56	76.85
B^3	73.10	74.52	76.30
CEAFE	48.19	50.20	56.61
CoNLL	59.97	62.76	69.92
English	PM	GB	GM
MD	75.38	75.3	86.16
MUC	67.58	67.29	78.70
B^3	70.26	69.70	72.67
CEAFE	45.87	45.27	53.23
CoNLL	61.24	60.75	68.20

Table 3: Performance on the shared task test set. Using predicted mentions (PM; i.e., the official evaluation), gold mentions boundaries (GB), and gold mentions (GM).

Compared to the results on the development set (cf. Table 2), we see a slight drop for Chinese and English, but a fairly big increase for Arabic. Given that Chinese and English have the biggest training sets, we speculate that the increase in Arabic might stem from the increased lexical coverage provided by training on both the training and the development sets.

9 Conclusion

We have presented a novel cluster-based coreference resolution algorithm. This algorithm was combined with conventional pair-wise resolution algorithms in a stacking approach. We applied our system to all three languages in the Shared Task, and obtained an official overall final score of 58.25 which was the second highest in the Shared Task.

Acknowledgments

This work was supported by the Deutsche Forschungsgemeinschaft (DFG) via the SFB 732 "Incremental Specification in Context", projects D4 (PI Helmut Schmid) and D8 (PI Jonas Kuhn).

References

Anders Björkelund and Pierre Nugues. 2011. Exploring lexicalized features for coreference resolution. In *Proceedings of the Fifteenth Conference on Computational Natural Language Learning: Shared Task*, pages 45–50, June.

Adriane Boyd, Whitney Gegg-Harrison, and Donna Byron. 2005. Identifying non-referential it: A machine learning approach incorporating linguistically motivated patterns. In *Proceedings of the ACL Workshop on Feature Engineering for Machine Learning in Natural Language Processing*, pages 40–47, June.

Jinho D. Choi and Martha Palmer. 2010. Robust Constituent-to-Dependency Conversion for English. In *Proceedings of 9th Treebanks and Linguistic Theories Workshop (TLT)*, pages 55–66.

Rong-En Fan, Kai-Wei Chang, Cho-Jui Hsieh, Xiang-Rui Wang, and Chih-Jen Lin. 2008. LIBLINEAR: A library for large linear classification. *Journal of Machine Learning Research*, 9:1871–1874.

Xiaoqiang Luo and Imed Zitouni. 2005. Multi-lingual coreference resolution with syntactic features. In *Proceedings of Human Language Technology Conference and Conference on Empirical Methods in Natural Language Processing*, pages 660–667, October.

Andrew Kachites McCallum. 2002. Mallet: A machine learning for language toolkit. http://mallet.cs.umass.edu.

Eugene W. Myers. 1986. An O(ND) difference algorithm and its variations. *Algorithmica*, 1:251–266.

Vincent Ng. 2010. Supervised noun phrase coreference research: The first fifteen years. In *Proceedings of the 48th Annual Meeting of the Association for Computational Linguistics*, pages 1396–1411, July.

Sameer Pradhan, Alessandro Moschitti, Nianwen Xue, Olga Uryupina, and Yuchen Zhang. 2012. CoNLL-2012 shared task: Modeling multilingual unrestricted coreference in OntoNotes. In *Proceedings of the Sixteenth Conference on Computational Natural Language Learning (CoNLL 2012)*.

Emili Sapena, Lluís Padró, and Jordi Turmo. 2010. A global relaxation labeling approach to coreference resolution. In *Coling 2010: Posters*, pages 1086–1094, August.

Wee Meng Soon, Hwee Tou Ng, and Daniel Chung Yong Lim. 2001. A machine learning approach to coreference resolution of noun phrases. *Computational Linguistics*, 27(4):521–544.

Yue Zhang and Stephen Clark. 2011. Syntactic processing using the generalized perceptron and beam search. *Computational Linguistics*, 37(1):105–151.

Combining the Best of Two Worlds: A Hybrid Approach to Multilingual Coreference Resolution

Chen Chen and **Vincent Ng**
Human Language Technology Research Institute
University of Texas at Dallas
Richardson, TX 75083-0688
{yzcchen,vince}@hlt.utdallas.edu

Abstract

We describe our system for the CoNLL-2012 shared task, which seeks to model coreference in OntoNotes for English, Chinese, and Arabic. We adopt a hybrid approach to coreference resolution, which combines the strengths of rule-based methods and learning-based methods. Our official combined score over all three languages is 56.35. In particular, our score on the Chinese test set is the best among the participating teams.

1 Introduction

The CoNLL-2012 shared task extends last year's task on coreference resolution from a monolingual to a multilingual setting (Pradhan et al., 2012). Unlike the SemEval-2010 shared task on Coreference Resolution in Multiple Languages (Recasens et al., 2010), which focuses on coreference resolution in European languages, the CoNLL shared task is arguably more challenging: it focuses on three languages that come from very different language families, namely English, Chinese, and Arabic.

We designed a system for resolving references in all three languages. Specifically, we participated in four tracks: the closed track for all three languages, and the open track for Chinese. In comparison to last year's participating systems, our resolver has two distinguishing characteristics. First, unlike last year's resolvers, which adopted either a rule-based method or a learning-based method, we adopt a *hybrid* approach to coreference resolution, attempting to combine the strengths of both methods. Second, while last year's resolvers did not exploit genre-specific information, we optimize our system's parameters with respect to each genre.

Our decision to adopt a hybrid approach is motivated by the observation that rule-based methods and learning-based methods each have their unique strengths. As shown by the Stanford coreference resolver (Lee et al., 2011), the winner of last year's shared task, many coreference relations in OntoNotes can be identified using a fairly small set of simple hand-crafted rules. On the other hand, our prior work on machine learning for coreference resolution suggests that coreference-annotated data can be profitably exploited to (1) induce lexical features (Rahman and Ng, 2011a, 2011b) and (2) optimize system parameters with respect to the desired coreference evaluation measure (Ng, 2004, 2009).

Our system employs a fairly standard architecture, performing mention detection prior to coreference resolution. As we will see, however, the parameters of these two components are optimized jointly with respect to the desired evaluation measure.

In the rest of this paper, we describe the mention detection component (Section 2) and the coreference resolution component (Section 3), show how their parameters are jointly optimized (Section 4), and present evaluation results on the development set and the official test set (Section 5).

2 Mention Detection

To build a mention detector that strikes a relatively good balance between precision and recall, we employ a two-step approach. First, in the *extraction* step, we identify named entities (NEs) and employ *language-specific* heuristics to extract mentions from syntactic parse trees, aiming to increase our upper bound on recall as much as possible. Then, in the *pruning* step, we aim to improve precision by employing both *language-specific* heuristic pruning and *language-independent* learning-based pruning. Section 2.1 describes the language-specific heuristics for extraction and pruning, and Section 2.2 describes our learning-based pruning method.

2.1 Heuristic Extraction and Pruning

English. During extraction, we create a candidate mention from a contiguous text span s if (1) s is a PRP or an NP in a syntactic parse tree; or (2) s corresponds to a NE that is not a PERCENT, MONEY, QUANTITY or CARDINAL. During pruning, we remove a candidate mention m_k if (1) m_k is embedded within a larger mention m_j such that m_j and m_k have the same head, where the head of a mention is detected using Collins's (1999) rules; (2) m_k has a quantifier or a partitive modifier; or (3) m_k is a singular common NP, with the exception that we retain mentions related to time (e.g., "today").

Chinese. Similar to English mention extraction, we create Chinese mentions from all NP and QP nodes in syntactic parse trees. During pruning, we remove a candidate mention m_k if (1) m_k is embedded within a larger mention m_j such that m_j and m_k have the same head, except if m_j and m_k appear in a newswire document since, unlike other document annotations, Chinese newswire document annotations do consider such pairs coreferent; (2) m_k is a NE that is a PERCENT, MONEY, QUANTITY and CARDINAL; or (3) m_k is an interrogative pronoun such as *"什么 [what]", "哪儿 [where]"*.

Arabic. We employ as candidate mentions all the NPs extracted from syntactic parse trees, removing those that are PERCENT, MONEY, QUANTITY or CARDINAL.

2.2 Learning-Based Pruning

While the heuristic pruning method identifies candidate mentions, it cannot determine which candidate mentions are likely to be coreferent. To improve pruning (and hence the precision of mention detection), we employ learning-based pruning, where we employ the training data to identify and subsequently discard those candidate mentions that are not likely to be coreferent with other mentions.

Language	Recall	Precision	F-Score
English	88.59	40.56	55.64
Chinese	85.74	42.52	56.85
Arabic	81.49	21.29	33.76

Table 1: Mention detection results on the development set obtained prior to coreference resolution.

Specifically, for each mention m_k in the test set that survives heuristic pruning, we compute its *mention coreference probability*, which indicates the likelihood that the *head noun* of m_k is coreferent with another mention. If this probability does not exceed a certain threshold t_C, we will remove m_k from the list of candidate mentions. Section 4 discusses how t_C is jointly learned with the parameters of the coreference resolution component to optimize the coreference evaluation measure.

We estimate the mention coreference probability of m_k from the training data. Specifically, since only non-singleton mentions are annotated in OntoNotes, we can compute this probability as the number of times m_k's head noun is annotated (as a gold mention) divided by the total number of times m_k's head noun appears. If m_k's head noun does not appear in the training set, we set its coreference probability to 1, meaning that we let it pass through the filter. In other words, we try to be conservative and do not filter any mention for which we cannot compute the coreference probability.

Table 1 shows the mention detection results of the three languages on the development set *after* heuristic extraction and pruning but *prior to* learning-based pruning and coreference resolution.

3 Coreference Resolution

Like the mention detection component, our coreference resolution component employs heuristics and machine learning. More specifically, we employ Stanford's multi-pass sieve approach (Lee et al., 2011) for heuristic coreference resolution, but since most of these sieves are unlexicalized, we seek to improve the multi-pass sieve approach by incorporating lexical information using machine learning techniques. As we will see below, while different sieves are employed for different languages, the way we incorporate lexical information into the sieve approach is the same for all languages.

3.1 The Multi-Pass Sieve Approach

A *sieve* is composed of one or more heuristic *rules*. Each rule extracts a coreference relation between two mentions based on one or more *conditions*. For example, one rule in Stanford's discourse processing sieve posits two mentions as coreferent if two conditions are satisfied: (1) they are both pronouns; and (2) they are produced by the same speaker.

Sieves are ordered by their precision, with the most precise sieve appearing first. To resolve a set of mentions in a document, the resolver makes multiple passes over them: in the *i*-th pass, it attempts to use only the rules in the *i*-th sieve to find an antecedent for each mention m_k. Specifically, when searching for an antecedent for m_k, its candidate antecedents are visited in an order determined by their positions in the associated parse tree (Haghighi and Klein, 2009). The partial clustering of the mentions created in the *i*-th pass is then passed to the *i*+1-th pass. Hence, later passes can exploit the information computed by previous passes, but a coreference link established earlier cannot be overridden later.

3.2 The Sieves

3.2.1 Sieves for English

Our sieves for English are modeled after those employed by the Stanford resolver (Lee et al., 2011), which is composed of 12 sieves.[1] Since we participated in the closed track, we re-implemented the 10 sieves that do not exploit external knowledge sources. These 10 sieves are listed under the "English" column in Table 2. Specifically, we leave out the Alias sieve and the Lexical Chain sieve, which compute semantic similarity using information extracted from WordNet, Wikipedia, and Freebase.

3.2.2 Sieves for Chinese

Recall that for Chinese we participated in both the closed track and the open track. The sieves we employ for both tracks are the same, except that we use NE information to improve some of the sieves in the system for the open track.[2] To obtain automatic NE annotations, we employ a NE model that we trained on the gold NE annotations in the training data.

[1]Table 1 of Lee et al.'s (2011) paper listed 13 sieves, but one of them was used for mention detection.

[2]Note that the use of NEs puts a Chinese resolver in the open track.

English	Chinese
Discourse Processing	Chinese Head Match
Exact String Match	Discourse Processing
Relaxed String Match	Exacth String Match
Precise Constructs	Precise Constructs
Strict Head Match A–C	Strict Head Match A–C
Proper Head Match	Proper Head Match
Relaxed Head Match	Pronouns
Pronouns	--

Table 2: Sieves for English and Chinese (listed in the order in which they are applied).

The Chinese resolver is composed of 9 sieves, as shown under the "Chinese" column of Table 2. These sieves are implemented in essentially the same way as their English counterparts except for a few of them, which are modified in order to account for some characteristics specific to Chinese or the Chinese coreference annotations. As described in detail below, we introduce a new sieve, the Chinese Head Match sieve, and modify two existing sieves, the Precise Constructs sieve, and the Pronoun sieve.

1. **Chinese Head Match sieve:** Recall from Section 2 that the Chinese newswire articles were coreference-annotated in such a way that a mention and its embedding mention can be coreferent if they have the same head. To identify these coreference relations, we employ the Same Head sieve, which posits two mentions m_j and m_k as coreferent if they have the same head and m_k is embedded within m_j. There is an exception to this rule, however: if m_j is a coordinated NP composed of two or more base NPs, and m_k is just one of these base NPs, the two mentions will not be considered coreferent (e.g., 查尔斯和戴安娜 *[Charles and Diana]* and 戴安娜 *[Diana]*).

2. **Precise Constructs sieve:** Recall from Lee et al. (2011) that the Precise Constructs sieve posits two mentions as coreferent based on information such as whether one is an acronym of the other and whether they form an appositive or copular construction. We incorporate additional rules to this sieve to handle specific cases of abbreviations in Chinese: (a) Abbreviation of foreign person names, e.g., 萨达姆・侯赛因 *[Saddam Hussein]* and 萨达姆 *[Saddam]*. (b) Abbreviation of Chinese person names, e.g.,

陈总统 *[Chen President] and* 陈水扁总统 *[Chen Shui-bian President]*. (c) Abbreviation of country names, e.g, 多国 *[Do country] and* 多米尼加 *[Dominica]*.

3. **Pronouns sieve:** The Pronouns sieve resolves pronouns by exploiting grammatical information such as the *gender* and *number* of a mention. While such grammatical information is provided to the participants for English, the same is not true for Chinese.

   To obtain such grammatical information for Chinese, we employ a simple method, which consists of three steps.

   First, we employ simple heuristics to extract grammatical information from those Chinese NPs for which such information can be easily inferred. For example, we can heuristically determine that the gender, number and animacy for 她 *[she]* is *{Female, Single and Animate}*; and for 它们 *[they]* is *{Unknown, Plural, Inanimate}*. In addition, we can determine the grammatical attributes of a mention by its named entity information. For example, a *PERSON* can be assigned the grammatical attributes *{Unknown, Single, Animate}*.

   Next, we bootstrap from these mentions with heuristically determined grammatical attribute values. This is done based on the observation that all mentions in the same coreference chain should agree in gender, number, and animacy. Specifically, given a training text, if one of the mentions in a coreference chain is heuristically labeled with grammatical information, we automatically annotate all the remaining mentions with the same grammatical attribute values.

   Finally, we automatically create *six* word lists, containing (1) animate words, (2) inanimate words, (3) male words, (4) female words, (5) singular words, and (6) plural words. Specifically, we populate these word lists with the grammatically annotated mentions from the previous step, where each element of a word list is composed of the head of a mention and a count indicating the number of times the mention is annotated with the corresponding grammatical attribute value.

   We can then apply these word lists to determine the grammatical attribute values of mentions in a test text. Due to the small size of these word lists, and with the goal of improving precision, we consider two mentions to be grammatically incompatible if for one of these three attributes, one mention has an *Unknown* value whereas the other has a known value.

As seen in Table 2, our Chinese resolver does not have the Relaxed String Match sieve, unlike its English counterpart. Recall that this sieve marks two mentions as coreferent if the strings after dropping the text following their head words are identical (e.g., *Michael Wolf*, and *Michael Wolf, a contributing editor for "New York"*). Since person names in Chinese are almost always composed of a single word and that heads are seldom followed by other words in Chinese, we believe that Relaxed Head Match will not help identify Chinese coreference relations. As noted before, cases of Chinese person name abbreviation will be handled by the Precise Constructs sieve.

3.2.3 Sieves for Arabic

We only employ one sieve for Arabic, the exact match sieve. While we experimented with additional sieves such as the Head Match sieve and the Pronouns sieve, we ended up not employing them because they do not yield better results.

3.3 Incorporating Lexical Information

As mentioned before, we improve the sieve approach by incorporating lexical information.

To exploit lexical information, we first compute lexical probabilities. Specifically, for each pair of mentions m_j and m_k in a test text, we first compute two probabilities: (1) the *string-pair* probability (SP-Prob), which is the probability that the strings of the two mentions, s_j and s_k, are coreferent; and (2) the *head-pair* probability (HP-Prob), which is the probability that the head nouns of the two mentions, h_j and h_k, are coreferent. For better probability estimation, we preprocess the training data and the two mentions by (1) downcasing (but not stemming) each English word, and (2) replacing each Arabic word w by a string formed by concatenating w with its lemmatized form, its Buckwalter form, and its vocalized Buckwalter form. Note that SP-Prob(m_j,m_k) (HP-

Prob(m_j,m_k)) is undefined if one or both of s_j (h_j) and s_k (h_k) do not appear in the training set.

Next, we exploit these lexical probabilities to improve the resolution of m_j and m_k by presenting two extensions to the sieve approach. The first extension aims to improve the *precision* of the sieve approach. Specifically, before applying any sieve, we check whether SP-Prob(m_j,m_k) $\leq t_{SPL}$ or HP-Prob(m_j,m_k) $\leq t_{HPL}$ for some thresholds t_{SPL} and t_{HPL}. If so, our resolver will bypass all of the sieves and simply posit m_j and m_k as not coreferent. In essence, we use the lexical probabilities to improve precision, specifically by positing two mentions as not coreferent if there is "sufficient" information in the training data for us to make this decision. Note that if one of the lexical probabilities (say SP-Prob(m_j,m_k)) is undefined, we only check whether the condition on the other probability (in this case HP(m_j,m_k) $\leq t_{HPL}$) is satisfied. If both of them are undefined, this pair of mentions will survive this filter and be processed by the sieve pipeline.

The second extension, on the other hand, aims to improve *recall*. Specifically, we create a new sieve, the **Lexical Pair** sieve, which we add to the end of the sieve pipeline and which posits two mentions m_j and m_k as coreferent if SP-Prob(m_j,m_k) $\geq t_{SPU}$ or HP-Prob(m_j,m_k) $\geq t_{HPU}$. In essence, we use the lexical probabilities to improve recall, specifically by positing two mentions as coreferent if there is "sufficient" information in the training data for us to make this decision. Similar to the first extension, if one of the lexical probabilities (say SP-Prob(m_j,m_k)) is undefined, we only check whether the condition on the other probability (in this case HP(m_j,m_k) $\geq t_{HPU}$) is satisfied. If both of them are undefined, the Lexical Pair sieve will not process this pair of mentions.

The four thresholds, t_{SPL}, t_{HPL}, t_{SPU}, and t_{HPU}, will be tuned to optimize coreference performance on the development set.

4 Parameter Estimation

As discussed before, we learn the system parameters to optimize coreference performance (which, for the shared task, is $Uavg$, the unweighted average of the three commonly-used evaluation measures, MUC, B^3, and $CEAF_e$) on the development set. Our system has two sets of tunable parameters. So far, we have seen one set of parameters, namely the five *lexical probability thresholds*, t_C, t_{SPL}, t_{HPL}, t_{SPU}, and t_{HPU}. The second set of parameters contains the *rule relaxation parameters*. Recall that each rule in a sieve may be composed of one or more *conditions*. We associate with condition i a parameter λ_i, which is a binary value that controls whether condition i should be removed or not. In particular, if λ_i=0, condition i will be dropped from the corresponding rule. The motivation behind having the rule relaxation parameters should be clear: they allow us to optimize the *hand-crafted* rules using machine learning. This section presents two algorithms for tuning these two sets of parameters on the development set.

Before discussing the parameter estimation algorithms, recall from the introduction that one of the distinguishing features of our approach is that we build *genre-specific* resolvers. In other words, for *each genre* of *each language*, we (1) learn the lexical probabilities from the corresponding training set; (2) obtain optimal parameter values Θ_1 and Θ_2 for the development set using parameter estimation algorithms 1 and 2 respectively; and (3) among Θ_1 and Θ_2, take the one that yields better performance on the development set to be the final set of parameter estimates for the resolver.

Parameter estimation algorithm 1. This algorithm learns the two sets of parameters in a sequential fashion. Specifically, it first tunes the lexical probability thresholds, assuming that all the rule relaxation parameters are set to one. To tune the five probability thresholds, we try all possible combinations of the five probability thresholds and select the combination that yields the best performance on the development set. To ensure computational tractability, we allow each threshold to have the following possible values. For t_C, the possible values are -0.1, 0, 0.05, 0.1, ..., 0.3; for t_{SPL} and t_{HPL}, the possible values are -0.1, 0, 0.05, 0.15, ..., 0.45; and for t_{SPU} and t_{HPU}, the possible values are 0.55, 0.65, ..., 0.95, 1.0 and 1.1. Note that the two threshold values -0.1 and 1.1 render a probability threshold useless. For example, if $t_C = -0.1$, that means all mentions will survive learning-based pruning in the mention detection component. As another example, if t_{SPU} and t_{HPU} are both 1.1, it means that the String Pair sieve will be useless because it will not posit any pair of mentions as coreferent.

Given the optimal set of probability thresholds, we tune the rule relaxation parameters. To do so, we apply the backward elimination feature selection algorithm, viewing each condition as a feature that can be removed from the "feature set". Specifically, all the parameters are initially set to one, meaning that all the conditions are initially present. In each iteration of backward elimination, we identify the condition whose removal yields the highest score on the development set and remove it from the feature set. We repeat this process until all conditions are removed, and identify the subset of the conditions that yields the best score on the development set.

Parameter estimation algorithm 2. In this algorithm, we estimate the two sets of parameters in an interleaved, iterative fashion, where in each iteration, we optimize exactly one parameter from one of the two sets. More specifically, (1) in iteration $2n$, we optimize the (n mod 5)-th lexical probability threshold while keeping the remaining parameters constant; and (2) in iteration $2n+1$, we optimize the (n mod m)-th rule relaxation parameter while keeping the remaining parameters constant, where $n = 1, 2, \ldots$, and m is the number of rule relaxation parameters. When optimizing a parameter in a given iteration, the algorithm selects the value that, when used in combination with the current values of the remaining parameters, optimizes the $Uavg$ value on the development set. We begin the algorithm by initializing all the rule relaxation parameters to one; t_C, t_{SPL} and t_{HPL} to -0.1; and t_{SPU} and t_{HPU} to 1.1. This parameter initialization is equivalent to the configuration where we employ all and only the hand-crafted rules as sieves and do not apply learning to perform any sort of optimization at all.

5 Results and Discussion

The results of our Full coreference resolver on the development set with optimal parameter values are shown in Table 3. As we can see, both the mention detection results and the coreference results (obtained via MUC, B^3, and $CEAF_e$) are expressed in terms of recall (R), precision (P), and F-measure (F). In addition, to better understand the role played by the two sets of system parameters, we performed ablation experiments, showing for each language-track combination the results obtained without tuning (1) the rule relaxation parameters ($-\lambda_i$'s); (2) the probability thresholds ($-t_j$'s); and (3) any of these parameters ($-\lambda_i$'s & t_j). Note that (1) we do not have any rule relaxation parameters for the Arabic resolver owing to its simplicity; and (2) for comparison purposes, we show the results of the Stanford resolver for English in the row labeled "Lee et al. (2011)".

A few points regarding the results in Table 3 deserve mention. First, these mention detection results are different from those shown in Table 1: here, the scores are computed over the mentions that appear in the non-singleton clusters in the coreference partitions produced by a resolver. Second, our reimplementation of the Stanford resolver is as good as the original one. Third, parameter tuning is comparatively less effective for Chinese, presumably because we spent more time on engineering the sieves for Chinese than for the other languages. Fourth, our score on Arabic is the lowest among the three languages, primarily because Arabic is highly inflectional and we have little linguistic knowledge of the language to design effective sieves. Finally, these results and our official test set results (Table 4), as well as our supplementary evaluation results on the test set obtained using gold mention boundaries (Table 5) and gold mentions (Table 6), exhibit similar performance trends.

Table 7 shows the optimal parameter values obtained for the Full resolver on the development set. Since there are multiple genres for English and Chinese, we show in the table the probability thresholds averaged over all the genres and the corresponding standard deviation values. For the rule relaxation parameters, among the 36 conditions in the English sieves and the 61 conditions in the Chinese sieves, we show the number of conditions being removed (when averaged over all the genres) and the corresponding standard deviation values. Overall, different conditions were removed for different genres.

To get a better sense of the usefulness of the probability thresholds, we show in Tables 8 and 9 some development set examples of correctly and incorrectly identified/pruned mentions and coreferent/non-coreferent pairs for English and Chinese, respectively. Note that no Chinese examples for t_C are shown, since its tuned value cor-

Language	Track	System	Mention Detect. R	P	F	MUC R	P	F	B-CUBED R	P	F	CEAF$_e$ R	P	F	Avg F
English	Closed	Full	74.8	75.6	**75.2**	65.6	67.3	**66.4**	69.1	74.7	**71.8**	49.8	47.9	**48.8**	**62.3**
		$-\lambda_i$'s	75.2	73.4	74.3	64.6	65.8	65.2	68.5	74.1	71.2	48.8	47.6	48.2	61.5
		$-t_j$'s	76.4	73.0	74.7	65.1	65.3	65.2	68.6	73.8	71.1	48.6	48.3	48.4	61.6
		$-\lambda_i$'s & t_j's	75.2	72.8	74.0	64.2	64.8	64.5	68.0	73.4	70.6	47.8	47.1	47.5	60.8
		Lee et al. (2011)	74.1	72.5	73.3	64.3	64.9	64.6	68.2	73.1	70.6	47.0	46.3	46.7	60.6
Chinese	Closed	Full	72.2	72.7	**72.4**	62.4	65.8	**64.1**	70.8	77.7	**74.1**	52.3	48.9	**50.5**	**62.9**
		$-\lambda_i$'s	71.3	72.8	71.9	61.8	66.7	64.2	70.2	78.2	74.0	52.2	47.6	49.9	62.6
		$-t_j$'s	72.7	71.1	71.9	62.3	64.8	63.5	70.7	77.1	73.8	51.2	48.8	50.0	62.4
		$-\lambda_i$'s & t_j's	71.7	71.4	71.5	61.5	65.1	63.3	70.0	77.6	73.6	51.3	47.9	49.5	62.1
Chinese	Open	Full	73.1	72.6	**72.9**	63.5	67.2	**65.3**	71.6	78.2	**74.8**	52.5	48.9	**50.7**	**63.6**
		$-\lambda_i$'s	72.5	73.1	72.8	63.2	67.0	65.1	71.3	78.1	74.5	52.4	48.7	50.4	63.3
		$-t_j$'s	72.8	72.5	72.7	63.5	66.5	65.0	71.4	77.8	74.5	51.9	48.9	50.4	63.3
		$-\lambda_i$'s & t_j's	72.4	72.5	72.4	63.0	66.3	64.6	71.0	77.8	74.3	51.7	48.5	50.1	63.0
Arabic	Closed	Full	56.6	64.5	**60.3**	40.4	42.8	**41.6**	58.9	62.7	**60.7**	40.4	37.8	**39.1**	**47.1**
		$-t_j$'s	52.0	64.3	57.5	33.1	40.2	36.3	53.4	67.9	59.8	41.9	34.2	37.6	44.6

Table 3: Results on the development set with optimal parameter values.

Language	Track	System	Mention Detect. R	P	F	MUC R	P	F	B-CUBED R	P	F	CEAF$_e$ R	P	F	Avg F
English	Closed	Full	75.1	72.6	73.8	63.5	64.0	63.7	66.6	71.5	69.0	46.7	46.2	46.4	59.7
Chinese	Closed	Full	71.1	72.1	71.6	59.9	64.7	62.2	69.7	77.8	73.6	53.4	48.7	51.0	62.2
Chinese	Closed	Full	71.5	73.5	72.4	62.5	67.1	64.7	71.2	78.4	74.6	53.6	49.1	51.3	63.5
Arabic	Closed	Full	56.2	64.0	59.8	38.1	40.0	39.0	60.6	62.5	61.5	41.9	39.8	40.8	47.1

Table 4: Official results on the test set.

Language	Track	System	Mention Detect. R	P	F	MUC R	P	F	B-CUBED R	P	F	CEAF$_e$ R	P	F	Avg F
English	Closed	Full	74.8	75.7	75.2	63.3	66.8	65.0	65.4	73.6	69.2	48.8	44.9	46.8	60.3
Chinese	Closed	Full	82.0	79.0	80.5	70.8	72.1	71.4	74.4	79.9	77.0	58.0	56.4	57.2	68.6
Chinese	Open	Full	82.4	80.1	81.2	73.5	74.3	73.9	76.3	80.5	78.3	58.2	57.3	57.8	70.0
Arabic	Closed	Full	57.2	62.6	59.8	38.7	39.2	39.0	61.5	61.8	61.7	41.6	40.9	41.2	47.3

Table 5: Supplementary results on the test set obtained using gold mention boundaries and predicted parse trees.

Language	Track	System	Mention Detect. R	P	F	MUC R	P	F	B-CUBED R	P	F	CEAF$_e$ R	P	F	Avg F
English	Closed	Full	80.8	100	89.4	72.3	89.4	79.9	64.6	85.9	73.8	76.3	46.4	57.7	70.5
Chinese	Closed	Full	84.7	100	91.7	76.6	92.4	83.8	73.0	91.4	81.2	83.6	57.9	68.4	77.8
Chinese	Open	Full	84.8	100	91.8	78.1	93.2	85.0	75.0	91.6	82.5	84.0	59.2	69.4	79.0
Arabic	Closed	Full	58.3	100	73.7	41.7	63.2	50.3	50.0	75.3	60.1	64.6	36.2	46.4	52.3

Table 6: Supplementary results on the test set obtained using gold mentions and predicted parse trees.

Language	Track	t_C Avg.	St.Dev.	t_{HPL} Avg.	St.Dev.	t_{SPL} Avg.	St.Dev.	t_{HPU} Avg.	St.Dev.	t_{SPU} Avg.	St.Dev.	Rule Relaxation Avg.	St.Dev.
English	Closed	−0.06	0.11	−0.04	0.08	−0.06	0.12	0.90	0.23	0.60	0.05	6.13	1.55
Chinese	Closed	−0.10	0.00	−0.08	0.06	0.00	0.95	1.01	0.22	0.88	0.27	4.67	1.63
Chinese	Open	−0.10	0.00	−0.08	0.06	−0.05	0.05	1.01	0.22	0.88	0.27	5.83	1.94
Arabic	Closed	0.05	0.00	0.00	0.00	−0.10	0.00	1.10	0.00	0.15	0.00	0.00	0.00

Table 7: Optimal parameter values.

responds to the case where no mentions should be pruned.

6 Conclusion

We presented a multilingual coreference resolver designed for the CoNLL-2012 shared task. We adopted

Parameter	Correct	Incorrect
t_C	no problem; the same	that; that idea
t_{HPL}	(people,that); (both of you,that)	(ours,they); (both of you,us)
t_{SPL}	(first,first); (the previous year,its)	(China,its); (Taiwan,its)
t_{HPU}	(The movie's,the film); (Firestone,the company's)	(himself,he); (My,I)
t_{SPU}	(Barak,the Israeli Prime Minister); (Kostunica,the new Yugoslav President)	(she,the woman); (Taiwan,the island)

Table 8: Examples of correctly & incorrectly identified/pruned English mentions and coreferent/non-coreferent pairs.

Parameter	Correct	Incorrect
t_C	---	---
t_{HPL}	(这个东西, 东西); (足够的钱, 钱)	(我们这儿人, 他们); (爸爸, 我)
t_{SPL}	(别人, 别人); (不少人, 不少人)	(台湾, 你们); (我国, 我)
t_{HPU}	(国内, 我们国内); (咱妈, 咱们妈)	(咱们妈, 她妈); (咱们, 咱)
t_{SPU}	(两岸, 海峡两岸); (大陆, 中国);	(中国, 中) ; (亚洲地区, 亚洲)

Table 9: Examples of correctly & incorrectly identified/pruned Chinese mentions and coreferent/non-coreferent pairs.

a hybrid approach to coreference resolution, which combined the advantages of rule-based methods and learning-based methods. Specifically, we proposed two extensions to Stanford's multi-pass sieve approach, which involved the incorporation of lexical information using machine learning and the acquisition of genre-specific resolvers. Experimental results demonstrated the effectiveness of these extensions, whether or not they were applied in isolation or in combination.

In future work, we plan to explore other ways to combine rule-based methods and learning-based methods for coreference resolution, as well as improve the performance of our resolver on Arabic.

Acknowledgments

We thank the two anonymous reviewers for their comments on the paper. This work was supported in part by NSF Grants IIS-0812261 and IIS-1147644.

References

Michael John Collins. 1999. *Head-Driven Statistical Models for Natural Language Parsing*. Ph.D. thesis, University of Pennsylvania, Philadelphia, PA.

Aria Haghighi and Dan Klein. 2009. Simple coreference resolution with rich syntactic and semantic features. In *Proceedings of the 2009 Conference on Empirical Methods in Natural Language Processing*, pages 1152--1161.

Heeyoung Lee, Yves Peirsman, Angel Chang, Nathanael Chambers, Mihai Surdeanu, and Dan Jurafsky. 2011. Stanford's multi-pass sieve coreference resolution system at the CoNLL-2011 shared task. In *Proceedings of the Fifteenth Conference on Computational Natural Language Learning: Shared Task*, pages 28--34.

Vincent Ng. 2004. Learning noun phrase anaphoricity to improve conference resolution: Issues in representation and optimization. In *Proceedings of the 42nd Meeting of the Association for Computational Linguistics*, pages 151--158.

Vincent Ng. 2009. Graph-cut-based anaphoricity determination for coreference resolution. In *Proceedings of the 2009 Conference of the North American Chapter of the Association for Computational Linguistics: Human Language Technologies*, pages 575--583.

Sameer Pradhan, Alessandro Moschitti, Nianwen Xue, Olga Uryupina, and Yuchen Zhang. 2012. CoNLL-2012 shared task: Modeling multilingual unrestricted coreference in OntoNotes, In *Proceedings of the Sixteenth Conference on Computational Natural Language Learning*.

Altaf Rahman and Vincent Ng. 2011a. Coreference resolution with world knowledge. In *Proceedings of the 49th Annual Meeting of the Association for Computational Linguistics: Human Language Technologies*, pages 814--824.

Altaf Rahman and Vincent Ng. 2011b. Narrowing the modeling gap: A cluster-ranking approach to coreference resolution. *Journal of Artificial Intelligence Research*, 40:469--521.

Marta Recasens, Lluís Màrquez, Emili Sapena, M. Antònia Martí, Mariona Taulé, Véronique Hoste, Massimo Poesio, and Yannick Versley. 2010. Semeval-2010 task 1: Coreference resolution in multiple languages. In *Proceedings of the 5th International Workshop on Semantic Evaluation*, pages 1--8.

Using Syntactic Dependencies to Solve Coreferences

Marcus Stamborg **Dennis Medved** **Peter Exner** **Pierre Nugues**
Lund University
Lund, Sweden
cid03mst@student.lu.se, dt07dm0@student.lth.se
Peter.Exner@cs.lth.se, Pierre.Nugues@cs.lth.se

Abstract

This paper describes the structure of the LTH coreference solver used in the closed track of the CoNLL 2012 shared task (Pradhan et al., 2012). The solver core is a mention classifier that uses Soon et al. (2001)'s algorithm and features extracted from the dependency graphs of the sentences.

This system builds on Björkelund and Nugues (2011)'s solver that we extended so that it can be applied to the three languages of the task: English, Chinese, and Arabic. We designed a new mention detection module that removes pleonastic pronouns, prunes constituents, and recovers mentions when they do not match exactly a noun phrase. We carefully redesigned the features so that they reflect more complex linguistic phenomena as well as discourse properties. Finally, we introduced a minimal cluster model grounded in the first mention of an entity.

We optimized the feature sets for the three languages: We carried out an extensive evaluation of pairs of features and we complemented the single features with associations that improved the CoNLL score. We obtained the respective scores of 59.57, 56.62, and 48.25 on English, Chinese, and Arabic on the development set, 59.36, 56.85, and 49.43 on the test set, and the combined official score of 55.21.

1 Introduction

In this paper, we present the LTH coreference solver used in the closed track of the CoNLL 2012 shared task (Pradhan et al., 2012). We started from an earlier version of the system by Björkelund and Nugues (2011), to which we added substantial improvements. As base learning and decoding algorithm, our solver extracts noun phrases and possessive pronouns and uses Soon et al. (2001)'s pairwise classifier to decide if a pair corefers or not. Similarly to the earlier LTH system, we constructed a primary feature set from properties extracted from the dependency graphs of the sentences.

2 System Architecture

The training and decoding modules consist of a mention detector, a pair generator, and a feature extractor. The training module extracts a set of positive and negative pairs of mentions and uses logistic regression and the LIBLINEAR package (Fan et al., 2008) to generate a binary classifier. The solver extracts pairs of mentions and uses the classifier and its probability output, $P_{coref}(\text{Antecedent, Anaphor})$, to determine if a pair corefers or not. The solver has also a post processing step to recover some mentions that do not match a noun phrase constituent.

3 Converting Constituents to Dependency Trees

Although the input to coreference solvers are pairs or sets of constituents, many systems use concepts from dependency grammars to decide if a pair is coreferent. The most frequent one is the constituent's head that solvers need then to extract using ad-hoc rules; see the CoNLL 2011 shared task (Pradhan et al., 2011), for instance. This can be tedious as we may have to write new rules for each new feature to incorporate in the classifier. That is why, instead of writing sets of rules applicable to specific types of dependencies, we converted all the constituents in the three corpora to generic dependency graphs before starting the training and solving steps. We used the LTH converter (Johansson and Nugues, 2007) for English, the Penn2Malt converter (Nivre, 2006) with the Chinese rules for Chinese[1], and the CATiB converter (Habash and Roth, 2009) for Arabic.

The CATiB converter (Habash and Roth, 2009) uses the Penn Arabic part-of-speech tagset, while the automatically tagged version of the CoNLL Arabic corpus uses a simplified tagset inspired by the English version of the Penn treebank. We translated these simplified POS tags to run the CATiB converter. We created a lookup table to map the simplified POS tags in the automatically annotated corpus to the Penn Arabic POS tags in the gold annotation. We took the most frequent association in the lookup table to carry out the translation. We then used the result to convert the constituents into dependencies. We translated the POS tags in the development set using a dictionary extracted from the gold training file and we translated the tags in the training file by a 5-fold cross-validation. We used this dictionary during both training and classifying since our features had a better performance with the Arabic tagset.

4 Mention Extraction

4.1 Base Extraction

As first step of the mention selection stage, we extracted all the noun phrases (NP), pronouns (PRP), and possessive pronouns (PRP$) for English and Arabic, with the addition of PN pronouns for Chinese. This stage is aimed at reaching a high recall of the mentions involved in the coreference chains and results in an overinclusive set of candidates. Table 1 shows the precision and recall figures for the respective languages when extracting mentions from the training set. The precision is significantly lower for Arabic than for English and Chinese.

4.2 Removal of the Pleonastic *it*

In the English corpus, the pronoun *it* in the first step of the mention extraction stage creates a high number of false positive mentions. We built a classifier to discard as many of these pleonastic *it* as possible from the mention list.

Language	Recall	Precision
English	92.17	32.82
English with named entities	94.47	31.61
Chinese	87.32	32.29
Arabic	87.22	17.64

Table 1: Precision and recall for the mention detection stage on the training set.

Feature name
HeadLex
HeadRightSiblingPOS
HeadPOS

Table 2: Features used by the pleonastic *it* classifier.

Table 2 shows the features we used to train the classifier and Table 3 shows the impact on the final system. We optimized the feature set using greedy forward and backward selections. We explored various ways of using the classifier: before, after, and during coreference resolving. We obtained the best results when we applied the pleonastic classifier during coreference solving and we multiplied the probability outputs from the two classifiers. We used the inequality:

$$P_{coref}(\text{Antecedent}, it) \times (1 - P_{pleo}(it)) > 0.4,$$

where we found the optimal threshold of 0.4 using a 5-fold cross-validation.

4.3 Named Entities

The simple rule to approximate entities to noun phrases and pronouns leaves out between $\sim$8% and $\sim$13 % of the entities in the corpora (Table 1). As the named entities sometimes do not match constituents, we tried to add them to increase the recall. We carried out extensive experiments for the three lan-

English	CoNLL score
Without removal	59.15
With removal	**59.57**

Table 3: Score on the English development set with and without removal of the pleonastic *it* pronouns.

[1]http://stp.lingfil.uu.se/ nivre/research/Penn2Malt.html

English	Total score
Without named entities	58.85
With named entities	**59.57**

Table 4: Impact on the overall score on the English development set by addition of named entities extracted from the corpus.

Language	Without pruning	With pruning
English	56.42	**59.57**
Chinese	50.94	**56.62**
Arabic	**48.25**	47.10

Table 5: Results on running the system on the development set with and without pruning for all the languages.

guages. While the named entities increased the score for the English corpus, we found that it lowered the results for Chinese and Arabic. We added all single and multiword named entities of the English corpus except the CARDINAL, ORDINAL, PERCENT, and QUANTITY tags. Table 1 shows the recall and precision for English and Table 4 shows the named entity impact on the overall CoNLL score on the development set.

4.4 Pruning

When constituents shared the same head in the list of mentions, we pruned the smaller ones. This increased the scores for English and Chinese, but lowered that of Arabic (Table 5). The results for the latter language are somewhat paradoxical; they are possibly due to errors in the dependency conversion.

5 Decoding

Depending on the languages, we applied different decoding strategies: For Chinese and Arabic, we used a closest-first clustering method as described by Soon et al. (2001) for pronominal anaphors and a best-first clustering otherwise as in Ng and Cardie (2002). For English, we applied a closest-first clustering for pronominal anaphors. For nonpronominal anaphors, we used an averaged best-first clustering: We considered all the chains before the current anaphor and we computed the geometric mean of the pair probabilities using all the mentions in a chain. We linked the anaphor to the maximal scoring chain or we created a new chain if the score was less than 0.5. We discarded all the remaining singletons.

As in Björkelund and Nugues (2011), we recovered some mentions using a post processing stage, where we clustered named entities to chains having strict matching heads.

English	Total score
Without extensions	57.22
With extensions	**59.57**

Table 6: Total impact of the extensions to the mention extraction stage on the English development set.

6 Features

We started with the feature set described in Björkelund and Nugues (2011) for our baseline system for English and with the feature set in Soon et al. (2001) for Chinese and Arabic. Due to space limitations, we omit the description of these features and refer to the respective papers.

6.1 Naming Convention

We denoted HD, the head word of a mention in a dependency tree, HDLMC and HDRMC, the left-most child and the right-most child of the head, HDLS and HDRS, the left and right siblings of the head word, and HDGOV, the governor of the head word.

From these tokens, we can extract the surface form, FORM, the part-of-speech tag, POS, and the grammatical function of the token, FUN, i.e. the label of the dependency edge of the token to its parent.

We used a naming nomenclature consisting of the role in the anaphora, where J- stands for the anaphor, I-, for the antecedent, F-, for the mention in the chain preceding the antecedent (previous antecedent), and A- for the first mention of the entity in the chain; the token we selected from the dependency graph, e.g. HD or HDLMC; and the value extracted from the token e.g. POS or FUN. For instance, the part-of-speech tag of the governor of the head word of the anaphor is denoted J-HDGOVPOS.

6.2 Combination of Features

In addition to the single features, we combined them to create bigram, trigram, and four-gram features. Table 7 shows the features we used, either single or in combination, e.g. I-HDFORM+J-HDFORM.

We emulated a simple cluster model by utilizing the first mention in the chain and/or the previous antecedent, e.g. A-EDITDISTANCE+F-EDITDISTANCE+EDITDISTANCE, where the edit distance of the anaphor is calculated for the first mention in the chain, previous antecedent, and antecedent.

6.3 Notable New Features

Edit Distance Features. We created edit distance-based features between pairs of potentially coreferring mentions: EDITDISTANCE is the character-based edit distance between two strings; EDITDISTANCEWORD is a word-level edit distance, where the symbols are the complete words; and PROPERNAMESIMILARITY is a character-based edit distance between proper nouns only.

Discourse Features. We created features to reflect the speaker agreement, i.e. when the pair of mentions corresponds to the same speaker, often in combination with the fact that both mentions are pronouns. For example, references to the first person pronoun *I* from a same speaker refer probably to a same entity; in this case, the speaker himself.

Document Type Feature. We created the I-HDFORM+J-HDFORM+DOCUMENTTYPE feature to capture the genre of different document types, as texts from e.g. the New Testament are likely to differ from internet blogs.

6.4 Feature Selection

We carried out a greedy forward selection of the features starting from Björkelund and Nugues (2011)'s feature set for English, and Soon et al. (2001)'s for Chinese and Arabic. The feature selection used a 5-fold cross-validation over the training set, where we evaluated the features using the arithmetic mean of MUC, BCUB, and CEAFE.

After reaching a maximal score using forward selection, we reversed the process using a backward elimination, leaving out each feature and removing the one that had the worst impact on performance. This backwards procedure was carried out until the score no longer increased. We repeated this forward-backward procedure until there was no increase in performance.

7 Evaluation

Table 7 shows the final feature set for each language combined with the impact each feature has on the score on the development set when being left out. A dash (—) means that the feature is not part of the feature set used in the respective language. As we can see, some features increase the score. This is due to the fact that the feature selection was carried out in a cross-validated manner over the training set.

Table 8 shows the results on the development and test sets as well as on the test set with gold mentions. For each language, the figures are overall consistent between the development and test sets across all the metrics. The scores improve very significantly with the gold mentions: up to more than 10 points for Chinese.

8 Conclusions

The LTH coreference solver used in the CoNLL 2012 shared task uses Soon et al. (2001)'s algorithm and a set of lexical and nonlexical features. To a large extent, we extracted these features from the dependency graphs of the sentences. The results we obtained seem to hint that this approach is robust across the three languages of the task.

Our system builds on an earlier system that we evaluated in the CoNLL 2011 shared task (Pradhan et al., 2011), where we optimized significantly the solver code, most notably the mention detection step and the feature design. Although not exactly comparable, we could improve the CoNLL score by 4.83 from 54.53 to 59.36 on the English corpus. The mention extraction stage plays a significant role in the overall performance. By improving the quality of the mentions extracted, we obtained a performance increase of 2.35 (Table 6).

Using more complex feature structures also proved instrumental. Scores of additional feature variants could be tested in the future and possibly increase the system's performance. Due to limited computing resources and time, we had to confine the search to a handful of features that we deemed most promising.

All features	En (+/-)	Zh (+/-)	Ar (+/-)
STRINGMATCH	-0.003	**-0.58**	**-1.79**
A-STRINGMATCH+STRINGMATCH	-0.11	—	—
DISTANCE	-0.19	-0.57	-0.24
DISTANCE+J-PRONOUN	0.03	—	—
I-PRONOUN	0.02	—	—
J-PRONOUN	0.02	—	—
J-DEMOSTRATIVE	-0.02	0.01	—
BOTHPROPERNAME	—	0.03	—
NUMBERAGREEMENT	**-0.23**	—	—
GENDERAGREEMENT	0.003	—	—
NUMBERBIGRAM	—	0.06	—
GENDERBIGRAM	-0.03	0.01	—
I-HDFORM	-0.16	—	-0.67
I-HDFUN	0.05	—	—
I-HDPOS	-0.02	—	-0.52
I-HDRMCFUN	0.003	—	—
I-HDLMCFORM	—	—	-0.05
I-HDLMCPOS	0.01	—	—
I-HDLSFORM	-0.08	—	-0.18
I-HDGOVFUN	0.06	—	—
I-HDGOVPOS	—	-0.003	-0.19
J-HDFUN	0.003	—	—
J-HDGOVFUN	0.03	—	—
J-HDGOVPOS	-0.05	—	—
J-HDRSPOS	—	—	-0.2
A-HDCHILDSETPOS	—	0.06	—
I-HDFORM+J-HDFORM	0.08	—	-0.57
A-HDFORM+J-HDFORM	—	—	-0.46
I-HDGOVFORM+J-HDFORM	—	-0.14	0.04
I-LMCFORM+J-LMCFORM	-0.07	-0.15	—
A-HDFORM+I-HDFORM+J-HDFORM	0.11	—	—
F-HDFORM+I-HDFORM+J-HDFORM	—	-0.1	—
I-HDPOS+J-HDPOS+I-HDFUN+J-HDFUN	—	-0.09	—
I-HDPOS+J-HDPOS+I-HDFORM+J-HDFORM	—	—	-0.05
I-HDFORM+J-HDFORM+SPEAKAGREE	—	-0.55	—
I-HDFORM+J-HDFORM+BOTHPRN+SPEAKAGREE	-0.11	—	—
I-HDGOVFORM+J-HDFORM+BOTHPRN+SPEAKAGREE	**-0.23**	—	—
A-HDFORM+J-HDFORM+SPEAKAGREE	0.04	—	—
I-HDFORM+J-HDFORM+DOCUMENTTYPE	-0.4	-0.18	—
SSPATHBERGSMALIN	-0.07	—	—
SSPATHFORM	—	—	-0.19
SSPATHFUN	-0.08	—	-0.14
SSPATHPOS	-0.1	-0.11	-0.53
DSPATHBERGSMALIN	—	—	0
DSPATHFORM	0.07	—	—
DSPATHFORM+DOCUMENTTYPE	0.03	—	—
DSPATHPOS	0.07	-0.06	0.05
EDITDISTANCE	-0.05	-0.16	0
EDITDISTANCEWORD	—	—	-0.25
A-EDITDISTANCE+EDITDISTANCE	—	—	-0.02
A-EDITDISTANCE+F-EDITDISTANCE	—	-0.01	-0.01
A-EDITDISTANCE+F-EDITDISTANCE+EDITDISTANCE	—	—	-0.09
EDITDISTANCEWORD+BOTHPROPERNAME	0.02	—	—
PROPERNAMESIMILARITY	-0.03	—	—
SEMROLEPROPJHD	0.01	—	—

Table 7: The feature sets for English, Chinese and Arabic, and for each feature, the degradation in performance when leaving out this feature from the set; the more negative, the better the feature contribution. We carried out all the evaluations on the development set. The table shows the difference with the official CoNLL score.

Metric/Corpus	Development set			Test set			Test set (Gold mentions)		
English	R	P	F1	R	P	F1	R	P	F1
Mention detection	74.21	72.81	73.5	75.51	72.39	73.92	78.17	100	87.74
MUC	65.27	64.25	64.76	66.26	63.98	65.10	71.22	88.12	78.77
BCUB	69.1	70.94	70.01	69.09	69.54	69.31	64.75	83.16	72.8
CEAFM	57.56	57.56	57.56	56.76	56.76	56.76	66.74	66.74	66.74
CEAFE	43.44	44.47	43.95	42.53	44.89	43.68	71.94	43.74	54.41
BLANC	75.36	77.41	76.34	74.03	77.28	75.52	78.68	81.47	79.99
CoNLL score			59.57			59.36			68.66
Chinese	R	P	F1	R	P	F1	R	P	F1
Mention detection	60.55	68.73	64.38	57.65	71.93	64.01	68.97	100	81.63
MUC	54.63	60.96	57.62	52.56	64.13	57.77	63.52	88.23	73.86
BCUB	66.91	74.4	70.46	64.43	77.55	70.38	63.54	88.12	73.84
CEAFM	55.09	55.09	55.09	55.57	55.57	55.57	65.60	65.60	65.60
CEAFE	44.65	39.25	41.78	47.90	38.04	42.41	72.56	42.01	53.21
BLANC	73.23	72.95	73.09	72.74	77.84	75.00	76.96	83.70	79.89
CoNLL score			56.62			56.85			66.97
Arabic	R	P	F1	R	P	F1	R	P	F1
Mention detection	55.54	61.7	58.46	56.1	63.28	59.47	56.13	100	71.9
MUC	39.18	43.76	41.34	39.11	43.49	41.18	41.99	69.78	52.43
BCUB	59.16	67.94	63.25	61.57	67.95	64.61	50.45	81.30	62.26
CEAFM	47.8	47.8	47.8	50.16	50.16	50.16	54.00	54.00	54.00
CEAFE	42.57	38.01	40.16	44.86	40.36	42.49	66.16	34.52	45.37
BLANC	62.44	67.18	64.36	66.80	66.94	66.87	67.37	73.46	69.87
CoNLL score			48.25			49.43			53.35

Table 8: Scores on the development set, test set, and test set with gold mentions for English, Chinese, and Arabic: recall R, precision P, and harmonic mean F1. The official CoNLL score is computed as the arithmetic mean of MUC, BCUB, and CEAFE.

Acknowledgments

This research was supported by Vetenskapsrådet, the Swedish research council, under grant 621-2010-4800, and the European Union's seventh framework program (FP7/2007-2013) under grant agreement no. 230902.

References

Anders Björkelund and Pierre Nugues. 2011. Exploring lexicalized features for coreference resolution. In *Proceedings of the Fifteenth Conference on Computational Natural Language Learning: Shared Task*, pages 45–50, Portland, Oregon, USA, June. Association for Computational Linguistics.

Rong-En Fan, Kai-Wei Chang, Cho-Jui Hsieh, Xiang-Rui Wang, and Chih-Jen Lin. 2008. LIBLINEAR: A library for large linear classification. *Journal of Machine Learning Research*, 9:1871–1874.

Nizar Habash and Ryan Roth. 2009. CATiB: The Columbia Arabic treebank. In *Proceedings of the ACL-IJCNLP 2009 Conference Short Papers*, pages 221–224, Suntec, Singapore, August. Association for Computational Linguistics.

Richard Johansson and Pierre Nugues. 2007. Extended constituent-to-dependency conversion for English. In Joakim Nivre, Heiki-Jaan Kaalep, Kadri Muischnek, and Mare Koit, editors, *NODALIDA 2007 Conference Proceedings*, pages 105–112, Tartu, May 25-26.

Vincent Ng and Claire Cardie. 2002. Improving machine laerning approaches to coreference resolution. In *Proceedings of the 40th Annual Meeting of the Association for Computational Linguistics*, pages 104–111.

Joakim Nivre. 2006. *Inductive Dependency Parsing*. Springer, Dordrecht, The Netherlands.

Sameer Pradhan, Lance Ramshaw, Mitchell Marcus, Martha Palmer, Ralph Weischedel, and Nianwen Xue. 2011. CoNLL-2011 shared task: Modeling unrestricted coreference in OntoNotes. In *Proceedings of the Fifteenth Conference on Computational Natural Language Learning: Shared Task*, pages 1–27, Portland, Oregon, USA, June. Association for Computational Linguistics.

Sameer Pradhan, Alessandro Moschitti, Nianwen Xue, Olga Uryupina, and Yuchen Zhang. 2012. CoNLL-2012 shared task: Modeling multilingual unrestricted coreference in OntoNotes. In *Proceedings of the Sixteenth Conference on Computational Natural Language Learning (CoNLL 2012)*, Jeju, Korea.

Wee Meng Soon, Hwee Tou Ng, and Daniel Chung Yong Lim. 2001. A machine learning approach to coreference resolution of noun phrases. *Computational Linguistics*, 27(4):521–544.

ICT: System Description for CoNLL-2012

Hao Xiong and Qun Liu
Key Lab. of Intelligent Information Processing
Institute of Computing Technology
Chinese Academy of Sciences
P.O. Box 2704, Beijing 100190, China
{xionghao, liuqun}@ict.ac.cn

Abstract

In this paper, we present our system description for the CoNLL-2012 coreference resolution task on English, Chinese and Arabic. We investigate a projection-based model in which we first translate Chinese and Arabic into English, run a publicly available coreference system, and then use a new projection algorithm to map the coreferring entities back from English into mention candidates detected in the Chinese and Arabic source. We compare to a baseline that just runs the English coreference system on the supplied parses for Chinese and Arabic. Because our method does not beat the baseline system on the development set, we submit outputs generated by the baseline system as our final submission.

1 Introduction

Modeling multilingual unrestricted coreference in the OntoNotes data is the shared task for CoNLL-2012. This is an extension of the CoNLL-2011 shared task and would involve automatic anaphoric mention detection and coreference resolution across three languages – English, Chinese and Arabic – using OntoNotes v5.0 corpus, given predicted information on the syntax, proposition, word sense and named entity layers. Automatic identification of coreferring entities and events in text has been an uphill battle for several decades, partly because it can require world knowledge which is not well-defined and partly owing to the lack of substantial annotated data.

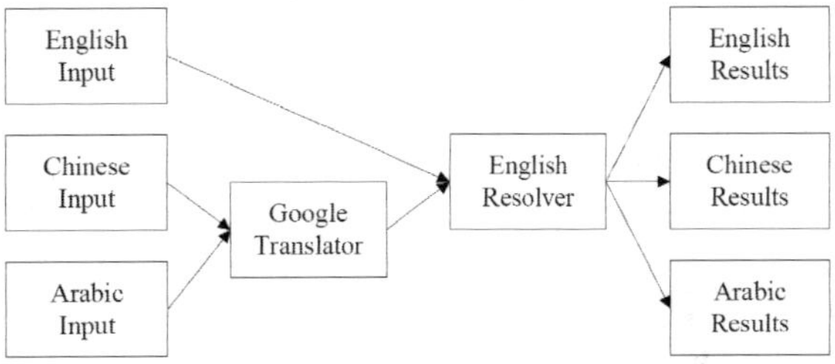

Figure 1: The overall process of our system, where we use Google Translator to translate Chinese and Arabic into English.

For more details, readers can refer to (Pradhan et al., 2012).

Before this year's task, researchers proposed two typical novel methods to address the problem of natural language processing across multiple languages: projection and joint learning (Rahman and Ng, 2012). Specific to this year's coreference resolution task, for projection based method, we could first develop a strong resolver or utilize a publicly available system on English, and translate other languages into English, eventually, we could project the coreferring entities resolved on English back into other language sides. Generally, a projection method is easier to develop since it doesn't need sentence alignment across multiple languages. Thus, in this year's task, we investigate a translation based model to resolve coreference on English, Chinese and Arabic. The whole process is illustrated in figure 1, in which we first use Google Translator to translate Chinese and Arabic into English, and we then employ a strong English coreference resolver to generate coreferring entities, after mapping entities from English into

Chinese and Arabic mention candidates, we could obtain coreferring entities for these languages.

Intuitively, the performance of coreference resolver on English should perform better than that on Chinese and Arabic since we have substantial corpus for English and coreference resolution on English is well studied compared to another two languages. Thus we could imagine that projecting the results from English into Chinese and Arabic should still beats the baseline system using monolingual resolution method. However, in our experiments, we obtain negative results on developing set that means our projection based model perform worse than the baseline system. According to our experimental results on developing set, finally, we submit results of baseline system in order to obtain better ranking.

The rest of this paper is organized as follows, in section 2, we will introduce our method in details, and section 3 is our experimental results, we draw conclusion in section 4.

2 Projection based Model

As the last section mentioned, we propose to use a projection based model to resolve coreference on multiple languages. The primary procedures of our method could be divided into three steps: first step is translation, where Google Translator is employed to translate Chinese and Arabic into English, second is coreference resolution for English, last is the projection of coreferring entities. Since the first step is clear that we extract sentences from Chinese and Arabic documents and translate them into English using Google Translator, hence in this section we will mainly describe the configuration of our English resolver and details of projection method.

2.1 English Resolver

In last year's evaluation task, the Standford Natural Language Processing Group ranked the first position and they also open their toolkit for research community, namely Standford CoreNLP (Lee et al., 2011) [1], better yet, their toolkit is optimized for CoNLL task. Thus we could use their toolkit as our English resolver and concentrate on bettering the projection of coreferring entities.

[1] http://nlp.stanford.edu/software/corenlp.shtml

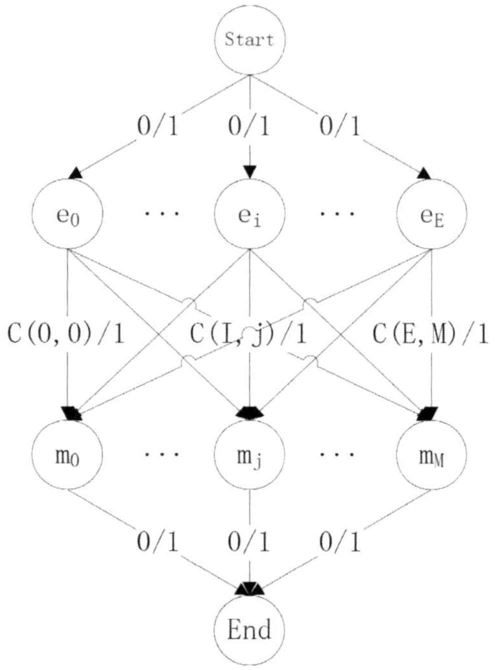

Figure 2: A minimum cost and maximum flow structure is used to solve the problem that mapping coreferring entities into each mention candidates with highest probability.

We use the basic running script that is "java -cp joda-time.jar:stanford-corenlp.jar:stanford-corenlp-models.jar:xom.jar -Xmx3g edu.stanford.nlp.pipeline.StanfordCoreNLP -filelist filelist.txt" to resolve the resolution, where "filelist" involves all documents need to be performed coreference resolution.

2.2 Projection of Coreferring Entities

After generating coreferring entities on English, the key step of our system is how to map them into mention candidates detected on Chinese and Arabic. For instance, assuming we translate Chinese documents into English and obtain coreferring entities e_1, e_2, e_i,.., e_E on translated English documents through aforementioned step, meanwhile, we consider all noun phrases(NP) in original Chinese documents and generate mention candidates m_1, m_2, m_j,.., m_M. Therefore, our task is to map each e_i into one mention candidate m_j with highest probability, and it can be obtained by the max-

Algorithm 1 Algorithm for computing similarity between two phrases in different languages.

1: **Input**: $w_{e_1}, .., w_{e_n}, w_{c_1}, .., w_{c_m}$, Phrase Table PT
2: $s[n] = [0, -\inf, .., -\inf]$
3: **for** $i \leftarrow 1..n$ **do**
4:     **for** $j \leftarrow 0..10$ **do**
5:         $s[i+j] = \max(s[i+j], s[i-1] + p(i, i+j))$
6: **Output:** $s[n]$ **V**

imization of the following formula,

$$\hat{P} = \sum_{e_i \in E, m_j \in M} \{a(i,j)b(j,i)p(i,j)\} \quad (1)$$

with constrains $\sum_{i,j}\{a(i,j)\} = 1$ and $\sum_{i,j}\{b(j,i)\} = 1$, where $p(i,j)$ is the probability of e_i mapping into m_j and $a(i,j)$ as well as $b(i,j)$ are integers guaranteeing each coreferring entity map into one mention and each mention has only one entity to be mapped into. To solve this problem, we reduce it as a Cost Flow problem since it is easier to understand and implement compared to other methods such as integer linear programming. Note that the number of mention candidates is theoretically larger than that of coreferring entities, thus this problem couldn't be reduced as the bipartite graph matching problem since it needs equal number of nodes in two parts.

Figure 2 shows the graph structure designed to solve this problem, where the symbols labeled on each edge is a two tuples(Cost,Flow), indicating the cost and flow for each edge. Since object of Cost Flow problem is to minimize the cost while maximizing the flows, thus we compute the $c(i,j)$ as $1 - p(i,j)$ in order to be consistent with the equation 1. To satisfy two constraints aforementioned, we set up two dummy nodes "Start" and "End", and connect "Start" to each entity e_i with cost 0 and flow 1 ensuring each entity is available to map one mention. We also link each mention candidate m_j to node "End" with the same value ensuring each mention could be mapped into by only one entity. Clearly, there is an edge with tuple $(1-p(i,j), 1)$ between each entity end mention indicating that each entity could map into any mention while with different probabilities. Thus, solving this Cost-Flow problem is equal to maximizing the equation 1 with two constraints. Since Cost-Flow problem is well studied, thus some algorithm can solve this problem in polynomial time (Ahuja et al., 1993). One may argue that we can modify translation decoder to output alignments between Chinese and translated English sentence, unfortunately, Google Translator API doesn't supply these information while its translation quality is obviously better than others for translating documents in OntoNotes, moreover, it is impossible to output alignment for each word since some translation rules used for directing translation include some unaligned words, thus an algorithm to map each entity into each mention is more applicable.

Clearly, another problem is how to compute $p(i,j)$ for each edge between entity and mention candidate. This problem could be casted as how to compute similarity of phrases across multiple languages. Formally, given an English phrases $w_{e_1}, .., w_{e_n}$ and a Chinese phrase $w_{c_1}, .., w_{c_m}$, the problem is how to compute the similar score S between them. Although we could compute lexical, syntactic or semantic similar score to obtain accurate similarity, here for simplicity, we just compute the lexical similarity using the phrase table extracted by a phrased-based machine translation decoder (Koehn et al., 2003). Phrase table is a rich resource that contains probability score for phrase in one language translated into another language, thus we could design a dynamic algorithm shown in Algorithm 1 to compute the similar score. Equation in line 5 is used to reserve highest similar score for its sub-phrases, and $p(i, i+j)$ is the similar score between sub-phrases $w_i, .., w_{i+j}$ and its translation. When we compute the score of the sub-phrases $w_i, .., w_{i+j}$, we literately pick one pt_i from PT and check whether $w_{c_1}, .., w_{c_m}$ involves pt_i's target side, if that we record its score until we obtain a higher score obtained by another pt_j and then update it. For instance, assuming the Chinese input sentence is "全球 第五 个 迪斯尼 乐园 即将 在 这里 向 公众 开放 。", and the Google translation of this sentence is "The world 's fifth Disneyland will soon open to the public . ". Following the aforementioned steps, we utilize English resolver to find a coreferring entity: "The world 's fifth Disneyland", and find two translation rules involving the former English phrase from the bilingual phrase table: "The world 's fifth Disneyland => 全球的第五个迪斯尼乐园 (probability=0.6) " and "The world 's fifth Disneyland => 全球第五个迪斯尼乐园 (probability=0.4)". Since the Chinese translation of both rules all contain the noun phrase "全球 第五 个 迪斯尼 乐园" in the original Chinese input, we thus add this noun phrase into the coreferring entities as the English resolve finding with the probability 0.6.

3 Experiments

3.1 English Results

In this section, we will report our experimental results in details. We use Standford CoreNLP toolkit to generate results for English. Table 1 lists the F-score obtained on developing set.

3.2 Chinese and Arabic Results

As last section mentioned, we first translate Chinese and Arabic into English and then use CoreNLP to resolve coreference on English. To obtain high translation quality, we use Google Translator Toolkit [2]. And to compute similarity score, we run Giza++(Och and Ney, 2003) [3], an open source toolkit for word alignment, to perform word alignment. For Chinese, we use 1 million bilingual corpus provided by NIST MT evaluation task to extract phrase table, and for Arabic its size is 2 million. Note that, we extract phrase table from English to Chinese and Arabic with maximum phrase length 10. The reason is that our algorithm check English phrase whose length is less than 10 tokens. To compare our results, we also use CoreNLP to generate results for Chinese and Arabic. Since CoreNLP use some syntactic knowledge to resolving coreference, it can also output coreferring entities for other languages. From table 2 we find that although CoreNLP is not designed for other languages, it still obtain acceptable scores and beat our projection based model. The main reason is that our method is coarse and obtain lower precision for mention detection, while CoreNLP use some manually written rules to detect mention candidates. Another explanation is that projection based model is hard to map some phrases back into original languages, such as "that, it, this". Moreover, translation quality for some corpus like web corpus is far from perfect, translation errors will surely affect the precision of coreference resolution. Thus, for the final testing set, we run the CoreNLP to generate the results.

3.3 Testing Results

Since CoreNLP beats our system in Chinese and Arabic, thus we run CoreNLP for all three languages. Table 3 lists the final results, and we also give results using golden parse tree for prediction in table 4. From these two tables, we find that for any language, the system using golden parse tree show better performance than the one using predicted system in term of each metric. The reason is that the CoreNLP resolve coreference on parse tree and employ some parse features to corefer. On the other hand, we could also see that the improvement is slight, because parsing errors affect little on finding mention candidates benefiting from high precision on noun phrase prediction. Finally, since we use an open source toolkit to generate results, unfortunately, we have no ranking in this task.

4 Conclusion

In this paper, we present a projection based model for coreference resolution. We first translate Chinese and Arabic into English, and then employ a strong English resolver to generate coreferring entities, after that a projection algorithm is designed to map coreferring entities into mention candidates detected in Chinese and Arabic. However, since our approach is coarse and due to limit time preparing for this task, the output generate by CoreNLP beats our results in three languages, thus we submit results generated by CoreNLP as our final submission.

Acknowledgments

The authors were supported by National Science Foundation of China, Contracts 90920004, and High-Technology R&D Program (863) Project No 2011AA01A207 and 2012BAH39B03. We thank organizers for their generous supplied resources and arduous preparation. We also thank anonymous reviewers for their thoughtful suggestions.

[2] http://www.google.cn/url?source=transpromo&rs=rsmf&q=http://translate.google.com/toolkit

[3] http://code.google.com/p/giza-pp/

	Mention	MUC	BCUB	CEAFE
CoreNLP	73.68%	64.58%	70.60%	46.64

Table 1: Experimental results on developing set(F-score) for English.

	Mention	MUC	BCUB	CEAFE
CoreNLP-Chinese	52.15%	38.16%	60.38%	34.58
Projection-Chinese	48.51%	32.31%	63.77%	24.72
CoreNLP-Arabic	52.97%	27.88%	60.75%	40.52
Projection-Arabic	42.68%	22.39%	62.18%	32.83

Table 2: Experimental results on developing set(F-score) for Chinese and Arabic using CoreNLP and our system.

	Mention	MUC	BCUB	CEAFE
CoreNLP-Chinese	49.82%	37.83%	60.30%	34.93
CoreNLP-Arabic	53.89%	28.31%	61.83%	42.97
CoreNLP-English	73.69%	63.82%	68.52%	45.36

Table 3: Experimental results on testing set(F-score) using predicted parse tree.

	Mention	MUC	BCUB	CEAFE
CoreNLP-Chinese	53.42%	40.60%	60.37%	35.75
CoreNLP-Arabic	55.17%	30.54%	62.36%	43.03
CoreNLP-English	75.58%	66.14%	69.55%	46.54

Table 4: Experimental results on testing set(F-score) using golden parse tree.

References

R.K. Ahuja, T.L. Magnanti, and J.B. Orlin. 1993. Network flows: theory, algorithms, and applications. 1993.

P. Koehn, F.J. Och, and D. Marcu. 2003. Statistical phrase-based translation. In *Proceedings of the 2003 Conference of the North American Chapter of the Association for Computational Linguistics on Human Language Technology-Volume 1*, pages 48–54. Association for Computational Linguistics.

H. Lee, Y. Peirsman, A. Chang, N. Chambers, M. Surdeanu, and D. Jurafsky. 2011. Stanford's multi-pass sieve coreference resolution system at the conll-2011 shared task. In *Proceedings of the Fifteenth Conference on Computational Natural Language Learning: Shared Task*, pages 28–34. Association for Computational Linguistics.

F.J. Och and H. Ney. 2003. A systematic comparison of various statistical alignment models. *Computational linguistics*, 29(1):19–51.

Sameer Pradhan, Alessandro Moschitti, Nianwen Xue, Olga Uryupina, and Yuchen Zhang. 2012. CoNLL-2012 shared task: Modeling multilingual unrestricted coreference in OntoNotes. In *Proceedings of the Sixteenth Conference on Computational Natural Language Learning (CoNLL 2012)*, Jeju, Korea.

Altaf Rahman and Vincent Ng. 2012. Translation-based projection for multilingual coreference resolution. In *NAACL 2012*.

A Mixed Deterministic Model for Coreference Resolution

Bo Yuan[1], Qingcai Chen, Yang Xiang, Xiaolong Wang[2]
Liping Ge, Zengjian Liu, Meng Liao, Xianbo Si
Intelligent Computing Research Center, Key Laboratory of Network Oriented Intelligent Computation, Computer Science and technology Department, Harbin Institute of Technology Shenzhen graduate School, Shenzhen, Guangdong, 518055, China
{yuanbo.hitsz[1], windseedxy, qingcai.chen, geliping123, autobotsonearth, dream2009gd, sixianbo}@gmail.com
wangxl@insun.hit.edu.cn[2]

Abstract

This paper presents a mixed deterministic model for coreference resolution in the CoNLL-2012 shared task. We separate the two main stages of our model, mention detection and coreference resolution, into several sub-tasks which are solved by machine learning method and deterministic rules based on multi-filters, such as lexical, syntactic, semantic, gender and number information. We participate in the closed track for English and Chinese, and also submit an open result for Chinese using tools to generate the required features. Finally, we reach the average F1 scores 58.68, 60.69 and 61.02 on the English closed task, Chinese closed and open tasks.

1 Introduction

The coreference resolution task is a complicated and challenging issue of natural language processing. Although many sub-problems, such as noun phrase to noun phrase and pronouns to noun phrase, are contained in this issue, it is interesting that humans do not get too confused when they determine whether two mentions refer to the same entity. We also believe that automatic systems should copy the human behavior (Kai-Wei et al., 2011). In our understanding, the basis for human making judgment on different sub-problems is different and limited. Although there are some complicated and ambiguous cases in this task, and we are not able to cover all the prior knowledge of human mind, which plays a vital role in his solution, the mixed deterministic model we constructed can solve a big part of this task. We present a mixed deterministic model for coreference resolution in the CoNLL-2012 shared task (Sameer et al., 2011).

Different methods such as Relaxation labeling (Emili et al., 2011), Best-Link (Kai-Wei et al., 2011), Entropy Guided Transformation Learning (Cicero et al., 2011) and deterministic models (Heeyoung et al., 2011), were attempted in the CoNLL-2011 shared task (Sameer et al., 2011). The system performance reported by the task shows that a big part of this task has been solved but some sub-problems need more exploration.

We also participate in the Chinese closed and open tracks. However, the lack of linguistic annotations makes it more difficult to build a deterministic model. Basic solutions such as Hobbs Algorithm and Center Theory have been listed in (Wang et al., 2002; Jun et al., 2007). The recent research on Chinese contains non-anaphors detection using a composite kernel (Kong Fang, et al., 2012(a)) and a tree kernel method to anaphora resolution of pronouns (Kong Fang et al., 2012(b)).

We accept the thought of Stanford (Karthik et al., 2010; Heeyoung et al., 2011). In Stanford system the coreference resolution task is divided into several problems and each problem is solved by rule based methods. For English we did some research on mention detection which uses Decision Tree to decide whether the mention 'it' should refer to some other mention. For Chinese we submit closed and open result. The lack of gender, number and name entities make it more difficult for the Chinese closed task and we try to extract information from the training data to help enhance the performance. For the open task, we use some dictionaries such as appellation dictionary, gender dictionary, geographical name dictionary and temporal word dictionary (Bo et al., 2009), and some tools such as conversion of pinyin-to-character and LTP which is a Chinese parser that can generate the features such as Part-of-Speech, Parse bit, Named Entities (Liu et al., 2011) to generate the similar information.

We describe the system architecture in section 2. Section 3 illustrates the mention detection process. Section 4 describes the core process of coreference resolution. In section 5, we show the results and discussion of several experiments. Finally, we give the conclusion of our work in section 6.

2 System Architecture

Our system mainly contains mention detection and coreference resolution. Recall is the determining factor in mention detection stage. The reason is that if some mention is missed in this stage, the coreference resolution part will miss the chains which contain this mention. Yet some mentions still need to be distinguished because in some cases they refer to no entity. For example 'it', in the sentence 'it + be + weather/ time', 'it' should refer to no entity. But the 'it' in the phrase 'give it to me' might refer to some entity. The coreference resolution module of our system follows the idea of Stanford. In the English task we did some more exploration on mention detection, pronoun coreference and partial match of noun phrases. The Chinese task is more complicated and because gender, number and name entities are not provided, the feature generation from the training data has to be added before the coreference resolution process. Some Chinese idiomatic usages are also considered in this stage.

3 Mention detection

All the NPs, pronouns and the phrases which are indexed as named entities are selected as candidates. NPs are extracted from the parse tree. Yet some mentions do not refer to any entity in some cases. In our system we attempt to distinguish these mentions in this stage. The reason is that the deterministic rules in coreference resolution part are not complete to distinguish these mentions. The methods below can also be added to the coreference resolution part as a pre-processing. For the conveniences of system design, we finish this work in this stage.

For English, the pronoun 'it' and NPs 'this, that, those and these' need to be distinguished. We take 'it' as an example to illustrate the process. First we use regular expressions to select 'it', which refers to no entity, such as 'it + be + weather/ time', 'it happened that' and 'it makes (made) sense that'. Second we use Decision Tree (C4.5) to classify the two kinds of 'it' based on the training data. The features contain the Part-of-Speech, Parse bit, Predicate Arguments of 'it', the word before and after 'it'. The number of total 'it' is 9697 and 4043 of them have an entity to refer to in the training data.

Category	Precision	Recall	F
no entity refered	0.576	0.596	0.586
entity refered	0.747	0.731	0.739
total	0.682	0.679	0.68

Table 1: Results of 'it' classification using C4.5

Table 1 shows the classification result of 'it' in the development data v4. The number of total 'it' is 1401 and 809 of them have an entity to refer to. The result is not perfect but can help enhance the performance of coreference resolution. However, the results of 'this, that, those and these' are not acceptable and we skip over these words. We did not do any process on 'verb' mention detection and coreference resolution.

In addition, we divide mentions into groups in which they are nested in position. And for mentions which have the same head word in one group, only the mentions with the longest span should be left (for the English task and a set of Chinese articles). For some Chinese articles of which names contain 'chtb', both in the training data and the development data, the nest is permitted based on the statistic results.

For Chinese we also attempt to train a model for pronouns '你'(you) and '那'(that). However, the results are not acceptable either since the features we select are not enough for the classifier.

After the mentions have been extracted, the related features of each mention are also extracted. We transform the 'conll' document into mention document. Each mention has basic features such as position, part-of-speech, parse tree, head word, speaker, Arguments, and the gender and number of head word. The head word feature is very important and regular expression can almost accomplish the process but not perfectly. Firstly, we extract the key NPs of a mention based on parse feature. Then the regular expressions are to extract the head word. For example, the mention:

(NP (DNP (LCP (NP (NP (NR 中国)) (NP (NN 大地))) (LC 上)) (DEG 的)) (NP (NR 二战)) (NP (NN 标志))) (NP (DNP (LCP (NP (NP (NR 中国)) (NP (NN 大地))) (LC 上)) (DEG 的)) (NP (NR 二战)) (NP (NN 标志)))

The key NPs of this mention is:

(NP (NR 二战)) (NP (NN 标志)) .The head word of this mention is: *NN 标志*

However, there are still some cases that need to be discussed. For example, the head word of 'the leader of people' should be 'leader', while the head word of 'the city of Beijing' should be 'city' and 'Beijing' for the mentions of 'the city' and 'Beijing' both have the same meaning with 'the city of Beijing'. Finally, we only found the words of 'city' and 'country' should be processed.

4 Coreference resolution

The deterministic rules are the core methods to solve the coreference resolution task. All the mentions in the same part can be seen as a list. The mentions which refer to the same entity will be clustered based on the deterministic rules. After all the clusters have generated, the merge program will merge the clusters into chains based on the position information. The mentions in one chain cannot be reduplicative in position. Basically the nested mentions are not allowed.

The process contains two parts NP-NP and NP-pronoun. Each part has several sub-problems to be discussed. First, the same process of English task and Chinese task will be illustrated. Then the different parts will be discussed separately.

4.1 NP-NP

Exact match: the condition of exact match is the two NP mentions which have no other larger parent mentions in position are coreferential if they are exactly the same. The stop words such as 'a', 'the', 'this' and 'that' have been removed.

Partial match: there are two conditions for partial match which are the two mentions have the same head word and one of them is a part of the other in form simultaneously.

Alias and abbreviation: some mentions have alias or abbreviation. For example the mentions 'USA' and 'America' should refer to the mention 'the United States'.

Similar match: there are three forms of this match. The first one is all the modifiers of two NPs are same and the head words are similar based on WordNet[1] which is provided for the English closed task. We only use the English synonym sets of the WordNet to solve the first form. The second one is the head words are same and the modifiers are not conflicted. The third form is that the head words and modifiers are all different. The result of similar match may be reduplicative with that of exact match and partial match. This would be eliminated by the merge process.

4.2 Pronoun - NP

There are seven categories of pronoun to NP in our system. For English second person, it is difficult to distinguish the plural form from singular form and we put them in one deterministic rule. For each kind of pronouns shown below, the first cluster is the English form and the second cluster is the Chinese form.

First Person (singular) = {'I', 'my', 'me', 'mine', 'myself'}{'我'}

Second Person= {'you', 'your', 'yours', 'yourself', 'yourselves'}{'你', '你们'}

Third Person (male) = {'he', 'him', 'his', 'himself'}{'他'}

Third Person (female) = {'she', 'her', 'hers', 'herself'}{'她'}

Third Person (object) = {'it', 'its', 'itself'}{'它'}

First Person (plural) = {'we', 'us', 'our', 'ours', 'ourselves'}{'我们'}

Third Person (plural) = {'they', 'them', 'their', 'theirs', 'themselves'}{'他们', '她们', '它们'}

In the Chinese task the possessive form of pronoun is not considered. For example, the mention '我们 的'(our) is a DNP in the parse feature and it contains two words '我们' and '的'. We only selected the NP '我们'as a mention. The reflexive pronouns are composed by two words which are the pronoun itself and the word '自己'.

---
[1] http://wordnet.princeton.edu/

For example, the mention '我 自己'(myself) is processed as '我'(I or me).

Gender, number and distance between pronoun and NP are the most important features for this part (Shane et al., 2006). We only allow pronoun to find NPs at first. We find out the first mention of which all the features are satisfied ahead of the pronoun. If there is no matching mention, search backward from the pronoun. For the first person and second person, we merged all the pronouns with the same form and the same speaker. If the context is a conversation of two speakers, the second person of a speaker should refer to the first person of the other speaker. The scene of multi-speakers conversation is too difficult to be solved.

In the Chinese task there are some other pronouns. The pronoun '双方'(both sides) should refer to a plural mention which contain '和'(and) in the middle. The pronoun '其' has similar meaning of third person and refers to the largest NP mention before it. The pronouns '这'(this), '那'(that), '这里'(here), '那里'(there) are not processed for we did not find a good solution.

However in some cases the provided gender and number are not correct or missing and we had to label these mentions based on the appellation words of the training data. For example, if the appellation word of a person is 'Mr.' or 'sir', the gender should be male.

4.3 Chinese closed task

For the Chinese closed task NE, the gender and number are not provided. We used regular patterns to generate these features from the training data.

In the NE (named entities) feature 'PERSON' is a very important category because most pronouns will refer to the person entity. To extract 'PERSON', we build a PERSON dictionary which contains all the PERSON mentions in training data, such as '先生'(Mr.) and '教授'(Professor). If the same mention appears in the test data, we believe it is a person entity. However, the PERSON dictionary cannot cover all the PERSON mentions. The appellation words are extracted before or after the person entity. When some appellation word appears in the test data, the NP mention before or after the appellation word should be a person entity, if they compose a larger NP mention.

The Gender feature was generated at the same time of the 'PERSON' generation. We separate the 'PERSON' dictionary and appellation dictionary into male cluster and female cluster by the pronouns in the same chain.

The generation of number feature is a little complicated. Since the Chinese word does not have plural form, the numerals and the quantifiers of the mention are the main basis to extract the number feature. We extract the numerals and the quantifiers from the training data and built regular expressions for determine the number feature of a mention in test data. Other determinative rules for number feature extraction are shown below:

If the word '们' appears in a mention tail, this mention is plural. For example '同学'(student) is singular and '同学们'(students) is plural.

If the word '和'(and) appears in the middle of a mention A, and the two parts separated by '和' are sub-mentions of A, mention A should be plural. Other words which have the similar meaning of '和', such as '同', '与' and '跟', are considered.

The time and date coreference resolution is also considered. The NP mentions which contain temporal words are processed separately since these categories of name entity are not provided. These temporal words are also extracted from training data. Since the head words of these mentions are themselves, the two time or date mentions are coreferential if they are the same or one must be a part of the other's tail. For example '今年九月'(this September) and '九月'(September) which are not nested should be coreferential.

4.4 Chinese open task

For the Chinese open task we use several tools to generate features we need.

NE generation: LTP is a Chinese parser that can generate the features such as Part-of-Speech, Parse bit, Named Entities (Liu et al., 2011). We only use LTP for the NE generation. However, the NE labels of LTP are different with that provided by the gold training data and need to be transformed. The difference of word segmentation between LTP and the provided data also made some errors. At last we find the NE feature from LTP does not perform well and it will be discussed in section 5.

The conversion of pinyin-to-character is also used in the Chinese open task. The speaker provided in the training data is given in pinyin form. The speaker might be the 'PERSON' mention in the context. When we determine the pronoun coreference, we need to know whether the speaker and the 'PERSON' mention are same.

Other tools used in open task contain appellation dictionary, gender dictionary, geographical name dictionary and temporal word dictionary (Bo et al., 2009). These dictionaries are more complete than those used in the closed task, although the enhancements are also limited.

5 Results and Discussion

Table 2 to table 4 show the results of English coreference resolution on the gold and auto development and the test data. The results of the auto development data and the test data are close and lower than that of the gold data. Since the deterministic rules can not cover all the cases, there is still an improvement if we could make the deterministic rules more complete.

Measure	R	P	F1
Mention detection	77.7	71.8	74.6
MUC	65.1	62.9	64
B^3	69.2	70.9	70.1
CEAF(E)	46.4	48.9	47.6
(CEAF(E)+MUC+B^3)/3			60.6

Table 2: Results of the English gold development data

Measure	R	P	F1
Mention detection	72.4	71.5	72
MUC	62.3	62.8	62
B^3	66.7	71.8	69.1
CEAF(E)	46.4	44.9	45.6
(CEAF(E)+MUC+B^3)/3			58.9

Table 3: Results of the English auto development data

Measure	R	P	F1
Mention detection	73.2	71.9	72.53
MUC	62.1	63	63
B^3	66.2	70.5	68.3
CEAF(E)	45.7	44.7	45.2
CEAF(M)	57.3	57.3	57.3
BLANC	72.1	76.9	74.2
(CEAF(E)+MUC+B^3)/3			58.68

Table 4: Results of English test data

The results of the closed Chinese performance on the gold and auto development and the test data are shown in table 5 to table 7. The performance of the auto development data and the test data has about 4% decline to that of the gold development on F1 of coreference resolution. It means the Chinese results are also partly affected by the parse feature. In fact we attempted to revise the parse feature of the auto development data using regular expressions. Yet the complicacy and unacceptable results made us abandon that.

Measure	R	P	F1
Mention detection	82.3	69.8	75.5
MUC	71.6	64.3	67.7
B^3	76.7	74.2	75.4
CEAF(E)	49	56.5	52.5
(CEAF(E)+MUC+B^3)/3			65.2

Table 5: Closed results of the Chinese gold development data

Measure	R	P	F1
Mention detection	74.2	66	70
MUC	63.6	60	61.7
B^3	73.1	73.5	73.3
CEAF(E)	47.3	50.6	48.9
(CEAF(E)+MUC+B^3)/3			61.3

Table 6: Closed results of the Chinese auto development data

Measure	R	P	F1
Mention detection	72.8	64.1	68.15
MUC	62.4	58.4	60.3
B^3	73.1	72.7	72.9
CEAF(E)	47.1	50.7	48.8
CEAF(M)	59.6	59.6	59.6
BLANC	73.7	78.2	75.8
(CEAF(E)+MUC+B^3)/3			60.69

Table 7: Closed results of the Chinese test data

The results of the open Chinese performance on the gold and auto development and the test data are shown in table 8 to table 10. The performance is similar with that of the closed task. However, the improvement between F1 of the open task and F1 of the closed task is limited. We also get the F1 of the closed and open test results using gold parser which are 66.46 and 66.38. The open result is even lower. This can be explained. The performance enhanced by the dictionaries we used for the open task are limited because the open dictionaries information which appears in the test data is not much more than that of the closed dictionaries which generated from the training data, although the total information of the former is much larger. The named entities generated by LTP have some errors such as person identification errors and will caused coreferential errors in Pronoun-NP stage. For the time we did not use LTP well and some other open tools such as Wikipedia and Baidu Baike should be applied in the open task.

Measure	R	P	F1
Mention detection	82.4	69.3	75.3
MUC	72.3	63.8	67.8
B^3	77.7	73.3	75.4
CEAF(E)	48.3	56.8	52.2
(CEAF(E)+MUC+B^3)/3			65.1

Table 8: Open results of the Chinese gold development data

Measure	R	P	F1
Mention detection	75.1	65.7	70.1
MUC	64.9	59.9	62.3
B^3	74.2	72.6	73.4
CEAF(E)	46.7	51.5	49
(CEAF(E)+MUC+B^3)/3			61.6

Table 9: Open results of the Chinese auto development data

Measure	R	P	F1
Mention detection	73.7	64	68.49
MUC	63.7	58.5	61
B^3	74	72.2	73.1
CEAF(E)	60.1	60.1	60.1
CEAF(M)	46.8	51.5	49
BLANC	74.3	78	76
(CEAF(E)+MUC+B^3)/3			61.02

Table 10: Open results of the Chinese test data

The results of the gold-mention-boundaries and gold-mentions data of the English and Chinese closed task are shown in table 11 and 12. Although the mention detection stage is optimized by the gold-mention-boundaries and gold-mentions data and the final performance is enhanced, there is still space to enhance in the coreference resolution stage. The recall of mention detection of gold-mentions is 99.8. This problem will be explored in our future work.

Data	R	P	F1
Mention detection(A)	75.7	70.8	73.2
gold-mention-boundaries			59.50
Mention detection(B)	80	100	88.91
gold-mentions			69.88

Table 11: Results of the English closed gold-mention-boundaries and gold-mentions data, (A) is the mention detection score of the gold-mention-boundaries and (B) is the score of the gold-mentions.

Data	R	P	F1
Mention detection(A)	82.9	66.9	74.02
gold-mention-boundaries			64.42
Mention detection(B)	81.7	99.8	89.85
gold-mentions			76.05

Table 12: Results of the Chinese closed gold-mention-boundaries and gold-mentions data

6 Conclusion

In this paper we described a mixed deterministic model for coreference resolution of English and Chinese. We start the mention detection from extracting candidates based on the parse feature. The pre-processing which contains static rules and decision tree is applied to remove the defective candidates. In the coreference resolution stage the task is divided into several sub-problems and for each sub-problem the deterministic rules are constructed based on limited features. For the Chinese closed task we use regular patterns to generate named entities, gender and number from the training data. Several tools and dictionaries are applied for the Chinese open task. The result is not as good as we supposed since the feature errors caused by these tools also made the coreferential errors.

However, a deeper error analysis is needed in the construction of deterministic rules. The feature of the predicate arguments is not used well. Although the open performance of the Chinese task is not good, we still believe that complete and accurate prior knowledge can help solve the task.

Acknowledgement

This work is supported in part by the National Natural Science Foundation of China (No. 61173075 and 60973076), ZTE Foundation and Science and Technology Program of Shenzhen.

References

Bo Yuan, Qingcai Chen, Xiaolong Wang, Liwei Han. 2009. Extracting Event Temporal Information based on Web. 2009 Second International Symposium on Knowledge Acquisition and Modeling, pages.346-350

Cicero Nogueira dos Santos, Davi Lopes Carvalho. 2011. Rule and Tree Ensembles for Unrestricted Coreference Resolution. Proceedings of the 15th Conference on Computational Natural Language Learning: Shared Task, pages 51–55.

Emili Sapena, Llu´ıs Padr´o and Jordi Turmo. 2011. RelaxCor Participation in CoNLL Shared Task on Coreference Resolution. Proceedings of the 15th Conference on Computational Natural Language Learning: Shared Task, pages 35–39.

Heeyoung Lee, Yves Peirsman, Angel Chang, Nathanael Chambers, Mihai Surdeanu, Dan Jurafsky. 2011. Stanford's Multi-Pass Sieve Coreference Resolution System at the CoNLL-2011 Shared Task. Proceedings of the 15th Conference on Computational Natural Language Learning: Shared Task, pages 28–34, Portland, Oregon.

Liu Ting, Che Wanxiang, Li Zhenghua. 2011. Language Technology Platform. Journal of Chinese Information Processing. 25(6): 53-62

Jun Lang, Bing Qin, Ting Liu, Sheng Li. 2007. Intra-document Coreference Resolution: The state of the art. Journal of Chinese Language and Computing. 17 (4):227-253

Kai-Wei Chang Rajhans Samdani. 2011. Inference Protocols for Coreference Resolution. Proceedings of the 15th Conference on Computational Natural Language Learning: Shared Task, pages 40–44, Portland, Oregon.

Karthik Raghunathan, Heeyoung Lee, Sudarshan Rangarajan, Nathanael Chambers, Mihai Surdeanu, Dan Jurafsky, Christopher Manning. 2010. A Multi-Pass Sieve for Coreference Resolution. In EMNLP.

Kong Fang, Zhu Qiaoming and Zhou Guodong. 2012(a). Anaphoricity determination for coreference resolution in English and Chinese languages. Computer Research and Development (Chinese).

Kong Fang and Zhou Guodong. 2012(b). Tree kernel-based pronoun resolution in English and Chinese languages. Journal of Software (Chinese). Accepted: 23(8).

Sameer Pradhan, Lance Ramshaw, Mitchell Marcus, Martha Palmer, Ralph Weischedel and Nianwen Xue.2011. CoNLL-2011 Shared Task: Modeling Unrestricted Coreference in OntoNotes. Proceedings of the Fifteenth Conference on Computational Natural Language Learning (CoNLL 2011). Portland, OR.

Sameer Pradhan and Alessandro Moschitti and Nianwen Xue and Olga Uryupina and Yuchen Zhang. 2012. CoNLL-2012 Shared Task: Modeling Multilingual Unrestricted Coreference in OntoNotes. Proceedings of the Sixteenth Conference on Computational Natural Language Learning (CoNLL 2012). Jeju, Korea.

Shane Bergsma and Dekang Lin. 2006. Bootstrapping Path-Based Pronoun Resolution Proceedings of the 21st International Conference on Computational Linguistics and 44th Annual Meeting of the ACL, pages 33–40, Sydney

Wang Houfeng. 2002. Survey: Computational Models and Technologies in Anaphora Resolution. Journal of Chinese Information Processing. 16(6): 9-17.

Simple Maximum Entropy Models for Multilingual Coreference Resolution

Xinxin Li, Xuan Wang, Xingwei Liao
Computer Application Research Center
Harbin Institute of Technology Shenzhen Graduate School
Shenzhen, China
lixxin2@gmail.com

Abstract

This paper describes our system participating in the CoNLL-2012 shared task: Modeling Multilingual Unrestricted Coreference in Ontonotes. Maximum entropy models are used for our system as classifiers to determine the coreference relationship between every two mentions (usually noun phrases and pronouns) in each document. We exploit rich lexical, syntactic and semantic features for the system, and the final features are selected using a greedy forward and backward strategy from an initial feature set. Our system participated in the closed track for both English and Chinese languages.

1 Introduction

In this paper, we present our system for the CoNLL-2012 shared task which aims to model coreference resolution for multiple languages. The task of coreference resolution is to group different mentions in a document into coreference equivalent classes (Pradhan et al., 2012). Plenty of machine learning algorithms such as Decision tree (Ng and Cardie, 2002), maximum entropy model, logistic regression (Björkelund and Nugues, 2011), Support Vector Machines, have been used to solve this problem. Meanwhile, the CoNLL-2011 shared task on English language show that a well-designed rule-based approach can achieve a comparable performance as a statistical one (Pradhan et al., 2011).

Our system treats coreference resolution problem as classification problem by determining whether every two mentions in a document has a coreference relationship or not. We use maximum entropy (ME) models to train the classifiers. Previous work reveal that features play an important role on coreference resolution problem, and many different kinds of features has been exploited. In this paper, we use many different lexical, syntactic and semantic features as candidate features, and use a greedy forward and backward approach for feature selection for ME models.

2 System Description

The framework of our system is shown in figure 1. It includes four components: candidate mention selection, training example generation, model generation, and decoding algorithm for test data. The details of each component as described below.

2.1 Candidate Mention Selection

In both training and test sets, our system only consider all noun phrases (NP) and pronouns (PRP, PRP$) as candidate mentions for both English and Chinese. The mentions in each sentence are obtained from given syntactic tree by their syntactic label. Other phrases in the syntactic tree are omitted due to their small proportion. For example, in the English training dataset, our candidate mentions includes about 91% of golden mentions.

2.2 Training Example Generation

There are many different training example generation algorithms, e.g., McCarthy and Lehnert's method, Soon et al.s method, Ng and Cardies method (Ng, 2005). For our baseline system, we choose Soon et al.'s method because it is easily understandable, implemented and popularly used. It

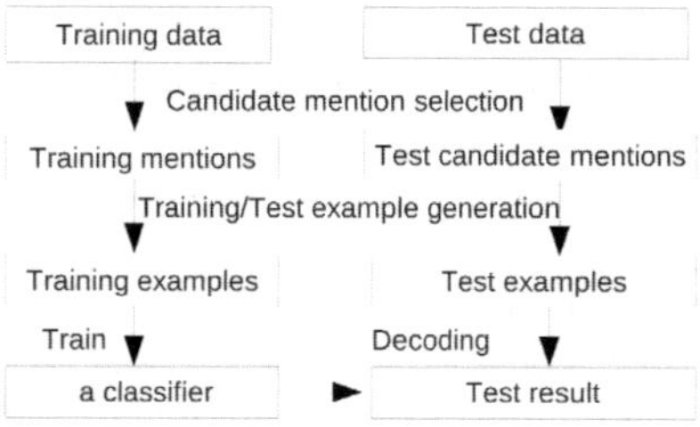

Figure 1: The framework of our coreference resolution system

selects pairs of two coreferent mentions as positive examples, and pairs between mentions among the two mentions and the last mention as negative examples.

2.3 Feature Selection

Rich and meaningful features are important for coreference resolution. Our system starts with Soon's 12 features as baseline features (Soon et al., 2001), and exploits many lexical, syntactic, and semantic features as candidate features. Totally 71 features are considered in our system, and summarized below:

- Distance features: sentence distance, distance in phrases, whether it's a first mention (Strube et al., 2002)
- Lexical features: string match, partial match, apposition, proper name match, head word match, partial head word match, minimum edit distance (Daumé III and Marcu, 2005)
- Grammatical features: pronoun, demonstrative noun phrase, embedded noun, gender agreement, number agreement (Soon et al., 2001)
- Syntactic features: same head, maximal NP, syntactic path (Yang et al., 2006)
- Semantic features: semantic class agreement, governing verb and its grammatical role, predicate (Ponzetto and Strube, 2006)

For English, the number agreement and gender agreement features can be obtained through the gender corpus provided. However, there is no corpus for Chinese. Our system obtains this information by collecting dictionaries for number and gender information from training dataset. For example, the pronoun "他" (he) denotes a male mention, and the noun phrase "女友" (girlfriend) represents a female mention. Similarly for number information, e.g., the mentions containing "和" (and), "群" (group) are plural. We use these words to build number and gender dictionaries, and determine the number and gender information of a new mention by checking whether one of the words in the dictionaries is in the mention.

For semantic class agreement feature in English, the relation between two mentions is extracted from WordNet 3.0 (Ng, 2007),(Miller, 1995). There is no corresponding dictionary for Chinese, so we keep it blank. The head word for each mention is selected by its dependency head, which can be extracted throught the conversion head rules (English [1] and Chinese [2]).

Maximum Entropy modeling is used to train the classifier for our system [3]. We employ a greedy forward and backward procedure for feature selection. The procedure is shown in Algorithm 1.

Algorithm 1 Greedy forward and backward feature selection

```
Initialization: all candidate features in set C
                Choose initial feature set c
                Compute F1 with features c
while forward || backward:
  while forward:
    for each feature f in C-c
      Compute F1 with features c+f
    if best(F1) increases:
      backward = true, c=c+f, continue forward
    else forward = false
  while backward:
    for each feature f in in c
      Compute F1 with features c-f
    if best(F1) increases:
      forward = true, c=c-f continue backward
    else backward = false
```

The algorithm will iterate forward and backward procedures until the performance does not improve. We use two initial feature sets: a blank set and Soon's baseline feature set. Both feature sets start

[1] http://w3.msi.vxu.se/ nivre/research/headrules.txt

[2] http://w3.msi.vxu.se/ nivre/research/chn_headrules.txt

[3] http://homepages.inf.ed.ac.uk/lzhang10/maxent.html

with a forward procedure.

2.4 Decoding

For every candidate mention pair, to determine their coreference relationship is simple because the probability whether they are coreferent can be obtained by our maximum entropy model. We can just set a threshold $\theta = 0.5$ and select the pairs with probability larger than θ. But usually it is hard for multiple mentions. Suppose there are three mentions A, B, C where the probability between A and B, A and C is larger than θ, but B and C is small. Thus choosing an appropriate decoding algorithm is necessary.

We use best-first clustering method for our system which for each candidate mention in a document, chooses the mention before it with best probability larger than threshold θ. The difference between English and Chinese is that we consider the coreference relationship of two mentions nested in Chinese, but not in English.

3 Experiments

3.1 Setting

Our system participates in the English and Chinese closed tracks with auto mentions. For both the English and Chinese datasets, we use gold annotated training data for training, and a portion of auto annotated development data for feature selection. Only part of development data is chosen because the evaluation procedure takes lot of time. To simplify, We only select one or two file in each directory as our development data.

The performance of the system is evaluated on MUC, B-CUBED, CEAF(M), CEAF(E), BLANC metrics. The official metric is calculated as $(MUC+B^3+CEAF)/3$.

3.2 Development set

Figures 2 and 3 show the performance on the English and Chinese development datasets using feature selection starting from a empty feature set and Soon's baseline feature set. The x-axis means the number of iterations with either forward or backward selection. The performance on Soon's baseline feature set for both languages are shown on 1st iteration. The performance from empty feature set starts on 2nd iteration. From these figures, we can see that

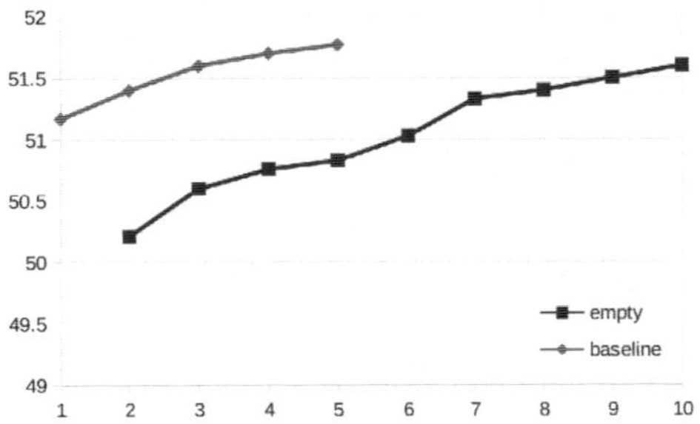

Figure 2: Performance of English development data with Feature selection

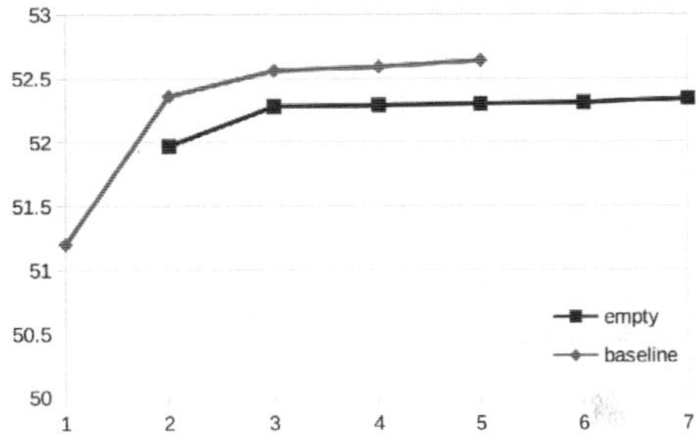

Figure 3: Performance of Chinese development data with Feature selection

using feature selection in both initial feature sets, the performance improves.

However the performance of our system is improved only on a few iteration. The best system for English stops at the 4th iteration with total 10 features left, which starts from Soon's baseline feature set. Similarly, the system for Chinese achieves its best performance at the 4th iteration with only 8 features. The phenomenon reveals that most of the features left for our system are still from Soon's baseline features, and our newly exploited lexical, syntactic, and semantic features are not well utilized.

Then we evaluate our model on the entire development data. The results are shown on Table 1. Comparing Figures 2, 3 and Table 1, we can observe that the performance on entire development data is lower than part one, about 1% decrease.

3.3 Test

For test data, we retrain our model on both gold training data and development data using the selected features. The final results for English and Chinese are shown in Table 2.

Model	English	Chinese
MUC	49.28	48.31
B^3	62.79	67.97
CEAF(M)	46.77	49.49
CEAF(E)	38.19	38.9
BLANC	66.31	68.91
Average	50.09	51.73

Table 1: Results on entire development data

Model	English	Chinese
MUC	48.27	48.09
B^3	61.37	68.31
CEAF(M)	44.83	49.92
CEAF(E)	36.68	38.89
BLANC	65.42	71.44
Official	48.77	51.76

Table 2: Results on test data

Comparing tables 2 and 1, we can observe that the performance for the Chinese test data is similar as the development data. The result seems reasonable because the model for testing use additional development data which is much smaller than training data. However, the result on English test data seem a little odd. The performance is about 1.4% less than that on the development data. The result needs further analysis.

4 Conclusion

In this paper, we presented our coreference resolution system which uses maximum entropy model to determine the coreference relationship between two mentions. Our system exploits many lexical, syntactic and semantic features. However, using greedy forward and backward feature selection strategy for ME model, these rich features are not well utilized. In future work we will analyze the reason for this phenomenon and extend these features to other machine learning algorithms.

References

Anders Björkelund and Pierre Nugues. 2011. Exploring lexicalized features for coreference resolution. In *Proceedings of the Fifteenth Conference on Computational Natural Language Learning: Shared Task*, pages 45–50, Portland, Oregon, USA, June. Association for Computational Linguistics.

Hal Daumé III and Daniel Marcu. 2005. A large-scale exploration of effective global features for a joint entity detection and tracking model. In *Proceedings of Human Language Technology Conference and Conference on Empirical Methods in Natural Language Processing*, pages 97–104, Vancouver, British Columbia, Canada, October. Association for Computational Linguistics.

George A. Miller. 1995. Wordnet: a lexical database for english. *Communications of the ACM*, 38:39–41, November.

Vincent Ng and Claire Cardie. 2002. Improving machine learning approaches to coreference resolution. In *Proceedings of the ACL*, pages 104–111.

Vincent Ng. 2005. Machine learning for coreference resolution: From local classification to global ranking. In *Proceedings of the 43rd Annual Meeting of the Association for Computational Linguistics (ACL'05)*, pages 157–164, Ann Arbor, Michigan, June. Association for Computational Linguistics.

Vincent Ng. 2007. Semantic class induction and coreference resolution. In *Proceedings of the 45th Annual Meeting of the Association of Computational Linguistics*, pages 536–543, Prague, Czech Republic, June. Association for Computational Linguistics.

Simone Paolo Ponzetto and Michael Strube. 2006. Exploiting semantic role labeling, wordnet and wikipedia for coreference resolution. In *Proceedings of the Human Language Technology Conference of the NAACL, Main Conference*, pages 192–199, New York City, USA, June. Association for Computational Linguistics.

Sameer Pradhan, Lance Ramshaw, Mitchell Marcus, Martha Palmer, Ralph Weischedel, and Nianwen Xue. 2011. Conll-2011 shared task: Modeling unrestricted coreference in ontonotes. In *Proceedings of the Fifteenth Conference on Computational Natural Language Learning: Shared Task*, pages 1–27, Portland, Oregon, USA, June. Association for Computational Linguistics.

Sameer Pradhan, Alessandro Moschitti, Nianwen Xue, Olga Uryupina, and Yuchen Zhang. 2012. CoNLL-2012 shared task: Modeling multilingual unrestricted coreference in OntoNotes. In *Proceedings of the Sixteenth Conference on Computational Natural Language Learning (CoNLL 2012)*, Jeju, Korea.

Wee Meng Soon, Hwee Tou Ng, and Daniel Chung Yong Lim. 2001. A machine learning approach to coreference resolution of noun phrases. *Comput. Linguist.*, 27:521–544, December.

Michael Strube, Stefan Rapp, and Christoph Müller. 2002. The influence of minimum edit distance on reference resolution. In *Proceedings of the ACL-02 conference on Empirical methods in natural language processing - Volume 10*, EMNLP '02, pages 312–319, Stroudsburg, PA, USA. Association for Computational Linguistics.

Xiaofeng Yang, Jian Su, and Chew Lim Tan. 2006. Kernel-based pronoun resolution with structured syntactic knowledge. In *Proceedings of the 21st International Conference on Computational Linguistics and 44th Annual Meeting of the Association for Computational Linguistics*, pages 41–48, Sydney, Australia, July. Association for Computational Linguistics.

UBIU for Multilingual Coreference Resolution in OntoNotes

Desislava Zhekova Sandra Kübler Joshua Bonner Marwa Ragheb Yu-Yin Hsu
Indiana University
Bloomington, IN, USA
{dzhekova, skuebler, jebonner, mragheb, hsuy}@indiana.edu

Abstract

The current work presents the participation of UBIU (Zhekova and Kübler, 2010) in the CoNLL-2012 Shared Task: Modeling Multilingual Unrestricted Coreference in OntoNotes (Pradhan et al., 2012). Our system deals with all three languages: Arabic, Chinese and English. The system results show that UBIU works reliably across all three languages, reaching an average score of 40.57 for Arabic, 46.12 for Chinese, and 48.70 for English. For Arabic and Chinese, the system produces high precision, while for English, precision and recall are balanced, which leads to the highest results across languages.

1 Introduction

Multilingual coreference resolution has been gaining considerable interest among researchers in recent years. Yet, only a very small number of systems target coreference resolution (CR) for more than one language (Mitkov, 1999; Harabagiu and Maiorano, 2000; Luo and Zitouni, 2005). A first attempt at gaining insight into the comparability of systems on different languages was accomplished in the SemEval-2010 Task 1: Coreference Resolution in Multiple Languages (Recasens et al., 2010). Six systems participated in that task, UBIU (Zhekova and Kübler, 2010) among them. However, since systems participated across the various languages rather irregularly, Recasens et al. (2010) reported that the data points were too few to allow for a proper comparison between different approaches. Further significant issues concerned system portability across the various languages and the respective language tuning, the influence of the quantity and quality of diverse linguistic annotations as well as the performance and behavior of various evaluation metrics.

The CoNLL-2011 Shared Task: Modeling Unrestricted Coreference in OntoNotes (Pradhan et al., 2011) targeted unrestricted CR, which aims at identifying nominal coreference but also event coreference, within an English data set from the OntoNotes corpus. Not surprisingly, attempting to include such event mentions had a detrimental effect on overall accuracy, and the best performing systems (e.g., (Lee et al., 2011)) did not attempt event anaphora. The current shared task extends the task definition to three different languages (Arabic, Chinese and English), which can prove challenging for rule-based approaches such as the best performing system from 2011 (Lee et al., 2011).

In the current paper, we present UBIU, a memory-based coreference resolution system, and its results in the CoNLL-2012 Shared Task. We give an overview of UBIU in Section 2. In Section 3, we present the system results, after which Section 4 lays out some conclusive remarks.

2 UBIU

UBIU (Zhekova and Kübler, 2010) is a coreference resolution system designed specifically for a multilingual setting. As shown by Recasens et al. (2010), multilingual coreference resolution can be approached by various machine learning methods since machine learning provides a possibility for robust abstraction over the variation of language phenomena and specificity. Therefore, UBIU employs a machine learning approach, memory-based learning (MBL) since it has proven to be a good solution to various natural language processing tasks (Daelemans and van den Bosch, 2005). We employ TiMBL (Daelemans et al., 2010), which uses k nearest neighbour classification to assign class labels to the targeted instances. The classifier settings we used were determined by a non-exhaustive search over the development data and are as follows: the *IB1* algorithm, similarity is computed based on weighted overlap, gain ratio is used for the relevance weights and the number of nearest neighbors is set to k=3 (cf. (Daelemans et al., 2010) for an explanation of the system parameters).

In UBIU, we use a pairwise mention model (Soon et al., 2001; Broscheit et al., 2010) since this model has proven more robust towards multiple languages (Wunsch, 2009) than more elaborate ones. We concentrate on nominal coreference resolution, i.e. we ignore the more unrestricted cases of event coreference. Below, we describe the modules used in UBIU in more detail.

2.1 Preprocessing

The preprocessing module oversees the proper formatting of the data for all modules applied in later stages during coreference resolution. During preprocessing, we use the speaker information, if provided, and replace all 1st person singular pronouns from the token position with the information provided in the speaker column and adjust the POS tag correspondingly.

2.2 Mention Detection

Mention detection is the process of detecting the phrases that are potentially coreferent and are thus considered candidates for the coreference process. Mention detection in UBIU is based on the parse and named entity information provided by the shared task. This step is crucial for the overall system performance, and we aim for high recall at this stage. Singleton mentions that are added in this step can be filtered out in later stages. However, if we fail to detect a mention in this stage, it cannot be added later. We predict a mention for each noun phrase and named entity provided in the data. Additionally, we extract mentions for possessive pronouns in English as only those did not correspond to a noun phrase in the syntactic structure provided by the task. In Arabic and Chinese, possessives are already marked as noun phrases.

	MD		
	R	P	F_1
Arabic	97.13	19.06	31.87
Chinese	98.33	31.64	47.88
English	96.73	30.75	46.67

Table 1: Mention detection (development set).

The system results on mention detection on the development set are listed in Table 1. The results show that we reach very high recall but low precision, as intended. The majority of the errors are due to discrepancies between noun phrases and named entities on the one hand and mentions on the other. Furthermore, since we do not target event coreference, we do not add mentions for the verbs in the data, which leads to a reduction of recall.

In all further system modules, we represent a mention by its head, which is extracted via heuristic methods. For Arabic, we select the first noun or pronoun while for Chinese and English, we extract the the pronoun or the last noun of a mention unless it is a common title. Additionally, we filter out mentions that correspond to types of named entities that in a majority of the cases in the training data are not coreferent (i.e. cardinals, ordinals, etc.).

One problem with representing mentions mostly by their head is that it is difficult to decide between the different mention spans of a head. Since automatic mentions are considered correct only if they match the exact span of a gold mention, we include all identified mention spans for every extracted head for classification, which can lead to losses in evaluation. For example, consider the instance from the development set in (1): the noun phrase *the Avenue of Stars* is coreferent and thus marked as a gold mention (key 7). UBIU extracts two different spans for the same head *Avenue*: *the Avenue* (MD 3) and *the Avenue of Stars* (MD 5).

(1)

token	POS	parse	key	MD	output
the	DT	(NP(NP*	(7	(3|(5	(9
Avenue	NNP	*)	-	3)	9)
of	IN	(PP*	-	-	-
Stars	NNPS	(NP*)))	7)	(4)|5)	-

Both mention spans are passed to the coreference resolver, together with additional features (i.e. men-

	MD	MUC	B^3	$CEAF_E$	Average
	F_1	F_1	F_1	F_1	F_1
long	100.0	100.0	100.0	100.0	100.0
short	50.00	0	66.66	66.66	44.44

Table 2: The scores for the short example in (1).

tion length, head modification, etc.) that will allow the resolver to distinguish between the spans. The classifier decides that the shorter mention is coreferent and that the longer mention is a singleton. In order to show the effect of this decision, we assume that there is one coreferent mention to *key 7*. We consider the two possible spans and show the respective scores in Table 2. The evaluation in Table 2 shows that providing the correct coreference link but the wrong, short mention span, *the Avenue*, has considerable effects to the overall performance. First, as defined by the task, the mention is ignored by all evaluation metrics leading to a decrease in mention detection and coreference performance. Moreover, the fact that this mention is ignored means that the second mention becomes a singleton and is not considered by MUC either, leading to an F_1 score of 0. This example shows the importance of selecting the correct mention span.

2.3 Singleton Classification

A singleton is a mention which corefers with no other mention, either because it does not refer to any entity or because it refers to an entity with no other mentions in the discourse. Because singletons comprise the majority of mentions in a discourse, their presence can have a substantial effect on the performance of machine learning approaches to CR, both because they complicate the learning task and because they heavily skew the proportion in the training data towards negative instances, which can bias the learner towards assuming no coreference relation between pairs of mentions. For this reason, information concerning singletons needs to be incorporated into the CR process so that such mentions can be eliminated from consideration.

Boyd et al. (2005), Ng and Cardie (2002), and Evans (2001) experimented with machine learning approaches to detect and/or eliminate singletons, finding that such a module provides an improvement in CR performance provided that the classifier does not eliminate non-singletons too frequently. Ng (2004) additionally compared various feature- and constraint-based approaches to incorporating singleton information into the CR pipeline. Feature-based approaches integrate information from the singleton classifier as features while constraint-based approaches filter singletons from the mention set. Following these works, we include a *k* nearest neighbor classifier for singleton mentions in UBIU with 19 commonly-used features described below. However, unlike Ng (2004), we use a combination of the feature- and constraint-based approaches to incorporate the classifier's results.

#	Feature Description
1	the depth of the mention in the syntax tree
2	the length of the mention
3	the head token of the mention
4	the POS tag of the head
5	the NE of the head
6	the NE of the mention
7	PR if the head is premodified, PO if it is not; UN otherwise
8	D if the head is in a definite mention; I otherwise
9	the predicate argument corresponding to the mention
10	left context token on position token -3
11	left context token on position token -2
12	left context token on position token -1
13	left context POS tag of token on position token -3
14	left context POS tag of token on position token -2
15	left context POS tag of token on position token -1
10	right context token on position token +1
11	right context token on position token +2
12	right context token on position token +3
13	right context POS tag of token on position token +1
14	right context POS tag of token on position token +2
15	right context POS tag of token on position token +3
16	the syntactic label of the mother node
17	the syntactic label of the grandmother node
18	a concatenation of the labels of the preceding nodes
19	C if the mention is in a PP; else I

Table 3: The features used by the singleton classifier.

Each training/testing instance represents a noun phrase or a named entity from the data together with features describing this phrase in its discourse. The list of features is shown in Table 3. The instances that are classified by the learner as singletons with a distance to their nearest neighbor below a threshold (i.e., half the average distance observed in the training data) are filtered from the mention set, and are thus not considered in the pairwise coreference classification. For the remainder of the mentions, the class that the singletons classifier has assigned to the instance is used as a feature in the coreference classifier. Experiments on the development set showed

		MD	MUC	B^3	$CEAF_E$	Average
		F_1	F_1	F_1	F_1	F_1
Arabic	+SC	58.36	34.75	58.26	37.39	**43.47**
	-SC	56.12	34.96	58.52	36.05	43.18
Chinese	+SC	52.30	42.70	61.11	32.86	**45.56**
	-SC	50.40	41.19	60.96	32.47	44.87
English	+SC	67.38	53.20	59.23	34.90	**49.11**
	-SC	65.55	51.57	59.18	34.38	48.38

Table 4: Evaluation of using (+SC) or not (-SC) the singleton classifier in UBIU on the development set.

that the most important features across all languages are the POS tag of the head word, definiteness, and the mother node in the syntactic representation. Information about head modification is helpful for English and Arabic, but not for Chinese.

The results of using the singleton classifier in UBIU on the development set are shown in Table 4. They show a moderate improvement for all evaluation metrics and all languages, with the exception of MUC and B^3 for Arabic. The most noticeable improvement can be observed in mention detection, which gains approx. 2% in all languages. A manual inspection of the development data shows that the version using the singleton classifier extracts a slightly higher number of coreferent mentions than the version without. However, the reduction of mentions that are never coreferent, which was the main goal of the singleton classifier, is also present in the version without the classifier, so that the results of the classifier only have a minimal influence on the final results.

2.4 Coreference Classification

Coreference classification is the process in which all identified mentions are paired up and features are extracted to build feature vectors that represent the mention pairs in their context. Each mention is represented in the feature vector by its syntactic head. The vectors for the pairs are then used by the memory-based learner TiMBL.

As anaphoric mentions, we consider all definite phrases; we then create a pair for each anaphor with each mention preceding it within a window of 10 (English, Chinese) or 7 (Arabic) sentences. We consider a shorter window of sentences for Arabic because of its NP-rich syntactic structure and its longer sentences, which leads to an increased number of possible mention pairs. The set of features that we use, listed in Table 5, is an extension of the set by Rahman and Ng (2009). Before classification, we apply a morphological filter, which excludes vectors that disagree in number or gender (applied only if the respective information is provided or can be deduced from the data).

Both the anaphor and the antecedent carry a label assigned to them by the singletons classifier. Yet, we consider as anaphoric only the heads of definite mentions. Including a feature representing the class assigned by the singletons classifier for each anaphor triggers a conservative learner behavior, i.e., fewer positive classes are assigned. Thus, to account for this behavior, we ignore those labels for the anaphor and include only one feature (no. 25 in Table 5) in the vector for the antecedent.

2.5 Postprocessing

In postprocessing, we create the equivalence classes of mentions that were classified as coreferent and

#	Feature Description
1	m_j - the antecedent
2	m_k - the mention (further m.) to be resolved
3	C if m_j is a pronoun; else I
4	C if m_k is a pronoun; else I
5	the concatenated values of feature 3 and feature 4
6	C if the m. are the same string; else I
7	C if one m. is a substring of the other; else I
8	C if both m. are pronominal and are the same string; else I
9	C if both are non-pronominal and are the same string; else I
10	C if both are pronouns; I if neither is a pronoun; else U
11	C if both are proper nouns; I if neither is; else U
12	C if both m. have the same speaker; I if they do not
13	C if both m. are the same named entity; I if they are not and U if they are not assigned a NE
14	token distance between m_j and m_k
15	sentence distance between m_j and m_k
16	normalised levenstein distance for both m.
17	PR if m_j is premodified, PO if it is not; UN otherwise
18	PR if m_k is premodified, PO if it is not; UN otherwise
19	the concatenated values for feature 17 and 18
20	D if m_j is in a definite m.; I otherwise
21	C if m_j is within the subject; I-within an object; U otherwise
22	C if m_k is within the subject; I-within an object; U otherwise
23	C if neither is embedded in a PP; I otherwise
24	C if neither is embedded in a NP; I otherwise
25	C if m_j has been classified as singleton; I otherwise
26	C if both are within ARG0-ARG4; I-within ARGM; else U
27	C if m_j is within ARG0-ARG4; I-within ARGM; else U
28	C if m_k is within ARG0-ARG4; I-within ARGM; else U
29	concatenated values for features 27 and 28
30	the predicate argument label for m_j
31	the predicate argument label for m_k
32	C if both m. agree in number; else I
33	C if both m. agree in gender; else I

Table 5: The features used by the coreference classifier.

		MD			MUC			B^3			$CEAF_E$			Average
		R	P	F_1	R	P	F_1	R	P	F_1	R	P	F_1	F_1
Automatic Mention Detection														
auto	Arabic	27.54	80.34	41.02	19.64	62.13	29.85	41.91	90.72	57.33	56.79	24.81	34.53	40.57
	Chinese	35.12	72.52	47.32	31.19	57.97	40.56	49.49	77.65	60.45	45.92	25.24	32.58	44.53
	English	65.78	68.49	67.11	54.28	52.79	53.52	62.26	54.90	58.35	33.52	34.96	34.22	48.70
gold	Arabic	28.00	82.21	41.78	15.47	45.92	23.15	39.22	84.86	53.65	55.10	24.22	33.65	36.82
	Chinese	37.84	74.84	50.27	33.95	60.29	43.44	50.95	77.28	61.41	46.68	26.13	33.50	46.12
	English	66.05	69.62	67.79	54.45	53.59	54.02	61.66	55.62	58.48	33.82	34.65	34.23	48.91
Gold Mention Boundaries														
auto	Arabic	27.48	75.53	40.29	18.75	56.47	28.16	42.67	89.25	57.74	55.53	25.36	34.82	40.24
	Chinese	36.97	73.98	49.30	32.09	58.30	41.39	49.43	77.38	60.32	46.35	25.71	33.07	44.93
	English	66.45	70.91	68.61	54.96	54.67	54.82	61.85	55.60	58.56	34.38	34.67	34.53	49.30
gold	Arabic	28.06	82.39	41.87	15.56	46.18	23.28	39.23	84.95	53.67	55.10	24.20	33.63	36.86
	Chinese	37.89	74.79	50.30	33.93	60.19	43.39	50.87	77.27	61.35	46.62	26.13	33.49	46.08
	English	65.82	71.72	68.65	54.68	55.51	55.09	61.22	56.59	58.82	34.85	34.04	34.44	49.45
Gold Mentions														
auto	Arabic	100	100	100	42.48	80.36	55.58	50.87	89.69	64.92	71.96	34.52	46.66	55.72
	Chinese	100	100	100	42.02	79.57	55.00	50.22	80.81	61.94	60.27	27.08	37.37	51.44
	English	100	100	100	68.38	78.11	72.92	63.04	58.60	60.74	52.64	37.10	43.53	59.06
gold	Arabic	100	100	100	45.58	73.27	56.20	52.27	82.35	63.95	70.17	37.54	48.91	56.35
	Chinese	100	100	100	44.12	80.89	57.10	51.79	80.53	63.04	60.37	27.69	37.96	52.70
	English	100	100	100	68.54	78.10	73.01	63.14	58.63	60.80	52.84	37.44	43.83	59.21

Table 6: UBIU system performance in the shared task.

insert the appropriate class/entity IDs in the data, removing mentions that constitute a class on their own – singletons. We bind all pronouns (except the ones that were labeled as singletons by the singleton classifier) that were not assigned an antecedent to the last seen subject and if such is not present to the last seen mention. We consider all positively classified instances in the clustering process.

3 Evaluation

The results of the final system evaluation are presented in Table 6. Comparing the results for mention detection (MD) on the development set (see Table 1, which shows MD before the resolution step) and the final test set (Table 6, showing MD after resolution and the deletion of singletons), we encounter a reversal of precision and recall tendencies (even though the results are not fully comparable since they are based on different data sets). This is due to the fact that during mention detection, we aim for high recall, and after coreference resolution, all mentions identified as singletons by the system are excluded from the answer set. Thus mentions that are coreferent in the key set but wrongly classified in the answer set are removed, leading to a decrease in recall. With regard to MD precision, a considerable increase is recorded, showing that the majority of the mentions that the system indicates as coreferent have the correct mention spans. Additionally, the problem of selecting the correct span (as described in Section 2) is another factor that has a considerable effect on precision at that stage – mentions that were accurately attached to the correct coreference chain are not considered if their span is not identical to the span of their counterparts in the key set.

Automatic Mention Detection In the first part in Table 6, we show the system scores for UBIU's performance when no mention information is provided in the data. We report both gold (using gold linguistic annotations) and auto (using automatically annotated data) settings. A comparison of the results shows that there are only minor differences between them with gold outperforming auto apart from Arabic for which there is a drop of 3.75 points in the gold setting. However, the small difference between all results shows that the quality of the automatic annotation is good enough for a CR system and that further improvements in the quality of the linguistic information will not necessarily improve CR.

If we compare results across languages, we see that Arabic has the lowest results. One of the reasons for this decreased performance can be found in the NP-rich syntactic structure of Arabic. This leads to a high number of identified mentions and in combination with the longer sentence length to a higher number of training/test instances. Another reason for the drop in performance for Arabic can be found in the lack of annotations expected by our system (named entities and predicted arguments) that were not provided by the task due to time constraints and the accuracy of the annotations. Further, Arabic is a morphologically rich language for which only the simplified standard POS tags were provided and not the gold standard ones that contain much richer and thus more helpful morphology information.

The results for Chinese and English are relatively close. We can also see that the $CEAF_E$ results are extremely close, with a difference of less than 1%. MUC, in contrast, shows the largest differences with more than 30% between Arabic and English in the gold setting. It is also noteworthy that the results for English show a balance between precision and recall while both Arabic and Chinese favor precision over recall in terms of mention detection, MUC, and B^3. The reasons for this difference between languages need to be investigated further.

Gold Mention Boundaries The results for this set of experiments is based on a version of the test set that contains the gold boundaries of all mentions, including singletons. Thus, we use these gold mention boundaries instead of the ones generated by our system. These experiments give us an insight on how well UBIU performs on selecting the correct boundaries. Since we do not expect the system's selection to be perfect, we would expect to see improved system performance given the correct boundaries. The results are shown in the second part of Table 6. As for using automatically generated mentions the tendencies in scores between gold and auto linguistic annotations are kept. A further comparison of the overall results between the two settings also shows only minor changes. The only exception is the auto setting for Arabic, for which we see drop in MD precision of approximately 5%. This also results in lower MUC and B^3 precision and $CEAF_E$ recall. The reasons for this drop in performance need to be investigated further. The fact that most results for both auto and gold settings change only sightly shows that having information about the correct mention boundaries is not very helpful. Thus, the system seems to have reached its optimal performance on selecting mention boundaries given the information that it has.

Gold Mentions The last set of experiments is based on a version of the test set that contains the gold mentions, i.e., all mentions that are coreferent, but without any information about the identity of the coreference chains. The results of this set of experiments gives us information about the quality of the coreference classifier. The results are shown in the third part of Table 6. Using gold parses leads to only minor improvement of the overall system performance, yet, in that case all languages, including Arabic, show consistent increase of results. Altogether, there is a major improvement of the scores in MD, MUC, and $CEAF_E$. The B^3 scores only show minor improvements, resulting from a slight drop in precision across languages. The results also show considerably higher precision than recall for MUC and B^3, and higher recall for $CEAF_E$. This means that the coreference decisions that the system makes are highly reliable but that it still has a preference for treating coreferent mentions as singletons.

A comparison across languages shows that providing gold mentions has a considerable positive effect on the system performance for Arabic since for that setting Chinese leads to lower overall scores. We assume that this is again due to the NP-rich syntactic structure of Arabic and the fact that providing the mentions decreases drastically the number of mentions the system works with and has to choose from during the resolution process.

4 Conclusion and Future Work

We presented the UBIU system for coreference resolution in a multilingual setting. The system performed reliably across all three languages of the CoNLL 2012 shared task. For the future, we are planning an in-depth investigation of the performance of the mention detection module and the singleton classifier, as well as in investigation into more complex models for coreference classification than the mention pair model.

Acknowledgments

This work is based on research supported by the US Office of Naval Research (ONR) Grant #N00014-10-1-0140. We would also like to thank Kiran Kumar for his help with tuning the system.

References

Adriane Boyd, Whitney Gegg-Harrison, and Donna Byron. 2005. Identifying non-referential it: A machine learning approach incorporating linguistically motivated patterns. In *Proceedings of the ACL Workshop on Feature Engineering for Machine Learning in Natural Language Processing*, FeatureEng '05, pages 40–47, Ann Arbor, MI.

Samuel Broscheit, Massimo Poesio, Simone Paolo Ponzetto, Kepa Joseba Rodriguez, Lorenza Romano, Olga Uryupina, Yannick Versley, and Roberto Zanoli. 2010. BART: A Multilingual Anaphora Resolution System. In *Proceedings of the 5th International Workshop on Semantic Evaluation (SemEval)*, pages 104–107, Uppsala, Sweden.

Walter Daelemans and Antal van den Bosch. 2005. *Memory-Based Language Processing*. Studies in Natural Language Processing. Cambridge University Press, Cambridge, UK.

Walter Daelemans, Jakub Zavrel, Ko van der Sloot, and Antal van den Bosch. 2010. TiMBL: Tilburg Memory Based Learner, version 6.3,reference guide. Technical Report ILK 10-01, Induction of Linguistic Knowledge, Computational Linguistics, Tilburg University.

Richard Evans. 2001. Applying machine learning toward an automatic classification of it. *Literary and Linguistic Computing*, 16(1):45 – 57.

Sanda M. Harabagiu and Steven J. Maiorano. 2000. Multilingual coreference resolution. In *Proceedings of ANLP 2000*, Seattle, WA.

Heeyoung Lee, Yves Peirsman, Angel Chang, Nathanael Chambers, Mihai Surdeanu, and Dan Jurafsky. 2011. Stanford's multi-pass sieve coreference resolution system at the CoNLL-2011 shared task. In *Proceedings of the Fifteenth Conference on Computational Natural Language Learning: Shared Task*, pages 28–34, Portland, OR.

Xiaoqiang Luo and Imed Zitouni. 2005. Multi-Lingual Coreference Resolution with Syntactic Features. In *Proceedings of HLT/EMNLP 2005*, Vancouver, Canada.

Ruslan Mitkov. 1999. Multilingual anaphora resolution. *Machine Translation*, 14(3-4):281–299.

Vincent Ng and Claire Cardie. 2002. Identifying anaphoric and non-anaphoric noun phrases to improve coreference resolution. In *Proceedings COLING '02*, pages 1–7, Taipei, Taiwan.

Vincent Ng. 2004. Learning noun phrase anaphoricity to improve coreference resolution: Issues in representation and optimization. In *Proceedings of the 42nd Annual Meeting on Association for Computational Linguistics*, ACL '04, Barcelona, Spain.

Sameer Pradhan, Lance Ramshaw, Mitchell Marcus, Martha Palmer, Ralph Weischedel, and Nianwen Xue. 2011. CoNLL-2011 shared task: Modeling unrestricted coreference in OntoNotes. In *Proceedings of CoNLL 2011*, Portland, OR.

Sameer Pradhan, Alessandro Moschitti, Nianwen Xue, Olga Uryupina, and Yuchen Zhang. 2012. CoNLL-2012 shared task: Modeling multilingual unrestricted coreference in OntoNotes. In *Proceedings of the Sixteenth Conference on Computational Natural Language Learning (CoNLL 2012)*, Jeju, Korea.

Altaf Rahman and Vincent Ng. 2009. Supervised models for coreference resolution. In *Proceedings of EMNLP*, pages 968–977, Singapore.

Marta Recasens, Lluís Màrquez, Emili Sapena, M. Antònia Martí, Mariona Taulé, Véronique Hoste, Massimo Poesio, and Yannick Versley. 2010. SemEval-2010 task 1: Coreference resolution in multiple languages. In *Proceedings of the 5th International Workshop on Semantic Evaluation*, pages 1–8, Uppsala, Sweden.

Wee Meng Soon, Hwee Tou Ng, and Daniel Chung Yong Lim. 2001. A machine learning approach to coreference resolution of noun phrases. *Computational Linguistics*, 27(4):521–544.

Holger Wunsch. 2009. *Rule-Based and Memory-Based Pronoun Resolution for German: A Comparison and Assessment of Data Sources*. Ph.D. thesis, Universität Tübingen.

Desislava Zhekova and Sandra Kübler. 2010. UBIU: A language-independent system for coreference resolution. In *Proceedings of the 5th International Workshop on Semantic Evaluation*, pages 96–99, Uppsala, Sweden.

Chinese Coreference Resolution via Ordered Filtering*

Xiaotian Zhang[1,2] **Chunyang Wu**[1,2] **Hai Zhao**[1,2†]
[1]Center for Brain-Like Computing and Machine Intelligence,
Department of Computer Science and Engineering, Shanghai Jiao Tong University
[2]MOE-Microsoft Key Laboratory for Intelligent Computing and Intelligent Systems
Shanghai Jiao Tong University
xtian.zh@gmail.com, chunyang506@sjtu.edu.cn, zhaohai@cs.sjtu.edu.cn

Abstract

We in this paper present the model for our participation (BCMI) in the CoNLL-2012 Shared Task. This paper describes a pure rule-based method, which assembles different filters in a proper order. Different filters handle different situations and the filtering strategies are designed manually. These filters are assigned to different ordered tiers from general to special cases. We participated in the Chinese and English closed tracks, scored 51.83 and 59.24 respectively.

1 Introduction

In this paper, we describes the approaches we utilized for our participation in the CoNLL-2012 Shared Task. This year's shared task targets at modeling coreference resolution for multiple languages. Following (Lee et al., 2011), we extends the methodology of deterministic coreference model, using manually designed rules to recognize expressions with corresponding entities. The deterministic coreference model (Raghunathan et al., 2010) has shown good performance in the shared task of CoNLL-2011. This kind of model focuses on filtering with ordered tiers: One filter is applied at one time, from highest to lowest precision. However, compared with learning approaches (Soon et al., 2001), since effective rules are quite heterogeneous in different languages, several filtering methods should be redesigned when different languages are considered. We modified the original Stanford English coreference system[1] to adapt to the Chinese scenario. For the English participation, we implemented the full strategies and interface of the semantic-based filters which are not obtained from the open source toolkit.

The rest of this paper is organized as follows: In Section 2, we review the related work; In Section 3, we describe the detail of our model of handling coreference resolution in Chinese; Experiment results are reported in Section 4 and the conclusion is presented in Section 5.

2 Related Work

Many existing works have been published on learning relation extractors via supervised (Soon et al., 2001) or unsupervised (Haghighi and Klein, 2010; Poon and Domingos, 2008) approaches. For involving semantics, (Rahman and Ng, 2011) proposed a coreference resolution model with world knowledge; By using word associations, (Kobdani et al., 2011) showed its effectiveness to coreference resolution. Compared

* This work was partially supported by the National Natural Science Foundation of China (Grant No. 60903119 and Grant No. 61170114), the National Research Foundation for the Doctoral Program of Higher Education of China under Grant No. 20110073120022, the National Basic Research Program of China (Grant No. 2009CB320901), the Science and Technology Commission of Shanghai Municipality (Grant No. 09511502400), and the European Union Seventh Framework Program (Grant No. 247619).

† Corresponding author.

[1]http://nlp.stanford.edu/software/dcoref.shtml

with machine learning methods, (Raghunathan et al., 2010) proposed rule-base models which have been witnessed good performance.

Researchers began to work on Chinese coreference resolution at a comparatively late date and most of them adopt a machine learning approach. (Guochen and Yunfei, 2005) based their Chinese personal pronoun coreference resolution system on decision trees and (Naiquan et al., 2009) realized a Chinese coreference resolution system based on maximum entropy model. (Weixuan et al., 2010) proposes a SVM-based approach to anaphora resolution of noun phrases in Chinese and achieves the F-measure of 63.3% in the evaluation on ACE 2005. (Guozhi et al., 2011) presented a model for personal pronouns anaphora resolution based on corpus,which using rule pretreatment combined with maximum entropy.

3 Model for Chinese

In general, we adapt Stanford English coreference system to Chinese by making necessary changes. The sketch of this deterministic model is to extract mentions and relevant information firstly; then several manually designed rules, or filtering sieves are applied to identify the coreference. Moreover, these sieves are utilized in a predesigned order, which are sorted from highest to lowest precision. The ordered filtering sieves are listed in Table 1.

Ordered Sieves
1. **Mention Detection Sieve**
2. **Discourse Processing Sieve**
3. Exact String Match Sieve
4. **Relaxed String Match Sieve**
5. Precise Constructs Sieve
6. **Head Matching Sieves**
7. **Proper Head Word Match Sieve**
8. **Pronouns Sieve**
9. Post-Processing Sieve

Table 1: Ordered filtering sieves for Chinese. Modified sieves are bold.

We remove the semantic-based sieves due to the resource constraints. The simplified version consists of nine filtering sieves. The bold ones in Table 1 are the modified sieves for Chinese. First of all, we adopt the head finding rules for Chinese used in (Levy and Manning, 2003), and this affects sieve 4, 6 and 7 which are all take advantage of the head words. And our change to other sieves are described as follows.

- **Mention Detection Sieve:** We in this sieve first extract all the noun phrases, pronouns (the words with part-of-speech (POS) tag **PN**), proper nouns (the words with POS tag **NR**) and named entities. Thus a mention candidate set is produced. We then refine this set by removing several types of candidates listed as follows:
  1. The *measure words*, a special word pattern in Chinese such as "一年" (a year of), "一吨" (a ton of).
  2. Cardinals, percents and money.
  3. A mention if a larger mention with the same head word exists.
- **Discourse Processing & Pronouns Sieve:** In these two sieves, we adapt the common pronouns to Chinese. It includes "你" (you), "我" (I or me),"他" (he or him),"她" (she or her),"它" (it),"你们" (plural of "you"), "我们" (we or us),"他们" (they, gender: male),"她们" (they, gender: female),"它们" (plural of "it") and relative pronoun "自己" (self). Besides these, we enrich the pronouns set by adding "咱", "咱们", "俺" and "俺们" which are more often to appear in spoken dialogs as first person pronouns and "您" which is used to show respect for "you" and the third person pronoun "其".

Besides, for mention processing of the original system, whether a mention is *singular* or *plural* should be given. Different from English POS tags, in Chinese plural nouns couldn't be distinguished from single nouns in terms of the POS. Therefore, we add two rules to judge whether a noun is plural or not.

- A noun that ends with "们" (plural marker for pronouns and a few animate nouns), and "等" (and so on) is plural.

- A noun phrase that involves the coordinating conjunction words such as " 和" (and) is plural.

4 Experiments

4.1 Modification for the English system

We implement the semantic-similarity sieves proposed in (Lee et al., 2011) with the WordNet. These modifications consider the alias sieve and lexical chain sieve. For the alias sieve, two mentions are marked as aliases if they appear in the same synset in WordNet. For the lexical chain sieve, two mentions are marked as coreference if linked by a WordNet lexical chain that traverses hypernymy or synonymy relations.

4.2 Numerical Results

Lang.	Coref	Anno.	R	P	F
Ch	Before	gold	87.78	40.63	55.55
		auto	80.37	38.95	52.47
	After	gold	69.56	62.77	65.99
		auto	65.02	59.76	62.28
En	Before	gold	93.65	42.32	58.30
		auto	88.84	40.17	55.32
	After	gold	77.49	74.59	76.01
		auto	72.88	74.53	73.69

Table 2: Performance of the mention detection component, before and after coreference resolution, with both gold and auto linguistic annotations on development set.

Lang.	R	P	F
Ch	61.11	62.12	61.61
En	75.23	72.24	73.71

Table 3: Performance of the mention detection component, after coreference resolution, with auto linguistic annotations on test set.

Table 2 shows the performance of mention detection both before and after the coreference resolution with gold and predicted linguistic annotations on development set. The performance of mention detection on test set is presented in Table 3. The recall is much higher than the precision so as to make sure less mentions are missed, and because spurious mentions will be left as singletons and removed at last, a low precision will not affect the final result. The performance of mention detection for Chinese is worse than that of English, and this is a direction for future improvement for Chinese.

	Metric	R	P	F1	avg F1
Ch	MUC	50.02	49.64	49.83	51.83
	BCUBED	65.81	65.50	65.66	
	CEAF (M)	49.88	49.88	49.88	
	CEAF (E)	40.39	43.47	41.88	
	BLANC	67.12	65.83	66.45	
En	MUC	64.08	63.57	63.82	59.24
	BCUBED	66.45	70.71	68.51	
	CEAF (M)	57.24	57.24	57.24	
	CEAF (E)	45.13	45.67	45.40	
	BLANC	71.12	77.92	73.95	

Table 5: Results on the official test set (closed track).

Our results on the development set for both languages are listed in Table 4 and the official test results are in Table 5. Avg F1 is the arithmetic mean of MUC, B3, and CEAFE.

We further examine the performance by testing on different data types (broadcast conversations, broadcast news, magazine articles, newswire, conversational speech, and web data) of the development set, and the results are shown in Table 6. The system do better on bn, mz, tc than bc, nw, wb for both Chinese and English. And it performs the worst on wb due to a relative lower recall in mention detection. For Chinese, we also compare the performance when handling the three different mention types, proper nominal, pronominal, and other nominal. Table 7 shows the scores output by the official scorer when only each kind of mentions are provided in the keys file and response file each time and both the quality of the coreference links among the nominal of each mention type and the corresponding performance of mention detection are presented. The performance of coreference resolution among proper nominal and pronominal is significant higher than that of other nominal which highly coincides with the results in Table 6.

Lang.	Setting	MUC R	MUC P	MUC F1	BCUBED R	BCUBED P	BCUBED F1	CEAF (E) R	CEAF (E) P	CEAF (E) F1	avg F1
Ch	AUTO	52.38	47.44	49.79	68.25	62.36	65.17	37.43	41.89	39.54	51.50
	GOLD	58.16	53.55	55.76	70.66	68.65	69.64	41.44	45.60	43.42	56.27
	GMB	63.60	87.63	73.70	62.71	88.32	73.34	74.08	42.83	54.28	67.11
En	AUTO	64.24	64.95	64.59	68.22	73.16	70.60	47.03	46.29	46.66	60.61
	GOLD	67.45	66.94	67.20	69.76	73.62	71.64	47.86	48.42	48.14	62.33
	GMB	71.78	90.55	80.08	65.45	88.95	75.41	77.42	46.47	58.08	71.19

Table 4: Results on the official development set (closed track). GMB stands for Gold Mention Boundaries

Lang.	Anno.	bc	bn	mz	nw	pt	tc	wb
Ch	AUTO	50.31	53.87	52.80	47.82	-	55.10	47.54
	GOLD	53.19	63.63	58.23	50.65	-	58.96	50.15
En	AUTO	59.26	62.40	63.17	57.57	65.24	60.91	56.88
	GOLD	60.34	64.51	64.36	59.71	67.07	62.44	58.47

Table 6: Results (Avg F1) on different data types of the development set (closed track).

Data Type	Proper nominal MD (Recall)	Proper nominal avg F1	Pronominal MD (Recall)	Pronominal avg F1	Other nominal MD (Recall)	Other nominal avg F1
bc	94.5 (550/582)	68.06	94.5 (1372/1452)	66.40	80.5 (1252/1555)	47.74
bn	96.7 (1213/1254)	67.46	97.8 (264/270)	77.39	83.7 (1494/1786)	53.51
mz	92.0 (526/572)	67.05	94.8 (91/96)	56.89	76.1 (834/1096)	53.68
nw	91.4 (402/440)	67.44	90.6 (29/32)	83.54	51.0 (1305/2559)	44.86
tc	100 (23/23)	95.68	84.5 (572/677)	61.96	71.2 (272/382)	53.88
wb	93.2 (218/234)	72.23	95.9 (397/414)	72.55	77.1 (585/759)	43.37
all	94.4 (2932/3105)	68.30	92.7 (2725/2941)	68.10	70.6 (5742/8137)	49.56

Table 7: Results (Recall of mention detection and Avg F1) on different data types and different mention types of the development set with linguistic annotations (closed track).

5 Conclusion

We presented the rule-base approach for the BCMI's participation in the shared task of CoNLL-2012. We extend the work by (Lee et al., 2011) and modified several tiers to adapt to Chinese. Numerical results show the effectiveness in the evaluation for Chinese and English. For the Chinese scenario, we firstly show it is possible to consider special POS-tags and common pronouns as indicators for improving the performance. This work could be extended by involving more feasible filtering tiers or utilizing some automatic rule generating methods.

References

Li Guochen and Luo Yunfei. 2005. 采用优先选择策略的中文人称代词的指代消解. (Personal pronoun coreference resolution in Chinese using a priority selection strategy). *Journal of Chinese Information Processings*, pages 24–30.

Dong Guozhi, Zhu Yuquan, and Cheng Xianyi. 2011. Research on personal pronoun anaphora resolution in chinese. *Application Research of Computers*, 28:1774–1776.

Aria Haghighi and Dan Klein. 2010. Coreference resolution in a modular, entity-centered model. In *Human Language Technologies: The 2010 Annual Conference of the North American Chapter of the Association for Computational Linguistics*, HLT '10, pages 385–393, Stroudsburg, PA, USA. Association for Computational Linguistics.

Hamidreza Kobdani, Hinrich Schütze, Michael Schiehlen, and Hans Kamp. 2011. Bootstrapping coreference resolution using word associations. In *Proceedings of the 49th Annual Meeting of the Association for Computational Linguistics: Human Language Technologies - Volume 1*, HLT '11, pages 783–792, Stroudsburg, PA, USA. Association for Computational Linguistics.

Heeyoung Lee, Yves Peirsman, Angel Chang, Nathanael Chambers, Mihai Surdeanu, and Dan Jurafsky. 2011. Stanford multi-pass sieve coreference resolution system at the conll-2011 shared task. In *Proceedings of the Fifteenth Conference on Computational Natural Language Learning: Shared Task*, pages 28–34, Portland, Oregon, USA, June. Association for Computational Linguistics.

Roger Levy and Christopher Manning. 2003. Is it harder to parse chinese, or the chinese treebank? In *Proceedings of the 41st Annual Meeting on Association for Computational Linguistics - Volume 1*, ACL '03, pages 439–446, Stroudsburg, PA, USA. Association for Computational Linguistics.

Hu Naiquan, Kong Fang, Wang Haidong, and Zhou Guodong. 2009. Realization on chinese coreference resolution system based on maximum entropy model. *Application Research of Computers*, pages 2948–2951.

Hoifung Poon and Pedro Domingos. 2008. Joint unsupervised coreference resolution with markov logic. In *Proceedings of the Conference on Empirical Methods in Natural Language Processing*, EMNLP '08, pages 650–659, Stroudsburg, PA, USA. Association for Computational Linguistics.

Karthik Raghunathan, Heeyoung Lee, Sudarshan Rangarajan, Nate Chambers, Mihai Surdeanu, Dan Jurafsky, and Christopher Manning. 2010. A multi-pass sieve for coreference resolution. In *Proceedings of the 2010 Conference on Empirical Methods in Natural Language Processing*, pages 492–501, Cambridge, MA, October. Association for Computational Linguistics.

Altaf Rahman and Vincent Ng. 2011. Coreference resolution with world knowledge. In *Proceedings of the 49th Annual Meeting of the Association for Computational Linguistics: Human Language Technologies - Volume 1*, HLT '11, pages 814–824, Stroudsburg, PA, USA. Association for Computational Linguistics.

Wee Meng Soon, Hwee Tou Ng, and Daniel Chung Yong Lim. 2001. A machine learning approach to coreference resolution of noun phrases. *Comput. Linguist.*, 27(4):521–544, December.

Tan Weixuan, Kong Fang, Wang Haidong, and Zhou Guodong. 2010. Svm-based approach to chinese anaphora resolution. *High Performance Computing Technology*, pages 30–36.

A Multigraph Model for Coreference Resolution

Sebastian Martschat, Jie Cai, Samuel Broscheit, Éva Mújdricza-Maydt, Michael Strube
Natural Language Processing Group
Heidelberg Institute for Theoretical Studies gGmbH
Heidelberg, Germany
(sebastian.martschat|jie.cai|michael.strube)@h-its.org

Abstract

This paper presents HITS' coreference resolution system that participated in the CoNLL-2012 shared task on multilingual unrestricted coreference resolution. Our system employs a simple multigraph representation of the relation between mentions in a document, where the nodes correspond to mentions and the edges correspond to relations between the mentions. Entities are obtained via greedy clustering. We participated in the closed tasks for English and Chinese. Our system ranked second in the English closed task.

1 Introduction

Coreference resolution is the task of determining which mentions in a text refer to the same entity. This paper describes HITS' system for the CoNLL-2012 Shared Task on multilingual unrestricted coreference resolution, where the goal is to build a system for coreference resolution in an end-to-end multilingual setting (Pradhan et al., 2012). We participated in the closed tasks for English and Chinese and focused on English. Our system ranked second in the English closed task.

Being conceptually similar to and building upon Cai et al. (2011b), our system is based on a directed multigraph representation of a document. A multigraph is a graph where two nodes can be connected by more than one edge. In our model, nodes represent mentions and edges are built from relations between the mentions. The entities to be inferred correspond to clusters in the multigraph.

Our model allows for directly representing any kind of relations between pairs of mentions in a graph structure. Inference over this graph can harness structural properties and the rich set of encoded relations. In order to serve as a basis for further work, the components of our system were designed to work as simple as possible. Therefore our system relies mostly on local information between pairs of mentions.

2 Architecture

Our system is implemented on top of the BART toolkit (Versley et al., 2008). To compute the coreference clusters in a document, we first extract a set of mentions $M = \{m_1, \ldots, m_n\}$ ordered according to their position in the text (Section 2.1). We then build a directed multigraph where the set of nodes is M and edges are induced by relations between mentions (Section 2.4). The relations we use in our system are coreference indicators like string matching or alias (Section 3). For every relation R, we compute a weight w_R using the training data (Section 2.3). We then assign the weight w_R to any edge that is induced by the relation R. Depending on distance and connectivity properties of the graph the weights may change (Section 2.4.1). Given the constructed graph with edge weights, we go through the mentions according to their position in the text and perform greedy clustering (Section 2.6). For Chinese, we employ spectral clustering (Section 2.5) as adopted in Cai et al. (2011b) before the greedy clustering step to reduce the number of candidate antecedents for a mention. The components of our system are described in the following subsections.

2.1 Mention Extraction

Noun phrases are extracted from the provided parse and named entity annotation layers. For embedded mentions with the same head, we only keep the mention with the largest span.

2.1.1 English

For English we identify eight different mention types: common noun, proper noun, personal pronoun, demonstrative pronoun, possessive pronoun, coordinated noun phrase, quantifying noun phrase (*some of ...*, *17 of ...*) and quantified noun phrase (*the armed men* in *one of the armed men*). The head for a common noun or a quantified noun is computed using the SemanticHeadFinder from the Stanford Parser[1]. The head for a proper noun starts at the first token tagged as a noun until a punctuation, preposition or subclause is encountered. Coordinations have the CC tagged token as head and quantifying noun phrases have the quantifier as head.

In a postprocessing step we filter out adjectival use of nations and named entities with semantic class *Money*, *Percent* or *Cardinal*. We discard mentions whose head is embedded in another mention's head. Pleonastic pronouns are identified and discarded via a modified version of the patterns used by Lee et al. (2011).

2.1.2 Chinese

For Chinese we detect four mention types: common noun, proper noun, pronoun and coordination. The head detection for Chinese is provided by the SunJurafskyChineseHeadFinder from the Standford Parser, except for proper nouns whose head is set to the mention's rightmost token.

The remaining processing is similar to the mention detection for English.

2.2 Preprocessing

We extract the information in the provided annotation layers and transform the predicted constituent parse trees into dependency parse trees. We work with two different dependency representations, one obtained via the converter implemented in Stanford's NLP suite[2], the other using LTH's constituent-to-dependency conversion tool[3]. For pronouns, we determine number and gender using tables containing a mapping of pronouns to their gender and number.

2.2.1 English

For English, number and gender for common nouns are computed via a comparison of head lemma to head and using the number and gender data of Bergsma and Lin (2006). Quantified noun phrases are always plural. We compute semantic classes via a WordNet (Fellbaum, 1998) lookup.

2.2.2 Chinese

For Chinese, we simply determine number and gender by searching for the corresponding designators, since plural mentions mostly end with 们, while 先生 (*sir*) and 女士 (*lady*) often suggest gender information. To identify demonstrative and definite noun phrases, we check whether they start with a definite/demonstrative indicator (e.g. 这 (*this*) or 那 (*that*)). We use lists of named entities extracted from the training data to determine named entities and their semantic class in development and testing data.

2.3 Computing Weights for Relations

We compute weights for relations using simple descriptive statistics on training documents. Since this is a robust approach to learning weights for the type of graph model we employ (Cai et al., 2011b; Cai et al., 2011a), we use only a fraction of the available training data. We took a random subset consisting of around 20% for English and 15% for Chinese of the training data. For every document in this set and every relation R, we go through the set M of extracted mentions and compute for every pair (m_i, m_j) with $i > j$ whether R holds for this pair. The weight w_R for R is then the number of coreferent pairs with R divided by the number of all pairs with R.

2.4 Graph Construction

The set of relations we employ consists of two subsets: negative relations R_- which enforce that no

[1] http://nlp.stanford.edu/software/lex-parser.shtml

[2] http://nlp.stanford.edu/software/stanford-dependencies.shtml

[3] http://nlp.cs.lth.se/software/treebank_converter/

edge is built between two mentions, and positive relations R_+ that induce edges. Again, we go through M in a left-to-right fashion. If for two mentions m_i, m_j with $i > j$ a negative relation R_- holds, no edge between m_i and m_j can be built. Otherwise we add an edge from m_i to m_j for every positive relation R_+ such that $R_+(m_i, m_j)$ is true. The structure obtained by this construction is a directed multigraph.

We handle copula relations similar to Lee et al. (2011): if m_i is *this* and the pair (m_i, m_j) is in a copula relation (like *This is the World*), we remove m_j and replace m_j in all edges involving it by m_i. For Chinese, we handle "role appositives" as introduced by Haghighi and Klein (2009) analogously.

2.4.1 Assigning Weights to Edges

Initially, any edge (m_i, m_j) induced by the relation R has the weight w_R computed as described in Section 2.3. If R is a transitive relation, we divide the weight by the number of mentions connected by this relation. This corresponds to the way edge weights are assigned during the spectral embedding in Cai et al. (2011b). If R is a relation sensitive to distance like compatibility between a common/proper noun and a pronoun, the weight is altered according to the distance between m_i and m_j.

2.4.2 An Example

We demonstrate the graph construction by a simple example. Consider a document consisting of the following three sentences.

> *Barack Obama and Nicolas Sarkozy met in Toronto yesterday. They discussed the financial crisis. Sarkozy left today.*

Let us assume that our system identifies *Barack Obama* (m_1), *Nicolas Sarkozy* (m_2), *Barack Obama and Nicolas Sarkozy* (m_3), *They* (m_4) and *Sarkozy* (m_5) as mentions. We consider these mentions and the relations N_Number, P_Nprn_Prn, P_Alias and P_Subject described in Section 3. The graph constructed according to the algorithm described in this section is displayed in Figure 1.

Observe the effect of the negative relation N_Number: while P_Nprn_Prn holds for the pair *Barack Obama* (m_1) and *They* (m_4), the mentions do not agree in number. Hence N_Number holds for this pair and no edge from m_4 to m_1 can be built.

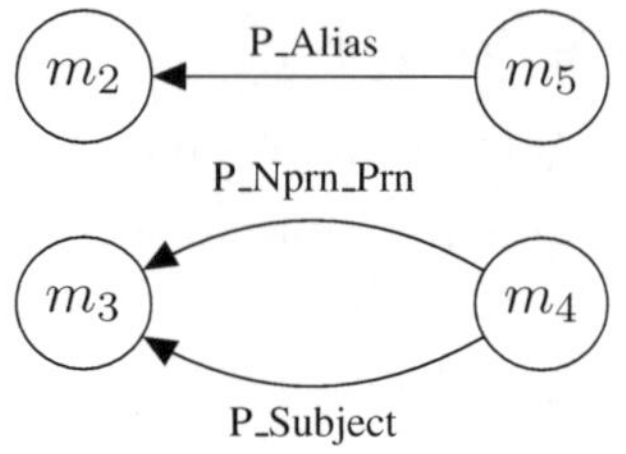

Figure 1: An example graph. Nodes represent mentions, edges are induced by relations between the mentions.

2.5 Spectral Clustering

For Chinese we apply spectral clustering before the final greedy clustering phase. In order to be able to apply spectral clustering, we make the graph undirected and merge parallel edges into one edge, summing up all weights. Due to the way edge weights are computed, the resulting undirected simple graph corresponds to the graph Cai et al. (2011b) use as input to the spectral clustering algorithm. Spectral clustering is now performed as in Cai et al. (2011b).

2.6 Greedy Clustering

To describe our clustering algorithm, we use some additional terminology: if there exists an edge from m to n we say that m is a *parent* of n and that n is a *child* of m.

In the last step, we go through the mentions from left to right. Let m_i be the mention in focus. For English, we consider all children of m_i as possible antecedents. For Chinese we restrict the possible antecedents to all children that are in the same cluster obtained by spectral clustering.

If m_i is a pronoun, we determine m_j such that the sum over all weights of edges from m_i to m_j is maximized. We then assign m_i and m_j to the same entity. In English, if m_i is a parent of a noun phrase m that embeds m_j, we instead assign m_i and m to the same entity.

For Chinese, all other noun phrases are assigned to the same entity as all their children in the cluster obtained by spectral clustering. For English, we are more restrictive: definites and demonstratives are assigned to the same cluster as their closest (according to the position of the mentions in the text) child.

Negative relations may also be applied as constraints in this phase. Before assigning m_i to the same entity as a set of mentions C, we check for every $m \in C$ and every negative relation R_- that we want to incorporate as a constraint whether $R_-(m_i, m)$ holds. If yes, we do not assign m_i to the same entity as the mentions in C.

2.7 Complexity

Our algorithms for weight computation, graph construction and greedy clustering look at all pairs of mentions in a document and perform simple calculations, which leads to a time complexity of $O\left(n^2\right)$ per document, where n is the number of mentions in a document. When performing spectral clustering, this increases to $O\left(n^3\right)$. Since we deal with at most a few hundred mentions per document, the cubic running time is not an issue.

3 Relations

In our system relations serve as templates for building or disallowing edges between mentions. We distinguish between positive and negative relations: negative relations disallow edges between mentions, positive relations build edges between mentions. Negative relations can also be used as constraints during clustering, while positive relations may also be applied as "weak" relations: in this case, we only add the induced edge when the two mentions under consideration are already included in the graph after considering all the non-weak relations.

Most of the relations presented here were already used in our system for last year's shared task (Cai et al., 2011b). The set of relations was enriched mainly to resolve pronouns in dialogue and to resolve pronouns that do not carry much information by themselves like *it* and *they*.

3.1 Negative Relations

(1) N_Gender, (2) N_Number: Two mentions do not agree in gender or number.

(3) N_SemanticClass: Two mentions do not agree in semantic class (only the *Object*, *Date* and *Person* top categories derived from WordNet (Fellbaum, 1998) are used).

(4) N_ItDist: The anaphor is *it* or *they* and the sentence distance to the antecedent is larger than one.

(5) N_BarePlural: Two mentions that are both bare plurals.

(6) N_Speaker12Prn: Two first person pronouns or two second person pronouns with different speakers, or one first person pronoun and one second person pronoun with the same speaker.

(7) N_DSprn: Two first person pronouns in direct speech assigned to different speakers.

(8) N_ContraSubjObj: Two mentions are in the subject and object positions of the same verb, and the anaphor is a non-possessive pronoun.

(9) N_Mod: Two mentions have the same syntactic heads, and the anaphor has a pre- or post-modifier which does not occur in the antecedent and does not contradict the antecedent.

(10) N_Embedding: Two mentions where one embeds the other, which is not a reflexive or possessive pronoun.

(11) N_2PrnNonSpeech: Two second person pronouns without speaker information and not in direct speech.

3.2 Positive Relations

(12) P_StrMatch_Npron, (13) P_StrMatch_Pron: After discarding stop words, if the strings of mentions completely match and are not pronouns, the relation P_StrMatch_Npron holds. When the matched mentions are pronouns, P_StrMatch_Pron holds.

(14) P_HeadMatch: If the syntactic heads of mentions match.

(15) P_Nprn_Prn: If the antecedent is not a pronoun and the anaphor is a pronoun. This relation is restricted to a sentence distance of 1.

(16) P_Alias: If mentions are aliases of each other (i.e. proper names with partial match, full names and acronyms, etc.).

(17) P_Speaker12Prn: If the speaker of the second person pronoun is talking to the speaker of the first person pronoun. The mentions contain only first or second person pronouns.

(18) P_DSPrn: If one mention is subject of a *speak* verb, and the other mention is a first person pronoun within the corresponding direct speech.

(19) P_ReflPrn: If the anaphor is a reflexive pronoun, and the antecedent is the subject of the sentence.

(20) P_PossPrn: If the anaphor is a possessive pronoun, and the antecedent is the subject of the sentence or the subclause.

(21) P_GPEIsA: If the antecedent is a Named Entity of *GPE* entity type and the anaphor is a definite expression of the same type.

(22) P_PossPrnEmbedding: If the anaphor is a possessive pronoun and is embedded in the antecedent.

(23) P_VerbAgree: If the anaphor is a pronoun and has the same predicate as the antecedent.

(24) P_Subject & (25) P_Object: If both mentions are subjects/objects (applies only if the anaphor is *it* or *they*).

(26) P_SemClassPrn: If the anaphor is a pronoun, the antecedent is not a pronoun, and both have semantic class *Person*.

For English, we used all relations except for (21) and (26). Relations (1), (2) and (10) were incorporated as constraints during greedy clustering. For Chinese, we used relations (1) – (6), (12) – (15), (21) and (26). (26) was incorporated as a weak relation.

4 Results

We submitted to the closed tasks for English and Chinese. The results on the English development set and testing set are displayed in Table 1 and Table 2 respectively. To indicate the progress we achieved within one year, Table 3 shows the performance of our system on the CoNLL '11 development data set compared to last year's results (Cai et al., 2011b). The *Overall* number is the average of MUC, B^3 and CEAF (E), MD is the mention detection score. Overall, we gained over 5% F1 some of which can be attributed to improved mention detection.

Metric	R	P	F1
MD	73.96	75.69	74.81
MUC	64.93	68.69	66.76
B^3	68.42	75.77	71.91
CEAF (M)	61.23	61.23	61.23
CEAF (E)	49.61	45.60	47.52
BLANC	77.81	80.75	79.19
Overall			62.06

Table 1: Results on the English CoNLL '12 development set

Metric	R	P	F1
MD	74.23	76.10	75.15
MUC	65.21	68.83	66.97
B^3	66.50	74.69	70.36
CEAF (M)	59.61	59.61	59.61
CEAF (E)	48.64	44.72	46.60
BLANC	73.29	78.94	75.73
Overall			61.31

Table 2: Results on the English CoNLL '12 testing set

Metric	R	P	F1	2011 F1
MD	70.84	73.08	71.94	66.28
MUC	60.80	65.09	62.87	55.19
B^3	68.37	75.89	71.94	68.52
CEAF (M)	60.42	60.42	60.42	54.44
CEAF (E)	50.40	46.11	48.16	43.19
BLANC	75.44	79.26	77.19	72.13
Overall			60.99	55.63

Table 3: Results on the English CoNLL '11 development set compared to Cai et al. (2011b)

Table 4 and Table 5 display our results on Chinese development data and testing data respectively.

Metric	R	P	F1
MD	52.45	71.50	60.51
MUC	45.90	67.07	54.50
B^3	58.94	84.26	69.36
CEAF (M)	53.60	53.60	53.60
CEAF (E)	50.73	34.24	40.89
BLANC	66.17	83.11	71.45
Overall			54.92

Table 4: Results on the Chinese CoNLL '12 development set

Metric	R	P	F1
MD	48.49	74.02	58.60
MUC	42.71	67.80	52.41
B^3	55.37	85.24	67.13
CEAF (M)	51.30	51.30	51.30
CEAF (E)	51.81	32.46	39.92
BLANC	63.96	82.81	69.18
Overall			53.15

Table 5: Results on the Chinese CoNLL '12 testing set

Because none of our team members has knowledge of the Arabic language we did not attempt to run our system on the Arabic datasets and therefore our official score for this language is considered to be 0. The combined official score of our submission is $(0.0 + 53.15 + 61.31)/3 = 38.15$. In the closed task our system was the second best performing system for English and the eighth best performing system for Chinese.

5 Error analysis

We did not attempt to resolve event coreference and did not incorporate world knowledge which is responsible for many recall errors our system makes.

Since we use a simple greedy strategy for clustering that goes through the mentions left-to-right, errors in clustering propagate, which gives rise to cluster-level inconsistencies. We observed a drop in performance when using more negative relations as constraints. A more sophisticated clustering strategy that allows a more refined use of constraints is needed.

5.1 English

Our detection of copula and appositive relations is quite inaccurate, which is why we limit the incorporation of copulas to cases where the antecedent is *this* and left appositives out.

We aim for high precision regarding the usage of the negative relation N_Modifier. This leads to some loss in recall. For example, our system does not assign *the just-completed Paralympics* and *the 12-day Paralympics* to the same entity. Such cases require a more involved reasoning scheme to decide whether the modifiers are actually contradicting each other.

Non-referring pronouns constitute another source of errors. While we improved detection of pleonastic *it* compared to last year's system, a lot of them are not filtered out. Our system also does not distinguish well between generic and non-generic uses of *you* and *we*, which hurts precision.

5.2 Chinese

Since each Chinese character carries its own meaning, there are multiple ways to express the same entity by combining different characters into a word. Both syntactic heads and modifiers can be replaced by similar words or by abbreviated versions. From 外省人 (*outside people*) to 外省 族群 (*outside ethnic group*) the head is replaced, while from 戴安娜 (*Diana*) to 美丽 迷人 的 戴妃 (*charming Di Princess*) the name is abbreviated.

Modifier replacement is more difficult to cope with, our system does not recognize that 重新 计票 作业 (*starting-over counting-votes job*) and 验票 作业 (*verifying-votes job*) are coreferent. It is also not trivial to separate characters from words (e.g. by separating 计 and 票) to resolve such cases, since it will introduce too much noise as a consequence. In order to tackle this problem, a smart scheme to propagate similarities from partial words to the entire mentions and a knowledge base upon which reliable similarities can be retrieved are necessary.

In contrast to English there is no strict enforcement of using definite noun phrases when referring to an antecedent in Chinese. Both 这次演说 (*the talk*) and 演说 (*talk*) can corefer with the antecedent 克林顿 在 河内 大选 的 演说 (*Clinton's talk during Hanoi election*). This makes it very difficult to distinguish generic expressions from referential ones. In the submitted version of our system, we simply ignore the nominal anaphors which do not start with definite articles or demonstratives.

6 Conclusions

In this paper we presented a graph-based model for coreference resolution. It captures pairwise relations between mentions via edges induced by relations. Entities are obtained by graph clustering. Discriminative information can be incorporated as negative relations or as constraints during clustering.

We described our system's architecture and the relations it employs, highlighting differences and similarities to our system from last year's shared task.

Designed to work as a basis for further work, our system works mainly by exploring the relationship between pairs of mentions. Due to its modular architecture, our system can be extended by components taking global information into account, for example for weight learning or clustering.

We focused on the closed task for English in which our system achieved competitive performance, being ranked second out of 15 participants.

Acknowledgments. This work has been funded by the Klaus Tschira Foundation, Heidelberg, Germany. The first and the second authors have been supported by a HITS PhD. scholarship.

References

Shane Bergsma and Dekang Lin. 2006. Bootstrapping path-based pronoun resolution. In *Proceedings of the 21st International Conference on Computational Linguistics and 44th Annual Meeting of the Association for Computational Linguistics,* Sydney, Australia, 17–21 July 2006, pages 33–40.

Jie Cai, Éva Mújdricza-Maydt, Yufang Hou, and Michael Strube. 2011a. Weakly supervised graph-based coreference resolution for clinical data. In *Proceedings of the 5th i2b2 Shared Tasks and Workshop on Challenges in Natural Language Processing for Clinical Data,* Washington, D.C., 20-21 October 2011. To appear.

Jie Cai, Éva Mújdricza-Maydt, and Michael Strube. 2011b. Unrestricted coreference resolution via global hypergraph partitioning. In *Proceedings of the Shared Task of the 15th Conference on Computational Natural Language Learning,* Portland, Oreg., 23–24 June 2011, pages 56–60.

Christiane Fellbaum, editor. 1998. *WordNet: An Electronic Lexical Database.* MIT Press, Cambridge, Mass.

Aria Haghighi and Dan Klein. 2009. Simple coreference resolution with rich syntactic and semantic features. In *Proceedings of the 2009 Conference on Empirical Methods in Natural Language Processing,* Singapore, 6–7 August 2009, pages 1152–1161.

Heeyoung Lee, Yves Peirsman, Angel Chang, Nathanael Chambers, Mihai Surdeanu, and Dan Jurafsky. 2011. Stanford's multi-pass sieve coreference resolution system at the CoNLL-2011 shared task. In *Proceedings of the Shared Task of the 15th Conference on Computational Natural Language Learning,* Portland, Oreg., 23–24 June 2011, pages 28–34.

Sameer Pradhan, Alessandro Moschitti, and Nianwen Xue. 2012. CoNLL-2012 Shared Task: Modeling multilingual unrestricted coreference in OntoNotes. In *Proceedings of the Shared Task of the 16th Conference on Computational Natural Language Learning,* Jeju Island, Korea, 12–14 July 2012. This volume.

Yannick Versley, Simone Paolo Ponzetto, Massimo Poesio, Vladimir Eidelman, Alan Jern, Jason Smith, Xiaofeng Yang, and Alessandro Moschitti. 2008. BART: A modular toolkit for coreference resolution. In *Companion Volume to the Proceedings of the 46th Annual Meeting of the Association for Computational Linguistics,* Columbus, Ohio, 15–20 June 2008, pages 9–12.

Incorporating Rule-based and Statistic-based Techniques for Coreference Resolution

Ruifeng Xu, Jun Xu, Jie Liu, Chengxiang Liu, Chengtian Zou, Lin Gui, Yanzhen Zheng, Peng Qu
Human Language Technology Group, Key Laboratory of Network Oriented Intelligent Computation, Shenzhen Graduate School, Harbin Institute of Technology, China
{xuruifeng.hitsz;hit.xujun;lyjxcz;matitalk;chsky.zou;monta3pt;zhyz.zheng;viphitqp@gmail.com}

Abstract

This paper describes a coreference resolution system for CONLL 2012 shared task developed by HLT_HITSZ group, which incorporates rule-based and statistic-based techniques. The system performs coreference resolution through the mention pair classification and linking. For each detected mention pairs in the text, a Decision Tree (DT) based binary classifier is applied to determine whether they form a coreference. This classifier incorporates 51 and 61 selected features for English and Chinese, respectively. Meanwhile, a rule-based classifier is applied to recognize some specific types of coreference, especially the ones with long distances. The outputs of these two classifiers are merged. Next, the recognized coreferences are linked to generate the final coreference chain. This system is evaluated on English and Chinese sides (Closed Track), respectively. It achieves 0.5861 and 0.6003 F1 score on the development data of English and Chinese, respectively. As for the test dataset, the achieved F_1 scores are 0.5749 and 0.6508, respectively. This encouraging performance shows the effectiveness of our proposed coreference resolution system.

1 Introduction

Coreference resolution aims to find out the different mentions in a document which refer to the same entity in reality (Sundheim and Beth, 1995; Lang et al. 1997; Chinchor and Nancy, 1998;). It is a core component in natural language processing and information extraction. Both rule-based approach (Lee et al. 2011) and statistic-based approach (Soon et al., 2001; Ng and Cardie, 2002; Bengtson and Roth, 2008; Stoyanov et al., 2009; Chen et al. 2011) are proposed in coreference resolution study. Besides the frequently used syntactic and semantic features, the more linguistic features are exploited in recent works (Versley, 2007; Kong et al. 2010).

CoNLL-2012 proposes a shared task, "Modeling multilingual unrestricted coreference in the OntoNotes" (Pradhan et al. 2012). This is an extension of the CoNLL-2011 shared task. The task involves automatic anaphoric mention detection and coreference resolution across three languages including English, Chinese and Arabic. HLT_HITSZ group participated in the Closed Track evaluation on English and Chinese side. This paper presents the framework and techniques of HLT_HITSZ system which incorporates both rule-based and statistic-based techniques. In this system, the mentions are firstly identified based on the provided syntactic information. The mention pairs in the document are fed to a Decision Tree based classifier to determine whether they form a coreference or not. The rule-based classifiers are then applied to recognize some specific types of coreference, in particular, the long distance ones. Finally, the recognized coreference are linked to obtain the final coreference resolution results. This system incorporates lexical, syntactical and semantic features. Especially for English, WordNet is used to provide semantic information of the mentions, such as semantic distance and the category of the mentions and so on. Other than the officially provided number and gender data, we generated some lexicons from the training dataset to obtain the values of some features. This system achieves 0.5861 and 0.6003 F_1 scores on English and Chinese development data, respectively, and 0.5749 and 0.6508 F_1 scores on English and Chinese testing data, respectively. The achieved encouraging performances show that the proposed incorporation of rule-based and statistic-based techniques is effective.

The rest of this report is organized as below. Section 2 presents the mention detection. Section 3 presents the coreference determination and Section 4 presents the coreference linking. The experimental results are given in Section 5 in detail. Finally, Section 6 concludes this report.

2 Mention Detection

In this stage, the system detects the mentions from the text. The pairs of these mentions in one document are regarded as the coreference candidates. Thus, the high recall is a more important target than higher precision for this stage. Corresponding to English and Chinese, we adopted different detection methods, respectively.

2.1 Mention Detection - English

HLT_HITSZ system chooses the marked noun phrase (NP), pronouns (PRP) and PRP$ in English data as the mentions. The system selects most named entities (NE) as the mentions but filter out some specific types. Firstly, the NEs which cannot be labeled either as NP or NML are filter out because there are too cases that the pairs of these NEs does not corefer even they are in the same form as shown in the training dataset. Second, the NEs of ORDINAL, PERCENT and MONEY types are filtered because they have very low coreference ratio (less than 2%). Furthermore, for the cases that NPs overlapping a shorter NP, normally, only the longer one are choose. An exception is that if the shorter NPs are in parallel structures with the same level to construct a longer NP. For example, for a NP "A and B", "A", "B" and "A and B" as regarded ed as three different mentions.

2.2 Mention Detection – Chinese

HLT_HITSZ system extracts all NPs and PNs as the mention candidates. For the NPs have the overlaps, we handle them in three ways: 1. For the cases that two NPs share the same tail, the longer NP is kept and the rest discarded; 2. For cases that the longer NP has a NR as its tail, the NPs which share the same tail are discarded; 3. In MZ and NW folders, they are many mentions nested marked as the nested co-referent mentions. The system selects the longest NP as mention in this stage while the other mention candidates in the longest NP will be recalled in the post processing stage.

3 Coreference Determination

Any pair of two detected mentions in one document becomes one coreference candidate. In this stage, the classifiers are developed to determine whether this pair be a coreference or not. During the generation of mention pairs, it is observed that linking any two mentions in one document as candidates leads to much noises. The statistical observation on the Chinese training dataset show that 90% corefered mention pairs are in the distance of 10 sentences. Similar results are found in the English training dataset while the context window is set to 5 sentences. Therefore, in this stage, the context windows for generating mention pairs as coreference candidates for English and Chinese are limited to 5 and 10 sentences, respectively.

3.1 The Statistic-based Coreference Determination

The same framework is adopted in the statistical-based coreference determination for English and Chinese, respectively, which is based on a machine learning-based statistical classifier and selected language-dependent features. Through transfer the examples in the training test into feature-valued space, the classifier is trained. This binary classifier will be applied to determine whether the input mention pair be a coreference or not. Here, we evaluated three machine learning based classifiers including Decision Tree, Support Vector Machines and Maximum Entropy on the training data while Decision Tree perform the best. Thus, DT classifier is selected. Since the annotations on the training data from different directory show some inconsistence, multiple classifiers corresponding to each directory are trained individually.

3.1.1 Features - English

51 features are selected for English coreference determination. The features are camped to six categories. Some typical features are listed below:

1. Basic features:
   (1) Syntactic type of the two mentions, includes NP, NE, PRP, PRP$. Here, only the NPs which do not contain any named entities or its head word isn't a named entity are considered as an NP while the others are discarded.
   (2) If one mention is a PRP or PRP$, use an ID to specify which one it is.
   (3) The sentence distance between two mentions.
   (4) Whether one mention is contained by another one.
2. Parsing features:
   (1) Whether two mentions belong to one NP.
   (2) The phrase distance between the two mentions.
   (3) The predicted arguments which the two mentions belong to.
3. Named entity related features:
   (1) If both of the two mentions may be considered as named entities, whether they have the same type.
   (2) If one mention is a common NP or PRP and another one can be considered as named entity, whether the words of the common NP or PRP can be used to refer this type of named entity. This knowledge is extracted from the training dataset.
   (3) Whether the core words of the two named entity type NP match each other.
4. Features for PRP:
   (1) If both mentions are PRP or PRP$, use an ID to show what they are. The PRP$ with the same type will be assigned the same ID, for example, *he*, *him* and *his*.
   (2) Whether the two mentions has the same PRP ID.
5. Semantic Features:
   (1) Whether the two mentions have the same headword.
   (2) Whether the two mentions belong to the same type. Here, we use WordNet to get three most common sense of each NP and compare the type they belong to.
   (3) The semantic distance between two mentions. WordNet is used here.
   (4) The natures of the two mentions, including number, gender, is human or not, and match each other or not. We use WordNet and a lexicon extracted from the gender and number file here.
6. Document features:
   (1) How many speakers in this document.
   (2) Whether the mention is the first or the last sentence of the document.
   (3) Whether the two mentions are from the same speaker.

3.1.2 Features - Chinese

There are 61 features adopted in Chinese side. Because of the restriction of closed crack, most of features use the position and POS information. It is mentionable that the ways for calculating the features values. For instance, the sentence distance is not the real sentence distance in the document. For instead, the value is the number of sentences in which there are at least one mention between the mention pair. This ignores the sentences of only modal particles.

The 61 features are camped into five groups. Some example features are listed below.

1. Basic information:
   (1) The matching degree of two mentions
   (2) The word distance of two mentions
   (3) The sentence distance of two mentions
2. Parsing information:
   (1) Predicted arguments which the two mentions belong to and corresponding layers.
3. POS features
   (1) Whether the mention is NR
   (2) Whether the two mentions are both NR and are matched
4. Semantic features:
   (1) Whether the two mention is related
   (2) Whether the two mentions corefer in the history. Since the restriction of closed track, we did not use any additional semantic resources. Here, we extract the co-reference history from the training set to obtain some semantic information, such as "NN 歹徒" and "NN 绑匪" corefered in the training data, and they are regarded as coreference in the testing data.
5. Document Features:

(1) Whether the two mentions have the same speaker.
(2) Whether the mention is a human.
(3) Whether the mention is the first mention in the sentence.
(4) Whether the sentence to which the mention belongs to is the first sentence.
(5) Whether the sentence to which the mention belongs to is the second sentence
(6) Whether the sentence to which the mention belongs to is the last sentence
(7) The number of the speakers in the document.

3.2 The Rule-based Coreference Determination

The rule-based classifier is developed to recognize some specific types of coreference and especially, the long distance ones.

3.2.1 Rule-based Classifier - English

To achieve a high precision, only the mention pairs of NE-NE (include NPs those can be considered as NE) or NP-NP types with the same string are classified here.

For the NE-NE pair, the classifier identifies their NE part from the whole NP, if their strings are the same, they are considered as coreference.

For the NP-NP pair, the pairs satisfy the following rules are regarded as coreference.

(1) The POS of the first word isn't "JJR" or "JJ".
(2) If NP has only one word, its POS isn't "NNS" or "NNPS".
(3) The NP have no word like "*every*", "*every-*", "*none*", "*no*", "*any*", "*some*", "*each*".
(4) If the two NP has article, they can't be both "*a*" or "*an*".

Additionally, for the PRP mention pairs, only "*I*", "*me*", "*my*" with the same speaker can be regarded as coreference.

3.2.2 Rule-based Classifier - Chinese

A rule-based classifier is developed to determine whether the mention pairs between PNs and mentions not PN corefer or not. For instance, the mention pairs between the PN "他" which is after a comma and the mention which is marked as ARG0 in the same sentence. In the sentence "埃斯特拉达 表示 ， 他 希望 上帝 能够 赐给 他 智慧", because the mention pair between "埃斯特拉达" and the first "他" match the mentioned above rule, it is classified as a positive one. The result on the development set shows that the rule-based classifier brings good improvement.

4 Coreference Chain Construction

4.1 Coreference Chain Construction-English

The evaluation on development data shows that the achieved precision of our system is better than recall. Thus, in this stage, we simply link every pair of mentions together if there is any links can link them together to generate the initial coreference chain. After that, the mentions have the distance longer than 5 sentences are observed. The NE-NE or NP-NP mention pairs between one known coreference and an observing mention with long distance are classified to determine they are corefered or not by using a set of rules. The new detected conference will be linked to the initial coreference chain.

4.2 Coreference Chain Construction-Chinese

The coreference chain construction for Chinese is similar to English. Furthermore, as mentioned above, in MZ and NW folders, there are many mentions nested marked as the nested co-referenced mentions. In this stage, HLT_HITSZ system generates the nested co-reference mentions for improving the analysis for these two folders. Additionally, the system uses some rules to improve the coreference chain construction. We find that the trained classifier performs poor in co-reference resolution related to Pronoun. So, most rules adopted here are related to these Pronouns: "自己", "我", "你", "他", "她", "两国", "双方", "其". We use these rules to bridge the chain of pronouns and the chain of other type.

Although high precision for NT co-reference cases are achieved through string matching, the recall is not satisfactory. It partially attributes to the fact that the flexible use of Chinese. For example, to express the year of 1980, we found "一九八零年", "一九八零", " 一九八o", "八零年", "1980 年". Similar situation happens for month (月, 月份) and day (日,号), we conclude most situations to several templates to improve the rule-based conference resolution.

5 Evaluation Results

5.1 Dataset

The status of training dataset, development dataset and testing dataset in CoNLL 2012 for English and Chinese are given in Table 1 and Table 2, respectively.

	Files	Sentence	Cluster	Coreference
Train	1,940	74,852	35,101	155,292
Development	222	9,603	4,546	19,156
Test	222	9,479	n/a	n/a

Table 1. Status of CoNLL 2012 dataset - English

	Files	Sentence	Cluster	Coreference
Train	1,391	36,487	28,257	102,854
Develop	172	6,083	3,875	14,383
Test	166	4,472	n/a	n/a

Table 2. Status of CoNLL 2012 dataset - Chinese

5.2 Evaluation on Mention Detection

Firstly, the mention detection performance is evaluated. The performance achieved on the development dataset (Gold/Auto) and test data on English and Chinese are given in Table 3 and Table 4, respectively. In which, Gold means the development dataset with gold manually annotation and Auto means the automatically generated annotations.

	Precision	Recall	F_1
Develop-Gold	0.8499	0.6716	0.7503
Develop-Auto	0.8456	0.6256	0.7192
Test	0.8455	0.6264	0.7196

Table 3. Performance on Mention Detection - English

	Precision	Recall	F_1
Develop-Gold	0.7402	0.7360	0.7381
Develop-Auto	0.6987	0.6429	0.6697
Test	0.7307	0.7502	0.7403

Table 4. Performance on Mention Detection - Chinese

Generally speaking, our system achieves acceptable mention detection performance, but further improvements are desired.

5.3 Evaluation on Coreference Resolution

The performance on coreference resolution is next evaluated. The achieved performances on the development data (Gold/Auto) and test dataset on English and Chinese are given in Table 5 and Table 6, respectively. It is shown that the OF performance drops 0.0309(Gold) and 0.0112(Auto) from development dataset to test dataset on English, respectively. On the contrary, the OF performance increases 0.0096(Gold) and 0.0505(Auto) from development dataset to test dataset on Chinese, respectively. Compared with the performance reported in CoNLL2012 shared task, our system achieves a good result, ranked 3rd, on Chinese. The results show the effectiveness of our proposed system.

	Precision	Recall	F_1
MUC	0.7632	0.6455	0.6994
BCUB	0.7272	0.6797	0.7027
CEAFE	0.3637	0.4840	0.4154
OF-Develop-Gold			0.6058
MUC	0.7571	0.5993	0.6691
BCUB	0.7483	0.6441	0.6923
CEAFE	0.3350	0.4865	0.3968
OF-Develop-Auto			0.5861
MUC	0.7518	0.5911	0.6618
BCUB	0.7329	0.6228	0.6734
CEAFE	0.3264	0.4829	0.3895
OF-Test			0.5749

Table 5. Performance on Coreference Resolution – English

	Precision	Recall	F_1
MUC	0.6892	0.6655	0.6771
BCUB	0.7547	0.7410	0.7478
CEAFE	0.4876	0.5105	0.4988
OF-Develop-Gold			0.6412
MUC	0.6535	0.5643	0.6056
BCUB	0.7812	0.6809	0.7276
CEAFE	0.4322	0.5101	0.4679
OF-Develop-Auto			0.6003
MUC	0.6928	0.6595	0.6758
BCUB	0.7765	0.7328	0.7540
CEAFE	0.5072	0.5390	0.6253
OF-Test(Gold parses)			0.6508
MUC	0.5502	0.6147	0.5807
BCUB	0.6839	0.7638	0.7216
CEAFE	0.5040	0.4481	0.4744
OF-Test-Predicted-mentions (Auto parses)			0.5922
MUC	0.6354	0.6873	0.6603
BCUB	0.7136	0.7870	0.7485
CEAFE	0.5390	0.4907	0.5137
OF-Test-Gold-mention-boundaries(Auto parses)			0.6408
MUC	0.6563	0.9407	0.7732
BCUB	0.6505	0.9123	0.7595
CEAFE	0.7813	0.4377	0.5611
OF-Test-Gold-mentions (Auto parses)			0.6979

Table 6. Performance on Coreference Resolution – Chinese

6 Conclusions

This paper presents the HLT_HITSZ system for CoNLL2012 shared task. Generally speaking, this system uses a statistic-based classifier to handle short distance coreference resolution and uses a rule-based classifier to handle long distance cases. The incorporation of rule-based and statistic-based techniques is shown effective to improve the performance of coreference resolution. In our future work, more semantic and knowledge bases will be incorporated to improve coreference resolution in open track.

Acknowledgement

This research is supported by HIT.NSFIR.201012 from Harbin Institute of Technology, China and China Postdoctoral Science Foundation No. 2011M500670.

References

B. Baldwin. 1997. CogNIAC: High Precision Coreference with Limited Knowledge and Linguistic Resources. Proceedings of Workshop on Operational Factors in Practical, Robust Anaphora Resolution for Unrestricted Texts.

E. Bengtson, D. Roth. 2008. Understanding the Value of Features for Coreference Resolution. Proceedings of EMNLP 2008, 294-303.

M. S. Beth M. 1995. Overview of Results of the MUC-6 Evaluation. Proceedings of the Sixth Message Understanding Conference (MUC-6)

W. P. Chen, M. Y. Zhang, B. Qin, 2011. Coreference Resolution System using Maximum Entropy Classifier. Proceedings of CoNLL-2011.

N. A. Chinchor. 1998. Overview of MUC-7/MET-2. Proceedings of the Seventh Message Understanding Conference (MUC-7).

F. Kong, G. D. Zhou, L. H. Qian, Q. M. Zhu. 2010. Dependency-driven Anaphoricity Determination for Coreference Resolution. Proceedings of COLING 2010, 599-607

J. Lang, B. Qin, T. Liu. 2007. Intra-document Coreference Resolution: The State of the Art. Journal of Chinese Language and Computing , 2007, 17(4) : 227-253.

H. Lee, Y. Peirsman, A. Chang, N. Chambers, M. Surdeanu, D. Jurafsky. 2011. Stanford's Multi-Pass Sieve Coreference Resolution System at the CoNLL-2011 Shared Task. Proceedings of CoNLL-2011.

V. Ng and C. Cardie. 2002. Improving Machine Learning Approaches to Coreference Resolution. Proceedings of ACL 2002.

W. M. Soon, H. T. Ng, and D. C. Y. Lim. 2001. A Machine Learning Approach to Coreference Resolution of Noun Phrases. Computational Linguistics, 27(4):521-544

S. Pradhan and A. Moschitti et al. 2012. CoNLL-2012 Shared Task: Modeling Multilingual Unrestricted Coreference in OntoNotes. Proceedings of CoNLL 2012

V. Stoyanov, N. Gilbert, C. Cardie, E. Riloff. 2009. Conundrums in Noun Phrase Coreference Resolution: Making Sense of the State-of-the-Art. Proceeding ACL 2009

Y. Versley. 2007. Antecedent Selection Techniques for High-recall Coreference Resolution. Proceedings of EMNLP/CoNLL 2007.

Y. Yang, N. W. Xue, P. Anick. 2011. A Machine Learning-Based Coreference Detection System For OntoNotes. Proceedings of CoNLL-2011.

Illinois-Coref: The UI System in the CoNLL-2012 Shared Task

Kai-Wei Chang Rajhans Samdani Alla Rozovskaya Mark Sammons Dan Roth
University of Illinois at Urbana-Champaign
{kchang10|rsamdan2|rozovska|mssammon|danr}@illinois.edu

Abstract

The CoNLL-2012 shared task is an extension of the last year's coreference task. We participated in the closed track of the shared tasks in both years. In this paper, we present the improvements of *Illinois-Coref* system from last year. We focus on improving mention detection and pronoun coreference resolution, and present a new learning protocol. These new strategies boost the performance of the system by 5% MUC F1, 0.8% BCUB F1, and 1.7% CEAF F1 on the OntoNotes-5.0 development set.

1 Introduction

Coreference resolution has been a popular topic of study in recent years. In the task, a system requires to identify denotative phrases ("mentions") and to cluster the mentions into equivalence classes, so that the mentions in the same class refer to the same entity in the real world.

Coreference resolution is a central task in the Natural Language Processing research. Both the CoNLL-2011 (Pradhan et al., 2011) and CoNLL-2012 (Pradhan et al., 2012) shared tasks focus on resolving coreference on the OntoNotes corpus. We also participated in the CoNLL-2011 shared task. Our system (Chang et al., 2011) ranked first in two out of four scoring metrics (BCUB and BLANC), and ranked third in the average score. This year, we further improve the system in several respects. In Sec. 2, we describe the Illinois-Coref system for the CoNLL-2011 shared task, which we take as the baseline. Then, we discuss the improvements on mention detection (Sec. 3.1), pronoun resolution (Sec. 3.2), and learning algorithm (Sec. 3.3). Section 4 shows experimental results and Section 5 offers a brief discussion.

2 Baseline System

We use the Illinois-Coref system from CoNLL-2011 as the basis for our current system and refer to it as the *baseline*. We give a brief outline here, but focus on the innovations that we developed; a detailed description of the last year's system can be found in (Chang et al., 2011).

The *Illinois-Coref* system uses a machine learning approach to coreference, with an inference procedure that supports straightforward inclusion of domain knowledge via constraints.

The system first uses heuristics based on Named Entity recognition, syntactic parsing, and shallow parsing to identify candidate mentions. A pairwise scorer $\mathbf{w}$ generates compatibility scores w_{uv} for pairs of candidate mentions u and v using extracted features $\phi(u, v)$ and linguistic constraints c.

$$w_{uv} = \mathbf{w} \cdot \phi(u, v) + c(u, v) + t, \quad (1)$$

where t is a threshold parameter (to be tuned). An inference procedure then determines the optimal set of links to retain, incorporating constraints that may override the classifier prediction for a given mention pair. A post-processing step removes mentions in singleton clusters.

Last year, we found that a *Best-Link* decoding strategy outperformed an *All-Link* strategy. The *Best-Link* approach scans candidate mentions in a document from left to right. At each mention, if certain conditions are satisfied, the pairwise scores of all previous mentions are considered, together with any constraints that apply. If one or more viable links is available, the highest-scoring link is selected and added to the set of coreference links. After the scan is complete, the transitive closure of edges is taken to generate the coreference clusters, each cluster corresponding to a single predicted entity in the document.

The formulation of this best-link solution is as follows. For two mentions u and v, $u < v$ indicates that the mention u precedes v in the document. Let y_{uv} be a binary variable, such that $y_{uv} = 1$ *only if* u and v are in the same cluster. For a document d, *Best-Link* solves the following formulation:

$$\begin{aligned} \arg\max_y \quad & \sum\nolimits_{u,v:u<v} w_{uv} y_{uv} \\ \text{s.t} \quad & \sum\nolimits_{u<v} y_{uv} \leq 1 \; \forall v, \\ & y_{uw} \in \{0,1\}. \end{aligned} \qquad (2)$$

Eq. (2) generates a set of connected components and the set of mentions in each connected component constitute an entity. Note that we solve the above *Best-Link* inference using an efficient algorithm (Bengtson and Roth, 2008) which runs in time quadratic in the number of mentions.

3 Improvements over the Baseline System

Below, we describe improvements introduced to the baseline *Illinois-Coref* system.

3.1 Mention Detection

Mention detection is a crucial component of an end-to-end coreference system, as mention detection errors will propagate to the final coreference chain. *Illinois-Coref* implements a high recall and low precision rule-based system that includes all noun phrases, pronouns and named entities as candidate mentions. The error analysis shows that there are two main types of errors.

Non-referential Noun Phrases. Non-referential noun phrases are candidate noun phrases, identified through a syntactic parser, that are unlikely to refer to any entity in the real world (e.g., “the same time”). Note that because singleton mentions are not annotated in the OntoNotes corpus, such phrases are not considered as mentions. Non-referential noun phrases are a problem, since during the coreference stage they may be incorrectly linked to a valid mention, thereby decreasing the precision of the system. To deal with this problem, we use the training data to count the number of times that a candidate noun phrase happens to be a gold mention. Then, we remove candidate mentions that frequently appear in the training data but never appear as gold mentions. Relaxing this approach, we also take the predicted head word and the words before and after the mention into account. This helps remove noun phrases headed by a preposition (e.g., the noun “fact” in the phrase “in fact”). This strategy will slightly degrade the recall of mention detection, so we tune a threshold learned on the training data for the mention removal.

Incorrect Mention Boundary. A lot of errors in mention detection happen when predicting mention boundaries. There are two main reasons for boundary errors: parser mistakes and annotation inconsistencies. A mistake made by the parser may be due to a wrong attachment or adding extra words to a mention. For example, if the parser attaches the relative clause inside of the noun phrase ”President Bush, who traveled to China yesterday” to a different noun, the algorithm will predict ”President Bush” as a mention instead of ”President Bush, who traveled to China yesterday”; thus it will make an error, since the gold mention also includes the relative clause. In this case, we prefer to keep the candidate with a larger span. On the other hand, we may predict ”President Bush at Dayton” instead of ”President Bush”, if the parser incorrectly attaches the prepositional phrase. Another example is when extra words are added, as in ”Today President Bush”.

A correct detection of mention boundaries is crucial to the end-to-end coreference system. The results in (Chang et al., 2011, Section 3) show that the baseline system can be improved from 55.96 avg F1 to 56.62 in avg F1 by using gold mention boundaries generated from a gold annotation of the parsing tree and the name entity tagging. However, fixing mention boundaries in an end-to-end system is difficult and requires additional knowledge. In the current implementation, we focus on a subset of mentions to further improve the mention detection stage of the baseline system. Specifically, we fix mentions starting with a stop word and mentions ending with a punctuation mark. We also use training data to learn patterns of inappropriate mention boundaries. The mention candidates that match the patterns are removed. This strategy is similar to the method used to remove non-referential noun phrases.

As for annotation inconsistency, we find that in a few documents, a punctuation mark or an apostrophe used to mark the possessive form are inconsistently added to the end of a mention. The problem results in an incorrect matching between the gold and predicted mentions and downgrades the performance of the learned model. Moreover, the incorrect mention boundary problem also affects the training phase because our system is trained on a union set of the predicted and gold mentions. To fix this problem, in the training phase, we perform a relaxed matching between predicted mentions and gold mentions and ignore the punctuation marks and mentions that start with one of the following: adverb, verb, determiner, and cardinal number. For example, we successfully match the predicted mention "now the army" to the gold mention "the army" and match the predicted mention "Sony 's" to the gold mention "Sony." Note that we cannot fix the inconsistency problem in the test data.

3.2 Pronoun Resolution

The baseline system uses an identical model for coreference resolution on both pronouns and non-pronominal mentions. However, in the literature (Bengtson and Roth, 2008; Rahman and Ng, 2011; Denis and Baldridge, 2007) the features for coreference resolution on pronouns and non-pronouns are usually different. For example, lexical features play an important role in non-pronoun coreference resolution, but are less important for pronoun anaphora resolution. On the other hand, gender features are not as important in non-pronoun coreference resolution.

We consider training two separate classifiers with different sets of features for pronoun and non-pronoun coreference resolution. Then, in the decoding stage, pronoun and non-pronominal mentions use different classifiers to find the best antecedent mention to link to. We use the same features for non-pronoun coreference resolution, as the baseline system. For the pronoun anaphora classifier, we use a set of features described in (Denis and Baldridge, 2007), with some additional features. The augmented feature set includes features to identify if a pronoun or an antecedent is a speaker in the sentence. It also includes features to reflect the document type. In Section 4, we will demonstrate the improvement of using separate classifiers for pronoun and non-pronoun coreference resolution.

Algorithm 1 Online Latent Structured Learning for Coreference Resolution

Loop until convergence:

For each document D_t and each $v \in D_t$

1. Let $u^* = \max_{u \in y(v)} \mathbf{w}^T \phi(u, v)$, and
2. $u' = \max_{u \in \{u<v\} \cup \{\emptyset\}} \mathbf{w}^T \phi(u, v) + \Delta(u, v, y(v))$
3. Let $\mathbf{w} \leftarrow \mathbf{w} + \eta \mathbf{w}^T (\phi(u', v) - \phi(u^*, v))$.

3.3 Learning Protocol for Best-Link Inference

The baseline system applies the strategy in (Bengtson and Roth, 2008, Section 2.2) to learn the pairwise scoring function $\mathbf{w}$ using the Averaged Perceptron algorithm. The algorithm is trained on mention pairs generated on a per-mention basis. The examples are generated for a mention v as

- Positive examples: (u, v) is used as a positive example where $u < v$ is the closest mention to v in v's cluster
- Negative examples: for all w with $u < w < v$, (w, v) forms a negative example.

Although this approach is simple, it suffers from a severe label imbalance problem. Moreover, it does not relate well to the best-link inference, as the decision of picking the closest preceding mention seems rather ad-hoc. For example, consider three mentions belonging to the same cluster: $\{m_1$: "President Bush", m_2: "he", m_3:"George Bush"$\}$. The baseline system always chooses the pair (m_2, m_3) as a positive example because m_2 is the closet mention of m_3. However, it is more proper to learn the model on the positive pair (m_1, m_3), as it provides more information. Since the *best links* are not given but are latent in our learning problem, we use an online latent structured learning algorithm (Connor et al., 2011) to address this problem.

We consider a structured problem that takes mention v and its preceding mentions $\{u \mid u < v\}$ as inputs. The output variables $y(v)$ is the set of antecedent mentions that co-refer with v. We define a latent structure $\mathbf{h}(v)$ to be the bestlink decision of v. It takes the value $\emptyset$ if v is the first mention

Method	Without Separating Pronouns					With Separating Pronouns				
	MD	MUC	BCUB	CEAF	AVG	MD	MUC	BCUB	CEAF	AVG
Binary Classifier (baseline)	70.53	61.63	69.26	43.03	57.97	73.24	64.57	69.78	44.95	59.76
Latent-Structured Learning	73.02	64.98	70.00	44.48	59.82	73.95	65.75	70.25	45.30	60.43

Table 1: The performance of different learning strategies for best-link decoding algorithm. We show the results with/without using separate pronoun anaphora resolver. The systems are trained on the TRAIN set and evaluated on the **CoNLL-2012 DEV** set. We report the F1 scores (%) on mention detection (MD) and coreference metrics (MUC, BCUB, CEAF). The column AVG shows the averaged scores of the three coreference metrics.

System	MD	MUC	BCUB	CEAF	AVG
Baseline	64.58	55.49	69.15	43.72	56.12
New Sys.	70.03	60.65	69.95	45.39	58.66

Table 2: The improvement of *Illinois-Coref*. We report the F1 scores (%) on the DEV set from **CoNLL-2011** shared task. Note that the CoNLL-2011 data set does not include corpora of bible and of telephone conversation.

in the equivalence class, otherwise it takes values from $\{u \mid u < v\}$. We define a loss function $\Delta(\mathbf{h}(v), v, y(v))$ as

$$\Delta(\mathbf{h}(v), v, y(v)) = \begin{cases} 0 & \mathbf{h}(v) \in y(v), \\ 1 & \mathbf{h}(v) \notin y(v). \end{cases}$$

We further define the feature vector $\phi(\emptyset, v)$ to be a zero vector and η to be the learning rate in Perceptron algorithm. Then, the weight vector $\mathbf{w}$ in (1) can be learned from Algorithm 1. At each step, Alg. 1 picks a mention v and finds the Best-Link decision u^* that is consistent with the gold cluster. Then, it solves a loss-augmented inference problem to find the best link decision u' with current model ($u' = \emptyset$ if the classifier decides that v does not have coreferent antecedent mention). Finally, the model $\mathbf{w}$ is updated by the difference between the feature vectors $\phi(u', v)$ and $\phi(u^*, v)$.

Alg. 1 makes learning more coherent with inference. Furthermore, it naturally solves the data imbalance problem. Lastly, this algorithm is fast and converges very quickly.

4 Experiments and Results

In this section, we demonstrate the performance of *Illinois-Coref* on the OntoNotes-5.0 data set. A previous experiment using an earlier version of this data can be found in (Pradhan et al., 2007). We first show the improvement of the mention detection system. Then, we compare different learning protocols for coreference resolution. Finally, we show the overall performance improvement of *Illinois-Coref* system.

First, we analyze the performance of mention detection before the coreference stage. Note that singleton mentions are included since it is not possible to identify singleton mentions before running coreference. They are removed in the post-processing stage. The mention detection performance of the end-to-end system will be discussed later in this section. With the strategy described in Section 3.1, we improve the F1 score for mention detection from 55.92% to 57.89%. Moreover, we improve the detection performance on short named entity mentions (name entity with less than 5 words) from 61.36 to 64.00 in F1 scores. Such mentions are more important because they are easier to resolve in the coreference layer.

Regarding the learning algorithm, Table 1 shows the performance of the two learning protocols with/without separating pronoun anaphora resolver. The results show that both strategies of using a pronoun classifier and training a latent structured model with a online algorithm improve the system performance. Combining the two strategies, the avg F1 score is improved by 2.45%.

Finally, we compare the final system with the baseline system. We evaluate both systems on the CoNLL-11 DEV data set, as the baseline system is tuned on it. The results show that *Illinois-Coref* achieves better scores on all the metrics. The mention detection performance after coreference resolution is also significantly improved.

Task	MD	MUC	BCUB	CEAF	AVG
English (Pred. Mentions)	74.32	66.38	69.34	44.81	60.18
English (Gold Mention Boundaries)	75.72	67.80	69.75	45.12	60.89
English (Gold Mentions)	100.00	85.74	77.46	68.46	77.22
Chinese (Pred Mentions)	47.58	37.93	63.23	35.97	45.71

Table 3: The results of our submitted system on the TEST set. The systems are trained on a collection of TRAIN and DEV sets.

4.1 Chinese Coreference Resolution

We apply the same system to Chinese coreference resolution. However, because the pronoun properties in Chinese are different from those in English, we do not train separate classifiers for pronoun and non-pronoun coreference resolution. Our Chinese coreference resolution on Dev set achieves 37.88% MUC, 63.37% BCUB, and 35.78% CEAF in F1 score. The performance for Chinese coreference is not as good as the performance of the coreference system for English. One reason for that is that we use the same feature set for both Chinese and English systems, and the feature set is developed for the English corpus. Studying the value of strong features for Chinese coreference resolution system is a potential topic for future research.

4.2 Test Results

Table 3 shows the results obtained on TEST, using the best system configurations found on DEV. We report results on both English and Chinese coreference resolution on predicted mentions with predicted boundaries. For English coreference resolution, we also report the results when using gold mentions and when using gold mention boundaries[1].

5 Conclusion

We described strategies for improving mention detection and proposed an online latent structure algorithm for coreference resolution. We also proposed using separate classifiers for making Best-Link decisions on pronoun and non-pronoun mentions. These strategies significantly improve the *Illinois-Coref* system.

[1]Note that, in Ontonotes annotation, specifying gold mentions requires coreference resolution to exclude singleton mentions. Gold mention boundaries are provided by the task organizers and include singleton mentions.

Acknowledgments This research is supported by the Defense Advanced Research Projects Agency (DARPA) Machine Reading Program under Air Force Research Laboratory (AFRL) prime contract no. FA8750-09-C-0181 and the Army Research Laboratory (ARL) under agreement W911NF-09-2-0053. Any opinions, findings, and conclusion or recommendations expressed in this material are those of the author(s) and do not necessarily reflect the view of the DARPA, AFRL, ARL or the US government.

References

E. Bengtson and D. Roth. 2008. Understanding the value of features for coreference resolution. In *EMNLP*.

K. Chang, R. Samdani, A. Rozovskaya, N. Rizzolo, M. Sammons, and D. Roth. 2011. Inference protocols for coreference resolution. In *CoNLL*.

M. Connor, C. Fisher, and D. Roth. 2011. Online latent structure training for language acquisition. In *IJCAI*.

P. Denis and J. Baldridge. 2007. A ranking approach to pronoun resolution. In *IJCAI*.

S. Pradhan, L. Ramshaw, R. Weischedel, J. MacBride, and L. Micciulla. 2007. Unrestricted Coreference: Identifying Entities and Events in OntoNotes. In *ICSC*.

S. Pradhan, L. Ramshaw, M. Marcus, M. Palmer, R. Weischedel, and N. Xue. 2011. CoNLL-2011 shared task: Modeling unrestricted coreference in OntoNotes. In *CoNLL*.

S. Pradhan, A. Moschitti, N. Xue, O. Uryupina, and Y. Zhang. 2012. CoNLL-2012 shared task: Modeling multilingual unrestricted coreference in OntoNotes. In *CoNLL*.

A. Rahman and V. Ng. 2011. Narrowing the modeling gap: a cluster-ranking approach to coreference resolution. *Journal of AI Research*, 40(1):469–521.

Hybrid Rule-based Algorithm for Coreference Resolution *

Heming Shou[1,2] **Hai Zhao**[1,2†]
[1]Center for Brain-Like Computing and Machine Intelligence,
Department of Computer Science and Engineering, Shanghai Jiao Tong University
[2]MOE-Microsoft Key Laboratory for Intelligent Computing and Intelligent Systems
Shanghai Jiao Tong University
shouhm@gmail.com, zhaohai@cs.sjtu.edu.cn

Abstract

This paper describes our coreference resolution system for the CoNLL-2012 shared task. Our system is based on the Stanford's *dcoref* deterministic system which applies multiple sieves with the order from high precision to low precision to generate coreference chains. We introduce the newly added constraints and sieves and discuss the improvement on the original system. We evaluate the system using OntoNotes data set and report our results of average F-score 58.25 in the closed track.

1 Introduction

In this paper, our coreference resolution system for CoNLL-2012 shared task (Pradhan et al., 2012) is summarized. Our system is an extension of Stanford's multi-pass sieve system, (Raghunathan et al., 2010) and (Lee et al., 2011), by adding novel constraints and sieves. In the original model , sieves are sorted in decreasing order of precision. Initially each mention is in its own cluster. Mention clusters are combined by satisfying the condition of each sieve in the scan pass. Through empirical studies, we proposed some extensions and algorithms for furthermore enhancing the performance.

Many other existing systems applied supervised or unsupervised (Haghighi and Klein, 2010) learning models. The classical resolution algorithm was proposed by (Soon et al., 2001). Semantic knowledge like word associations was involved by (Kobdani et al., 2011). Most of the supervised learning models in CoNLL-2011 shared task (Chang et al., 2011)(Björkelund and Nugues, 2011) used classifiers (Maximum Entropy or SVM) to train the models for obtaining the pairwise mention scores. However, the training process usually takes much longer time than unsupervised or deterministic systems. In contrast, (Raghunathan et al., 2010) proposed a rule-based model which obtained competitive result with less time.

Two considerable extensions to the Stanford model in this paper are made to guarantee higher precision and recall. First, we recorded error patterns from outputs of the original Stanford system and found that the usual errors are mention boundary mismatches, pronoun mismatches and so on. To avoid the irrational coreference errors, we added some constraints to the mention detection for eliminating some unreasonable mention boundary mismatches. Second, we added some constraints in the coreference sieves based on the errors on the training set and the development set.

We participated in the closed track and received an official F-score (unweighted mean of MUC, BCUBED and CEAF(E) metric) of 58.25 for English. The system with our extensions is briefly introduced in Section 2. We report our evaluation results and discuss in Section 3.

*This work was partially supported by the National Natural Science Foundation of China (Grant No. 60903119 and Grant No. 61170114), the National Research Foundation for the Doctoral Program of Higher Education of China under Grant No. 20110073120022, the National Basic Research Program of China (Grant No. 2009CB320901) and the European Union Seventh Framework Program (Grant No. 247619).

† corresponding author

2 System Architecture

The original Stanford system consists of three stages: mention detection, coreference resolution and post-processing. The mention detection stage is for extracting mentions with a relative high recall. The coreference resolution stage uses multiple sieves to generate coreference clusters. The post-processing stage makes the output compatible with the shared task and OntoNotes specifications (Pradhan et al., 2007), e.g. removing singletons, appositive, predicate nominatives and relative pronouns.

2.1 Mention Detection

Our system mainly focuses on making extensions for mention detection and coreference resolution. From error analysis, we found that mention boundaries caused many precision and recall errors. For example, for the gold mention *Robert H. Chandross, an economist for Lloyd's Bank in New York*, the original system only extracts *Robert H. Chandross* as the mention and links it with *he* in the following sentence. This mismatch leads to both precision and recall errors since the mention with longer boundary is not detected but the shorter one is used. Another example which omits *today* in the phrase for the predicted mention is mentioned in (Lee et al., 2011) and this boundary mismatch also accounts for precision and recall errors. Some other examples may be like this: *Auto prices had a big effect in the PPI, and at the CPI level they won't*, the gold mentions are *Auto prices*, *the PPI*, *the CPI level* and *they* while the original system only finds out *auto prices*. Considering these boundary mismatches, it is not hard for us to categorize the error types.

By observation, most boundary problems happen in the following cases:

- The predicted mention is embedded in the gold mention.
- The gold mention is embedded in the predicted mention.
- Some gold mentions are totally omitted.

It is very rare for the case that predicted mention overlaps with the gold mention but no one includes the other.

For the first and second cases, some analysis and constraint about prefix and postfix of phrases are applied to get predicted mentions as precise as gold mentions. For the example mentioned above, the clause *,an economist ...* which modifies the person *Robert H. Chandross* is annexed to the person name mention. We also append time and other modifiers to the original mention. As for the third case, we allow more pronouns and proper nouns to be added to the list of mentions.

2.2 Sieve Coreference

Like the constraints on the extension to the mention detection stage, our system also generates error reports for the sieve passes. While our system is rule-based and it also works without training data sets, some statistical information is also helpful to detect and avoid errors.

The first extension we used is a direct way to utilize the training data and the development data. We simply record the erroneous mention pairs in the train and development sets with distance and sieve information. One of the most common errors is that when mentions with particular types appear twice in the same sentence, the original system often puts them into the same cluster. For example, there are often two or more *you* or person names in the dialogue, however, the different occurrences are treated as coreference which produces precision errors. To address this problem, we convert proper nouns to type designator, e.g. *Paul* as *Man Name*. Then we use the formatted error pairs as constraints on the sieve passes since some pairs mostly cause precision errors. If the checking pair matches up some records in the errors with the same sieve information and the error frequency is over a threshold, we must discard this pair in this sieve pass.

Another difference between our system and the Stanford system is the semantic similarity sieve. For each sieve pass, the current clusters are built by stronger sieves (sieves in the earlier passes). The Stanford system selects the most representative mention from a mention cluster to query for semantic information. The preference order is:

1. mentions headed by proper nouns
2. mentions headed by common nouns

3. nominal mentions

4. pronominal mentions

In our system, we not only select the most representative one but compare all the types above, i.e, select the longest string in each type of this cluster. When applying semantic sieves, we also compare representative mention for each type and make synthesized decisions by the number of types which have similar semantic meanings.

We also made some modifications on the sieves and their ordering in the original system. For *Proper Head Word Match* mentioned in (Lee et al., 2011), the Pronoun distance which indicates sentence distance limit between a pronoun and its antecedent. We change the value from 3 to 2.

3 Experiments and Results

Table 1: CoNLL-2012 Shared Task Test Results

Metric	Recall	Precision	F1
MD	75.35	72.08	73.68
MUC	63.46	62.39	62.92
BCUBED	65.31	68.90	67.05
CEAF(M)	55.68	55.68	55.68
CEAF(E)	44.20	45.35	44.77
BLANC	69.43	75.08	71.81
OFFICIAL	-	-	58.25

Table 2: Comparison between original system and our system on the development set

metric	original	our system
MUC F	61.64	62.31
MUC P	58.65	59.58
MUC R	64.95	65.29
BCUBED F	68.61	69.87
BCUBED P	67.23	68.81
BCUBED R	70.04	70.97

Our system enhanced the precision and recall of the original system of (Lee et al., 2011). The table 1. shows the official result for the CoNLL-2012 shared task. The recall of our mention detection approach is 75.35% while the precision is 72.08%. The final official score 58.25 is the unweighed mean of MUC, BCUBED and CEAF(E). Although the test set is different from that of the previous year, comparing with the original system, our result of MD and MUC shows that our improvement is meaningful. The table 2. indicates the improvement from our system over the original system evaluated by the development set. Since experiments with semantic knowledge like WordNet and Wikipedia cannot give better performance, we omit the semantic function for generating test result. Our explanation is that the predicted mentions are still not precise enough and the fuzziness of the semantic knowledge might cause conflicts with our sieves. If the semantic knowledge tells that two mentions are similar and possibly can be combined while they do not satisfy the sieve constraints, it will be very hard to make a decision since we cannot find an appropriate threshold to let the semantic suggestion pass through.

4 Conclusion

In this paper we made a series of improvements on the existing Stanford system which only uses deterministic rules. Since the rules are high dimensional, i.e., the rules that are adopted in the system may depend on the states of the ongoing clustering process, it is not feasible to apply it in the statistical learning methods since take the intermediate results into consideration will be. The experimental results show that our improvements are effective. For this task, we added constraints on the mention detection stage and the coreference resolution stage. We also added new sieves and conduct a group of empirical studies on semantic knowledge. Our results give a demonstration that the deterministic model for coreference resolution is not only simple and competitive but also has high extendibility.

References

Anders Björkelund and Pierre Nugues. 2011. Exploring lexicalized features for coreference resolution. In *Proceedings of the Fifteenth Conference on Computational Natural Language Learning: Shared Task*, pages 45–50, Portland, Oregon, USA, June. Association for Computational Linguistics.

Kai-Wei Chang, Rajhans Samdani, Alla Rozovskaya, Nick Rizzolo, Mark Sammons, and Dan Roth. 2011. Inference protocols for coreference resolution. In *Proceedings of the Fifteenth Conference on Computation-*

al Natural Language Learning: Shared Task, pages 40–44, Portland, Oregon, USA, June. Association for Computational Linguistics.

Aria Haghighi and Dan Klein. 2010. Coreference resolution in a modular, entity-centered model. In *Human Language Technologies: The 2010 Annual Conference of the North American Chapter of the Association for Computational Linguistics*, pages 385–393, Los Angeles, California, June. Association for Computational Linguistics.

Hamidreza Kobdani, Hinrich Schuetze, Michael Schiehlen, and Hans Kamp. 2011. Bootstrapping coreference resolution using word associations. In *Proceedings of the 49th Annual Meeting of the Association for Computational Linguistics: Human Language Technologies*, pages 783–792, Portland, Oregon, USA, June. Association for Computational Linguistics.

Heeyoung Lee, Yves Peirsman, Angel Chang, Nathanael Chambers, Mihai Surdeanu, and Dan Jurafsky. 2011. Stanford's multi-pass sieve coreference resolution system at the conll-2011 shared task. In *Proceedings of the Fifteenth Conference on Computational Natural Language Learning: Shared Task*, pages 28–34, Portland, Oregon, USA, June. Association for Computational Linguistics.

Sameer S. Pradhan, Lance A. Ramshaw, Ralph M. Weischedel, Jessica MacBride, and Linnea Micciulla. 2007. Unrestricted coreference: Identifying entities and events in ontonotes. In *ICSC*, pages 446–453.

Sameer Pradhan, Alessandro Moschitti, Nianwen Xue, Olga Uryupina, and Yuchen Zhang. 2012. CoNLL-2012 shared task: Modeling multilingual unrestricted coreference in OntoNotes. In *Proceedings of the Sixteenth Conference on Computational Natural Language Learning (CoNLL 2012)*, Jeju, Korea.

Karthik Raghunathan, Heeyoung Lee, Sudarshan Rangarajan, Nathanael Chambers, Mihai Surdeanu, Dan Jurafsky, and Christopher Manning. 2010. A multi-pass sieve for coreference resolution. In *Proceedings of EMNLP 2010*.

Wee Meng Soon, Hwee Tou Ng, and Daniel Chung Yong Lim. 2001. A machine learning approach to coreference resolution of noun phrases. *Comput. Linguist.*, 27(4):521–544, December.

BART goes multilingual: The UniTN / Essex submission to the CoNLL-2012 Shared Task

Olga Uryupina[‡] **Alessandro Moschitti**[‡] **Massimo Poesio**[‡†]
[‡]University of Trento
[†] University of Essex
uryupina@gmail.com, moschitti@disi.unitn.it, massimo.poesio@unitn.it

Abstract

This paper describes the UniTN/Essex submission to the CoNLL-2012 Shared Task on the Multilingual Coreference Resolution. We have extended our CoNLL-2011 submission, based on BART, to cover two additional languages, Arabic and Chinese. This paper focuses on adapting BART to new languages, discussing the problems we have encountered and the solutions adopted. In particular, we propose a novel entity-mention detection algorithm that might help identify nominal mentions in an unknown language. We also discuss the impact of basic linguistic information on the overall performance level of our coreference resolution system.

1 Introduction

A number of high-performance coreference resolution (CR) systems have been created for English in the past decades, implementing both rule-based and statistical approaches. For other languages, however, the situation is far less optimistic. For Romance and German languages, several systems have been developed and evaluated, in particular, at the SemEval-2010 track 1 on Multilingual Coreference Resolution (Recasens et al., 2010). For other languages, individual approaches have been proposed, covering specific subparts of the task, most commonly pronominal anaphors (cf., for example, (Iida and Poesio, 2011; Arregi et al., 2010) and many others).

Two new languages, Arabic and Chinese, have been proposed for the CoNLL-2012 shared task (Pradhan et al., 2012). They present a challenging problem: the systems are required to provide entity mention detection (EMD) and design a proper coreference resolver for both languages. At UniTN/Essex, we have focused on these parts of the task, relying on a modified version of our last-year submission for English.

Most state-of-the-art full-scale coreference resolution systems rely on hand-written rules for the mention detection subtask.[1] For English, such rules may vary from corpus to corpus, reflecting specifics of particular guidelines (e.g. whether nominal premodifiers can be mentions, as in MUC, or not, as in most other corpora). However, for each corpus, such heuristics can be adjusted in a straightforward way. Creating a robust rule-based EMD module for a new language, on the contrary, is a challenging issue that requires substantial linguistic knowledge.

In this paper, we advocate a novel approach, recasting parse-based EMD as a statistical problem. We consider a node-filtering model that does not rely on any linguistic expertise in a given language. Instead, we use tree kernels (Moschitti, 2008; Moschitti, 2006) to induce a classifier for mention NP-nodes automatically from the data.

Another issue to be solved when designing a coreference resolution system for a new language is a possible lack of relevant linguistic information. Most state-of-the-art CR algorithms rely on relatively advanced linguistic representations of mentions. This can be seen as a remarkable shift

[1]Statistical EMD approaches have been proved useful for ACE-style coreference resolution, where mentions are basic units belonging to a restricted set of semantic types.

from knowledge-lean approaches of the late nineties (Harabagiu and Maiorano, 1999). In fact, modern systems try to account for complex coreference links by incorporating lexicographic and world knowledge, for example, using WordNet (Harabagiu et al., 2001; Huang et al., 2009) or Wikipedia (Ponzetto and Strube, 2006). For languages other than English, however, even the most basic properties of mentions can be intrinsically difficult to extract. For example, Baran and Xue (2011) have shown that a complex algorithm is needed to identify the `number` property of Chinese nouns.

Both Arabic and Chinese have long linguistic traditions and therefore most grammar studies rely on terminology that can be very confusing for an outsider. For example, several works on Arabic (Hoyt, 2008) mention that nouns can be made definite with the suffix "Al-", but this is not a semantic, but syntactic definiteness. Without any experience in Arabic, one can hardly decide how such "syntactic definiteness" might affect coreference.

In the present study, we have used the information provided by the CoNLL organizers to try and extract at least some linguistic properties of mentions for Arabic and Chinese. We have run several experiments, evaluating the impact of such very basic knowledge on the performance level of a coreference resolution system.

The rest of the paper is organized as follows. In the next section we briefly describe the general architecture and the system for English, focusing on the adjustments made after the last year competition. Section 3 is devoted to new languages: we first discuss our EMD module and then describe the procedures for extracting linguistic knowledge. Section 4 discusses the impact of our solutions to the performance level of a coreference resolver. The official evaluation results are presented in Section 5.

2 BART

Our CoNLL submission is based on BART (Versley et al., 2008). BART is a modular toolkit for coreference resolution that supports state-of-the-art statistical approaches to the task and enables efficient feature engineering. BART has originally been created and tested for English, but its flexible modular architecture ensures its portability to other languages and domains.

The BART toolkit has five main components: preprocessing pipeline, mention factory, feature extraction module, decoder and encoder. In addition, an independent *LanguagePlugin* module handles all the language specific information and is accessible from any component.

The architecture is shown in Figure 1. Each module can be accessed independently and thus adjusted to leverage the system's performance on a particular language or domain.

The preprocessing pipeline converts an input document into a set of linguistic layers, represented as separate XML files. The mention factory uses these layers to extract mentions and assign their basic properties (number, gender etc). The feature extraction module describes pairs of mentions $\{M_i, M_j\}$, $i < j$ as a set of features. At the moment we have around 45 different feature extractors, encoding surface similarity, morphological, syntactic, semantic and discourse information. Note that no language-specific information is encoded in the extractors explicitly: a language-independent representation, provided by the Language Plugin, is used to compute feature values. For CoNLL-2012, we have created two additional features: `lemmata-match` (similar to string match, but uses lemmata instead of tokens) and `number-agreement-du` (similar to commonly used number agreement features, but supports dual number).

The encoder generates training examples through a process of sample selection and learns a pairwise classifier. Finally, the decoder generates testing examples through a (possibly distinct) process of sample selection, runs the classifier and partitions the mentions into coreference chains.

2.1 Coreference resolution in English

The English track at CoNLL-2012 can be considered an extension of the last year's CoNLL task. New data have been added to the corpus, including two additional domains, but the annotation guidelines remain the same.

We have therefore mainly relied on the CoNLL-2011 version of our system (Uryupina et al., 2011) for the current submission, providing only minor adjustments. Thus, we have modified our preprocess-

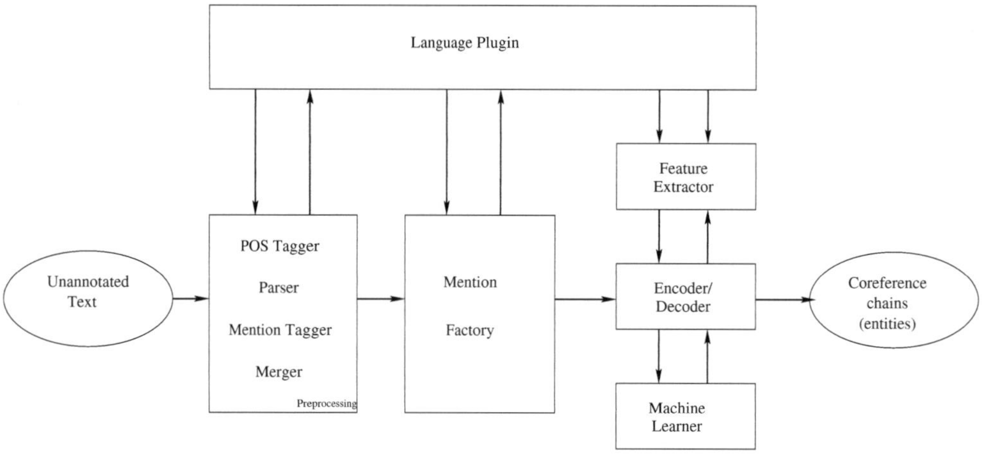

Figure 1: BART architecture

ing pipeline to operate on the OntoNotes NE-types, mapping them into MUC types required by BART. This allows us to participate in the closed track, as no external material is used any longer.

Since last year, we have continued with our experiments on multi-objective optimization, proposed in our CoNLL-2011 paper (Uryupina et al., 2011). We have extended the scope of our work to cover different machine learning algorithms and their parameters (Saha et al., 2011). For CoNLL-2012, we have re-tested all the solutions of our optimization experiments, picking the one with the highest score on the current development set.

Finally, our recent experiments on domain selection (Uryupina and Poesio, 2012) suggest that, at least for some subparts of OntoNotes, a system might benefit from training a domain-specific model. We have tested this hypothesis on the CoNLL-2012 data and have consequently trained domain-specific classifiers for the *nw* and *bc* domains.

3 Coreference resolution in Arabic and Chinese

We have addressed two main issues when developing our coreference resolvers for Arabic and Chinese: mention detection and extraction of relevant linguistic properties of our mentions.

3.1 Mention detection

Mention detection is rarely considered to be a separate task. Only very few studies on coreference resolution report on their EMD techniques. Existing corpora of coreference follow different approaches to mention annotation: this includes defining mention boundaries (basic vs. maximal NPs), alignment procedures (strict vs. relaxed with manually annotated minimal spans vs. relaxed with automatically extracted heads), the position on singleton and/or non-referential mentions (annotated vs. not).

The CoNLL-2011/2012 guidelines take a very strict view on mention boundaries: only the maximal spans are annotated and no approximate matching is allowed. Moreover, the singleton mentions (i.e. not participating in coreference relations) are not marked. This makes the mention detection task for OntoNotes extremely challenging, especially for the two new languages: on the one hand, one has to provide exact boundaries; on the other hand, it is hard to learn such information explicitly, as not all the candidate mentions are annotated.

Most CoNLL-2011 systems relied on hand-written rules for the mention detection subtask. This was mainly possible due to the existence of well-studied and thoroughly documented head-detection rules for English, available as a description for reimplementing (Collins, 1999) or as a downloadable package. Consider the following example:

(1) ..((the rising price)$_{NP_2}$ of (food)$_{NP_3}$)$_{NP_1}$..

In this fragment, three nominal phrases can be identified, with the first one ("the rising price of food") spanning over the two others ("the rising price") and ("food"). According to the OntoNotes annotation guidelines, the second noun phrase cannot be a mention, because it is embedded in an upper NP and they share the same head noun. The third noun phrase, on the contrary, could be a mention—even though it's embedded in another NP, their heads are different. Most CoNLL-2011 participants used as a backbone a heuristic discarding embedded noun phrases.

For less-known languages, however, this heuristic is only applicable as long as we can compute an NP's head reliably. Otherwise it's hard to distinguish between candidate mentions similar to NP_1 and to NP_2 in the example above.

A set of more refined heuristics is typically applied to discard or add some specific types of mentions. For example, several studies (Bergsma and Yarowsky, 2011) have addressed the issue of detecting expletive pronouns in English. Again, in the absence of linguistic expertise, one can hardly engineer such heuristics for a new language manually.

We have investigated the possibility of learning mention boundaries automatically from the OntoNotes data. We recast the problem as an NP-node filtering task: we analyze automatically computed parse trees and consider all the NP-nodes to be candidate instances to learn a classifier of correct vs. incorrect mention nodes. Clearly, this approach cannot account for mentions that do not correspond to NP-nodes. However, as Table 1 shows, around 85-89% of all the mentions, both for Arabic and Chinese, are NP-nodes.

	train		development	
	NP-nodes	%	NP-nodes	%
Arabic	24068	87.23	2916	87.91
Chinese	88523	85.96	12572	88.52

Table 1: NP-nodes in OntoNotes for Arabic and Chinese: total numbers and percentage of mentions.

We use tree kernels (Moschitti, 2008; Moschitti, 2006) to induce a classifier that labels an NP node and a part of the parse tree that surrounds it as $\pm$mention. Two integer parameters control the selection of the relevant part of the parse tree, allowing for pruning the nodes that are far above or far below the node of interest.

Our classifier is supposed to decide whether an NP-node is a mention of a real-world object. Such mentions, however, are annotated in OntoNotes as positive instances only when they corefer with some other mentions. The classifier works as a preprocessor for a CR system and therefore has no information that would allow it to discriminate between singleton vs. non-singleton mentions. One can investigate possibilities for joint EMD and CR to alleviate the problem. We have adopted a simpler solution: we tune a parameter (cost factor) that controls the precision/recall trade-off to bias the classifier strongly towards recall.

We use a small subset (1-5%) of the training data to train the EMD classifier. We tune the EMD parameters to optimize the overall performance: we run the classifier to extract mentions for the whole training and development sets, run the coreference resolver and record the obtained result (CoNLL score). The whole set of parameters to be tuned comprise: the size of the training set for EMD, the precision-recall trade-off, and two pruning thresholds.

3.2 Extracting linguistic properties

All the features implemented in BART use some kind of linguistic information from the mentions. For example, the `number-agreement` feature first extracts the `number` properties of individual mentions. For a language supported by BART, such properties are computed by the MentionFactory. For a new language, they should be provided as a part of the mention representation computed by some external preprocessing facilities. The only obligatory mention property is its span— the sequence of relevant token ids—all the properties discussed below are optional.

The following properties have been extracted for new languages directly from the CoNLL table:

- sentence id
- sequence of lemmata
- speaker (Chinese only)

Coordinations have been determined by analyzing the sequence of PoS tags: any span containing a coordinate conjunction is a coordination. They are always considered plural and unspecified for gender, their heads correspond to their entire spans.

For non-coordinate NPs, we extract the head nouns using simple heuristics. In Arabic, the first noun in a sequence is a head. In Chinese, the last one is a head. If no head can be found through this heuristic, we try the same method, but allow for pronouns to be heads, and, as a default, consider the whole span to be the head.

Depending on the PoS tag of the head noun, we classify a mention as an NE, a pronoun or a nominal (default). For named entities, no further mention properties have been extracted.

We have compiled lists of pronouns for both Arabic and Chinese from the training and development data. For Arabic, we use gold PoS tags to classify pronouns into subtypes, person, number and gender. For Chinese, no such information is available, so we have consulted several grammar sketches and lists of pronouns on the web. We do not encode clusivity[2] and honorifics.[3]

For Arabic, we extract the gender and number properties of nominals in the following way. First, we have processed the gold PoS tags to create a list of number and gender affixes. We compute the properties of our mentions by analyzing the affixes of their heads. In a number of constructions, however, the gender is not marked explicitly, so we have compiled a gender dictionary for Arabic lemmata on the training and development data. If the gender cannot be computed from affixes, we look it up in the dictionary.

Finally, we have made an attempt at computing the definiteness of nominal expressions. For Arabic, we consider as definites all mentions with definite head nouns (prefixed with "Al") and all the idafa constructs with a definite modifier.[4] We could not compute definiteness for Chinese reliably.

[2]In some dialects of Chinese, a distinction is made between the first person plural inclusive ("you and me") and the first person exclusive ("me and somebody else") pronouns.

[3]In Chinese, different pronouns should be used addressing different persons, reflecting the relative social status of the speaker and the listener.

[4]Idafa-constructs are syntactic structures, conveying, very roughly speaking, genitive semantics, commonly used in Arabic. Their accurate analysis requires some language-specific processing.

4 Evaluating the impact of kernel-based mention detection and basic linguistic knowledge

To adopt our system to new languages, we have focused on two main issues: EMD and extraction of linguistic properties. In this section we discuss the impact of each factor on the overall performance. Table 2 summarizes our evaluation experiments. All the figures reported in this section are CoNLL scores (averages of MUC, B^3 and $CEAF_e$) obtained on the development data.

To evaluate the impact of our kernel-based EMD (TKEMD), we compare its performance against two baselines. The lower bound, "allnp", considers all the NP-nodes in a parse tree to be candidate mentions. The upper bound, "goldnp" only considers gold NP-nodes to be candidate mentions. Note that the upper bound does not include mentions that do not correspond to NP-nodes at all (around 12% of all the mentions in the development data, cf. Table 1 above).

We have created three versions of our coreference resolver, using different amounts of linguistic knowledge. The baseline system (Table 2, first column) relies only on mention spans. The system itself is a reimplementation of Soon et al. (2001), but, clearly, only the string-matching feature can be computed without specifying mention properties.

A more advanced version of the system (second column) uses the same model and the same feature set, but relies on mention properties, extracted as described in Section 3.2 above. The final version (third column) makes use of all the features implemented in BART. We run a greedy feature selection algorithm, starting from the string matching and adding features one by one, until the performance stops increasing.

For Chinese, our EMD approach has proved to be useful, bringing around 1.5-2% improvement over the "allnp" baseline for all the versions of the coreference resolver. The module for extracting mention properties has only brought a moderate improvement. This is not surprising, as we have not been able to extract many relevant linguistic properties, especially for nominals. We believe that an improvement can be achieved on the Chinese data by incorporating more linguistic information.

	baseline	+linguistics	+linguistics +features
		Arabic	
allnp	45.47	46.15	46.32
TKEMD	46.98	47.44	49.07
goldnp	51.08	63.27	64.55
		Chinese	
allnp	50.72	51.04	51.40
TKEMD	53.10	53.33	53.53
goldnp	57.78	57.30	57.98

Table 2: Evaluating the impact of EMD and linguistic knowledge: CoNLL F-score.

For Arabic, the linguistic properties could potentially be very helpful: on gold NPs, our linguistically rich system outperforms its knowledge-lean counterpart by 13 percentage points. Unfortunately, this improvement is mirrored only partially on the fully automatically acquired mentions.

5 Official results

Table 3 shows the official results obtained by our system at the CoNLL-2012 competition.

Metric	Recall	Precision	F-score
	English		
MUC	61.00	60.78	60.89
BCUBED	63.59	68.48	65.95
CEAF (M)	52.44	52.44	52.44
CEAF (E)	41.42	41.64	41.53
BLANC	67.40	72.83	69.65
	Arabic		
MUC	41.33	41.66	41.49
BCUBED	65.77	69.23	67.46
CEAF (M)	50.82	50.82	50.82
CEAF (E)	42.43	42.13	42.28
BLANC	65.58	70.56	67.69
	Chinese		
MUC	45.62	63.13	52.97
BCUBED	59.17	80.78	68.31
CEAF (M)	52.40	52.40	52.40
CEAF (E)	48.47	34.52	40.32
BLANC	68.72	80.76	73.11

Table 3: BART performance at CoNLL-2012: official results on the test set.

6 Conclusion

In this paper we have discussed our experiments on adapting BART to two new languages, Chinese and Arabic, for the CoNLL-2012 Shared Task on the Multilingual Coreference Resolution. Our team has some previous experience with extending BART to cover languages other than English, in particular, Italian and German. For those languages, however, most of our team members had at least an advanced knowledge, allowing for more straightforward engineering and error analysis. Both Arabic and Chinese present a challenge: they require new mention detection algorithms, as well as special language-dependent techniques for extracting mention properties.

For Arabic, we have proposed several simple adjustments to extract basic morphological information. As our experiments show, this can potentially lead to a substantial improvement. The progress, however, is hindered by the mention detection quality: even though our TKEMD module outperforms the lower bound baseline, there is still a lot of room for improvement, that can be achieved after a language-aware error analysis.

For Chinese, the subtask of extracting relevant linguistic information has turned out to be very challenging. We believe that, by elaborating on the methods for assigning linguistic properties to nominal mentions and combining them with the TKEMD module, one can boost the performance level of a coreference resolver.

7 Acknowledgments

The research described in this paper has been partially supported by the European Community's Seventh Framework Programme (FP7/2007-2013) under the grants #247758: ETERNALS – Trustworthy Eternal Systems via Evolving Software, Data and Knowledge, and #288024: LIMOSINE – Linguistically Motivated Semantic aggregation engiNes.

References

Olatz Arregi, Klara Ceberio, Arantza Díaz De Illarraza, Iakes Goenaga, Basilio Sierra, and Ana Zelaia. 2010. A first machine learning approach to pronominal anaphora resolution in Basque. In *Proceedings of the 12th Ibero-American conference on Advances in artificial intelligence*, IBERAMIA'10, pages 234–243, Berlin, Heidelberg. Springer-Verlag.

Elizabeth Baran and Nianwen Xue. 2011. Singular or plural? Exploiting parallel corpora for Chinese number prediction. In *Proceedings of the Machine Translation Summit XIII*.

Shane Bergsma and David Yarowsky. 2011. NADA: A robust system for non-referential pronoun detection. In *Proceedings of the Discourse Anaphora and Anaphor Resolution Colloquium*, Faro, Portugal, October.

Michael Collins. 1999. *Head-Driven Statistical Models for Natural Language Parsing*. Ph.D. thesis, University of Pennsylvania.

Sanda Harabagiu and Steven Maiorano. 1999. Knowledge-lean coreference resolution and its relation to textual cohesion and coherence. In *Proceedings of the ACL Workshop On The Relation Of Discourse/Dialogue Structure And Reference*.

Sanda Harabagiu, Răzvan Bunescu, and Steven Maiorano. 2001. Text and knowledge mining for coreference resolution. In *Proceedings of the 2nd Meeting of the North American Chapter of the Association for Computational Linguistics*, pages 55–62.

Frederick Hoyt. 2008. The Arabic noun phrase. In *The Encyclopedia of Arabic Language and Linguistics*. Leiden:Brill.

Zhiheng Huang, Guangping Zeng, Weiqun Xu, and Asli Celikyilmaz. 2009. Effectively exploiting WordNet in semantic class classification for coreference resolution. In *Proceedings of the Conference on Empirical Methods in Natural Language Processing*.

Ryu Iida and Massimo Poesio. 2011. A cross-lingual ILP solution to zero anaphora resolution. In *Proceedings of the 49th Annual Meeting of the Association for Computational Linguistics*, pages 804–813.

Alessandro Moschitti. 2006. Efficient convolution kernels for dependency and constituent syntactic trees. In *Proceedings of European Conference on Machine Learning*, pages 318–329.

Alessandro Moschitti. 2008. Kernel methods, syntax and semantics for relational text categorization. In *Proceeding of the International Conference on Information and Knowledge Management*, NY, USA.

Simone Paolo Ponzetto and Michael Strube. 2006. Exploiting semantic role labeling, WordNet and Wikipedia for coreference resolution. In *Human Language Technology Conference of the North American Chapter of the Association of Computational Linguistics*, pages 192–199.

Sameer Pradhan, Alessandro Moschitti, Nianwen Xue, Olga Uryupina, and Yuchen Zhang. 2012. CoNLL-2012 shared task: Modeling multilingual unrestricted coreference in OntoNotes. In *Proceedings of the Sixteenth Conference on Computational Natural Language Learning (CoNLL 2012)*, Jeju, Korea.

Marta Recasens, Lluís Màrquez, Emili Sapena, M.Antònia Martí, Mariona Taulé, Véronique Hoste, Massimo Poesio, and Yannick Versley. 2010. SemEval-2010 Task 1: Coreference resolution in multiple languages. In *Proceedings of the 5th International Workshop on Semantic Evaluations (SemEval-2010)*, Uppsala, Sweden.

Sriparna Saha, Asif Ekbal, Olga Uryupina, and Massimo Poesio. 2011. Single and multi-objective optimization for feature selection in anaphora resolution. In *Proceedings of the International Joint Conference on Natural Language Processing*.

Wee Meng Soon, Hwee Tou Ng, and Daniel Chung Yong Lim. 2001. A machine learning approach to coreference resolution of noun phrases. *Computational Linguistic*, 27(4):521–544.

Olga Uryupina and Massimo Poesio. 2012. Domain-specific vs. uniform modeling for coreference resolution. In *Proceedings of the Language Resources and Evaluation Conference*.

Olga Uryupina, Sriparna Saha, Asif Ekbal, and Massimo Poesio. 2011. Multi-metric optimization for coreference: The UniTN / IITP / Essex submission to the 2011 CONLL shared task. In *Proceedings of the Fifteenth Conference on Computational Natural Language Learning (CoNLL 2011)*.

Yannick Versley, Simone Paolo Ponzetto, Massimo Poesio, Vladimir Eidelman, Alan Jern, Jason Smith, Xiaofeng Yang, and Alessandro Moschitti. 2008. BART: a modular toolkit for coreference resolution. In *Proceedings of the 46th Annual Meeting of the Association for Computational Linguistics on Human Language Technologies*, pages 9–12.

Learning to Model Multilingual Unrestricted Coreference in OntoNotes

Baoli LI
Department of Computer Science
Henan University of Technology
1 Lotus Street, High&New Technology
Industrial Development Zone, Zhengzhou,
Henan, China, 450001
csblli@gmail.com

Abstract

Coreference resolution, which aims at correctly linking meaningful expressions in text, is a much challenging problem in Natural Language Processing community. This paper describes the multilingual coreference modeling system of Web Information Processing Group, Henan University of Technology, China, for the CoNLL-2012 shared task (closed track). The system takes a supervised learning strategy, and consists of two cascaded components: one for detecting mentions, and the other for clustering mentions. To make the system applicable for multiple languages, generic syntactic and semantic features are used to model coreference in text. The system obtained combined official score 41.88 over three languages (Arabic, Chinese, and English) and ranked 7th among the 15 systems in the closed track.

1 Introduction

Coreference resolution, which aims at correctly linking meaningful expressions in text, has become a central research problem in natural language processing community with the advent of various supporting resources (e.g. corpora and different kinds of knowledge bases). OntoNotes (Pradhan et al. 2007), compared to MUC (Chinchor, 2001; Chinchor and Sundheim, 2003) and ACE (Doddington et al. 2000) corpora, is a large-scale, multilingual corpus for general anaphoric coreference that covers entities and events not limited to noun phrases or a limited set of entity types. It greatly stimulates the research on this challenging problem – Coreference Resolution. Moreover, resources like WordNet (Miller, 1995) and the advancement of different kinds of syntactic and semantic analysis technologies, make it possible to do in-depth research on this topic, which is demanded in most of natural language processing applications, such as information extraction, machine translation, question answering, summarization, and so on.

Our group is exploring how to extract information from grain/cereal related Chinese text for business intelligence. This shared task provides a good platform for advancing our research on IE related topics. We experiment with a machine learning strategy to model multilingual coreference for the CoNLL-2012 shared task (Pradhan et al. 2012). Two steps are taken to detect coreference in text: mention detection and mention clustering. We consider mentions that correspond to a word or an internal node in a syntactic tree and ignore the rest mentions, as we think a mention should be a valid meaningful unit of a sentence. Maximal entropy algorithm is used to model what a mention is and how two mentions link to each other. Generic features are designed to facilitate these modeling.

Our official submission obtained combined official score 41.88 over three languages (Arabic, Chinese, and English), which ranked the system 7th among 15 systems participating the closed track. Our system performs poor on the Arabic data, and has relatively high precision but low recall.

The rest of this paper is organized as follows. Section 2 gives the overview of our system, while Section 3 discusses the first component of our system for mention detection. Section 4 explains how our system links mentions. We present our experiments and analyses in Section 5, and conclude in Section 6.

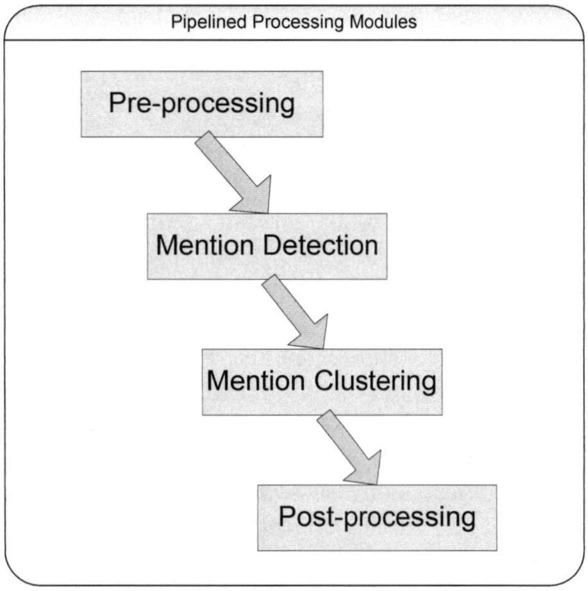

Figure 1. System Architecture.

2 System Description

Figure 1 gives the architecture of our CoNLL-2012 system, which consists of four pipelined processing modules: pre-processing, mention detection, mention clustering, and post-processing.

Pre-processing: this module reads in the data files in CoNLL format and re-builds the syntactic and semantic analysis trees in memory.

Mention Detection: this module chooses potential sub-structures on the syntactic parsing trees and determines whether they are real mentions.

Mention Clustering: this module compares pairs of mentions and links them together.

Post-processing: this module removes singleton mentions and produces the final results.

To facilitate the processing, the data files of the same languages are combined together to form big files for training, development, and test respectively.

Compared to the CoNLL-2011 shared task, the task of this year focuses on the multilingual capacity of a corefernece resolution system. We plan to take a generic solution for different languages rather than customized approach to some languages with special resources. In other words, our official system didn't take any special processing for data of different languages but used the same strategy and feature sets for all three languages.

Stanford's Rule-based method succeeded in resolving the coreferences in English text last year (Pradhan et al. 2011; Lee et al. 2011). Therefore, we planed to incorporate the results of a rule-based system (simple or complex as the Stanford's system) if available and derive some relevant features for our machine learning engine. However, due to limited time and resources, we failed to implement in our official system such a solution integrating rules within the overall statistical model.

Intuitively, mentions are meaningful sub-structures of sentences. We thus assume that a mention should be a word or a phrasal sub-structure of a parsing tree. Mention detection modules focus on these mentions and ignore others that do not correspond to a valid phrasal sub-structure.

A widely used machine learning algorithm in solving different NLP problems, Maximal Entropy (Berger et al.1996), is used to model mentions and detect links between them. Compared with Naive Bayes algorithm, Maximum entropy does not assume statistical independence of the different features. In our system, Le Zhang's maximum entropy package (Zhang, 2006) is integrated.

In the following two sections, we will detail the two critical modules: mention detection and mention clustering.

3 Mention Detection

This module determines all mentions in text. We take the assumption that a mention should be a valid sub-structure of a sentence.

3.1 Methods

We first choose potential mentions in text and then use statistical machine learning method to make final decisions.

From the train and development datasets, we could obtain a list of POS and syntactic structure tags that a mention usually has. For example, below is given such a list for English data:

```
POS_TAG    "NP" /*145765*/
POS_TAG    "NML" /*910*/
POS_TAG    "S" /*207*/
POS_TAG    "VP" /*189*/
POS_TAG    "ADVP" /*75*/
POS_TAG    "FRAG" /*73*/
POS_TAG    "WHNP" /*67*/
POS_TAG    "ADJP" /*65*/
POS_TAG    "QP" /*62*/
POS_TAG    "INTJ" /*40*/
POS_TAG    "PP" /*16*/
POS_TAG    "SBAR" /*10*/
POS_TAG    "WHADVP" /*7*/
POS_TAG    "UCP" /*5*/
//POS_TAG    "SINV" /*1*/
//POS_TAG    "SBARQ" /*1*/
//POS_TAG    "RRC" /*1*/
//POS_TAG    "SQ" /*1*/
//POS_TAG    "LST" /*1*/
SYN_TAG    "PRP$" /*14734*/
SYN_TAG    "NNP" /*3642*/
SYN_TAG    "VB" /*733*/
SYN_TAG    "VBD" /*669*/
SYN_TAG    "VBN" /*384*/
SYN_TAG    "VBG" /*371*/
SYN_TAG    "NN" /*306*/
SYN_TAG    "VBZ" /*254*/
SYN_TAG    "VBP" /*235*/
SYN_TAG    "PRP" /*137*/
SYN_TAG    "CD" /*132*/
SYN_TAG    "DT" /*77*/
SYN_TAG    "IN" /*64*/
SYN_TAG    "NNS" /*57*/
SYN_TAG    "JJ" /*52*/
SYN_TAG    "RB" /*19*/
SYN_TAG    "NNPS" /*17*/
SYN_TAG    "UH" /*7*/
SYN_TAG    "CC" /*7*/
SYN_TAG    "NFP" /*5*/
SYN_TAG    "XX" /*4*/
SYN_TAG    "MD" /*3*/
SYN_TAG    "JJR" /*2*/
SYN_TAG    "POS" /*2*/
//SYN_TAG    "FW" /*1*/
//SYN_TAG    "ADD" /*1*/
```

We remove tags rarely occurring in the datasets, such as FW and ADD for English and consider all words and syntactic structures of the rest categories as potential mentions.

To make a decision about whether a potential mention is a real one or not, we use a maximal entropy classifier with a set of generic features concerning the word or sub-structure itself and its syntactic and semantic contexts.

3.2 Features

The features we used in this step for each potential word or sub-structure include:

a. Source and Genre of a document; Speaker of a sentence;
b. Level of the Node in the syntactic parsing tree;
c. Named entity tag of the word or sub-structure;
d. Its head predicates and types;
e. Syntactic tag path to the root;
f. Whether it's part of a mention, named entity, or an argument;
g. Features from its parent: syntactic tag, named entity tag, how many children it has, whether the potential word or sub-structure is the left most child of it, the right most child, or middle child; binary syntactic tag feature;
h. Features from its direct left and right siblings: their syntactic tags, named entity tags, and binary syntactic tag features;
i. Features from its children: its total token length, words, pos tags, lemma, frameset ID, and word sense, tag paths to the left and right most child;
j. Features from its direct neighbor (before and after) tokens: words, pos tags, lemma, frameset ID, and word sense, and binary features of pos tags;

4 Mention Clustering

This component clusters the detected mentions into group.

4.1 Methods

For each pair of detected mentions, we determine whether they could be linked together with a maximal entropy classifier. The clustering takes a best-of-all strategy and works as the following algorithm:

INPUT: a list of mentions;
OUTPUT: a splitting of the mentions into groups;
ALGORIHTM:

1. For each detected mention *ANAP* from the last to the first:

1.1 Find its most likely linked antecedant *ANTE* before *ANAP*

1.2 if FOUND

1.2.1 link all anaphors of *ANAP* to *ANTE;*

1.2.2 link *ANAP* to *ANTE*

Figure 2. Algorithm for Clustering Detected Mentions

We used the probability value of the maximal entropy classifier's output for weighting the links between mentions.

4.2 Features

The features we used in this step include:

a. Source and Genre of a document; Speaker of a sentence;
b. Sentence distance between the potential antecedent and anaphor;
c. Syntactic tag of them, whether they are leaf node or not in the parsing tree;
d. Syntactic tag bi-grams of them, and whether their syntactic tags are identical;
e. Named entity tags of them, bi-gram of these tags, and whether they are identical;
f. Syntactic tag path to root of them, bi-gram of these paths, and whether they are identical;
g. Whether they are predicates;
h. Features of anaphor: Its head predicates and types, words, pos tags, the words and pos tags of the left/right 3 neighbor tokens, and bi-grams;
i. Features of antecedent: Its head predicates and types, words, pos tags, the words and pos tags of the left/right 3 neighbor tokens, and bi-grams;
j. The number of identical words of the antecedent and the anaphor;
k. The number of identical words in the neighbors (3 tokens before and after) of the antecedent and the anaphor.

The above features include not only those suggested by Soon et al. (2001), but also some context features, such as words within and out of the antecedent and the anaphor, and the overlapping number of the context words. Features about Gender and number agreements are not considered in our official system, as we failed to work out a generic solution to include them for all data of three different languages.

5 Experiments

5.1 Datasets

The datasets of the CoNLL-2012 shared task contain three languages: Arabic (ARB), Chinese (CHN), and English (ENG). No predicted names and propositions are provided in the Arabic data, while no predicted names are given in the Chinese data.

Tables 1 and 2 show statistical information of both training and development datasets for each language.

Language		# of Doc.	# of Sent.	# of Ment.	# of mentions that do not correspond to a valid phrasal sub-structure
ARB	Dev	44	950	3,317	262(7.9%)
	Train	359	7,422	27,590	2,176(7.9%)
CHN	Dev	252	6,083	14,183	677(4.8%)
	Train	1,810	36,487	102,854	6,345(6.2%)
ENG	Dev	343	9,603	19,156	661(3.5%)
	Train	2,802	75,187	155,560	4,639(3.0%)

Table 1. Statistical information of the three language datasets (train and development) (part 1).

Language		# of sentences per document		# of tokens per sentence	
		Avg.	Max	Avg.	Max
ARB	Dev	21.59	41	29.82	160
	Train	20.67	78	32.70	384
CHN	Dev	24.14	144	18.09	190
	Train	20.16	283	20.72	242
ENG	Dev	28.00	127	16.98	186
	Train	26.83	188	17.28	210

Table 2. Statistical information of the three language datasets (train and development) (part 2).

The total size of the uncompressed original data is about 384MB. The English dataset is the largest one containing 3,145 documents (343+2802), 84,790 sentences, and 174,716 mentions. The Arabic dataset is the smallest one containing 403 documents, 8,372 sentences, and 30,907 mentions. In the Arabic datasets, about 7.9% mentions do not correspond to a valid phrasal sub-structure. This number of the Chinese dataset is 6%, while that of English 3%. These small percentages verify that our assumption that a mention is expected to be a valid phrasal sub-structure is reasonable.

The average numbers of sentences in a document in the three language datasets are roughly 21, 22, and 27 respectively, while the longest document that has 283 sentences is found in the Chinese train dataset. The average numbers of tokens in a sentence in the three language datasets are roughly 31, 19, and 17 respectively, while the longest sentence with 384 tokens is found in the Arabic train dataset.

5.2 Experimental Results

For producing the results on the test datasets, we combined both train and development datasets for training maximal entropy classifiers.

The official score adopted by CoNLL-2012 is the unweighted average of scores on three languages, while for each language, the score is derived by averaging the three metrics MUC (Vilain et al. 1995), B-CUBED (Bagga and Baldwin, 1998), and CEAF(E) (Constrained Entity Aligned F-measure)(Luo, 2005) as follows:

$$\text{OFFICIAL SCORE} = \frac{\text{MUC} + \text{B-CUBED} + \text{CEAF (E)}}{3}$$

Our system achieved the combined official score 42.32 over three languages (Arabic, Chinese, and English). On each of the three languages, the system obtained scores 33.53, 46.27, and 45.85 respectively. It performs poor on the Arabic dataset, but equally well on the Chinese and English datasets.

Tables 3, 4, and 5 give the detailed results on three languages respectively.

Metric	Recall	Precision	F1
MUC	**10.77**	**55.60**	**18.05**
B-CUBED	**36.17**	**93.34**	**52.14**
CEAF (M)	37.03	37.03	37.03
CEAF (E)	**55.45**	**20.95**	**30.41**
BLANC[1]	52.91	73.93	54.12
OFFICIAL SCORE	NA	NA	**33.53**

Table 3. Official results of our system on the Arabic test dataset.

[1] For this metric, please refer to (Recasens and Hovy, 2011).

Metric	Recall	Precision	F1
MUC	**32.48**	**71.44**	**44.65**
B-CUBED	**45.51**	**86.06**	**59.54**
CEAF (M)	45.70	45.70	45.70
CEAF (E)	**55.11**	**25.24**	**34.62**
BLANC	64.99	76.63	68.92
OFFICIAL SCORE	NA	NA	**46.27**

Table 4. Official results of our system on the Chinese test dataset.

Metric	Recall	Precision	F1
MUC	**39.12**	**72.57**	**50.84**
B-CUBED	**43.03**	**80.06**	**55.98**
CEAF (M)	41.97	41.97	41.97
CEAF (E)	**49.44**	**22.30**	**30.74**
BLANC	64.01	66.86	65.24
OFFICIAL SCORE	NA	NA	**45.85**

Table 5. Official results of our system on the English test dataset.

Comparing the detailed scores, we found that our submitted system performs much poor on the MUC metric on the Arabic data. It can only recover 10.77% valid mentions. As a whole, the system works well in precision perspective but poor in recall perspective.

Language	Recall	Precision	F1
Arabic	18.17	80.43	29.65
Chinese	36.60	87.01	51.53
English	45.78	86.72	59.93

Table 6. Mention Detection Scores on the test datasets.

Table 6 shows the official mention detection scores on the test datasets, which could be regarded as the performance upper bounds (MUC metric) of the mention clustering component. Taking the mention detection results as a basis, the mention clustering component could achieve roughly 60.88 (18.05/29.65), 86.65 (44.65/51.53), and 84.83 (50.84/59.93) for the Arabic, Chinese, and English data respectively. It seems that the performance of the whole system is highly bottlenecked by that of the mention detection component. However, it may not be true as the task requires removing singleton mentions that do not refer to any other mentions. To examine how singleton mentions affect the final scores, we conducted additional experiments on the development datasets. Table 7 shows the mention detection scores on the dev datasets. When we include the singletons, the mention detection scores become 59, 63.75, and 71.27 from 31.46, 53.99, and 59.16 for the three language datasets respectively. They are reasonable and close to those that we can get at the mention clustering component. These analyses tell us that the requirement of removing singletons for scoring may deserve further study. At the same time, we realize that to get better performance we may need to re-design the feature sets (e.g. including more useful features like gender and number) and try some more powerful machine learning algorithms such as linear classification or Tree CRF (Bradley and Guestrin, 2010).

Language	Recall		Precision		F1	
	-Sing	+Sing	-Sing	+Sing	-Sing	+Sing
Arabic	19.42	47.58	82.88	77.61	31.46	59
Chinese	39.05	53.78	87.43	78.24	53.99	63.75
English	44.9	65.2	86.67	78.58	59.16	71.27

Table 7. Mention Detection Scores on the development (Dev) datasets. "-Sing" means without singletons, which is required by the task specification, while "+Sing" means including singletons.

	With gold mention boundaries (39.26)			With gold mentions (50.65)		
	ARB	**CHN**	**ENG**	**ARB**	**CHN**	**ENG**
MUC	**11.30**	**38.70**	**38.21**	**33.31**	**66.13**	**60.45**
B-CUBED	**54.25**	**59.27**	**59.51**	**53.74**	**66.84**	**57.18**
CEAF (M)	33.68	41.06	39.30	42.25	57.50	47.82
CEAF (E)	**28.84**	**31.86**	**31.39**	**34.81**	**46.83**	**36.58**
BLANC	51.46	61.47	61.33	57.96	73.47	67.12
MD Score	29.78	51.90	51.08	52.58	77.73	72.75
Official Score	**31.46**	**43.28**	**43.04**	**40.62**	**59.93**	**51.40**

Table 8. F1 scores of the two supplementary submissions with additional gold mention boundaries and gold mentions respectively.

Besides the official submission for the task with predicted data, we also provide two supplementary submissions with gold mention boundaries and gold mentions respectively. Table 8 summarizes the scores of these two submissions.

With gold mentions, our official system does achieve better performance with gain of 8.77 (50.65-41.88). On Chinese data, we get the highest score 61.61. However, the system performs worse when the gold mention boundaries are available. The F1 score drops 2.62 from 41.88 to 39.26. We guess that more candidate mentions bring more difficulties for the maximal entropy classifier to make decisions. The best-of-all strategy may not be a good choice when a large number of candidates are available. More efforts are required to explore the real reason behind the results.

6 Conclusions

In this paper, we describe our system for the CoNLL-2012 shared task – Modeling Multilingual Unrestricted Coreference in OntoNotes (closed track). Our system was built on machine learning strategy with a pipeline architecture, which integrated two cascaded components: mention detection and mention clustering. The system relies on successful syntactic analyses, which means that only valid sub-structures of sentences are considered as potential mentions.

Due to limited time and resources, we had not conducted thorough enough experiments to derive optimal solutions, but the system and the involvement in this challenge do provide a good foundation for further study. It's a success for us to finish all the submissions on time. In the future, we plan to focus on those mentions that do not correspond to a syntactic structure and consider introducing virtual nodes for them. We may also explore different strategies when linking an anaphor and its antecedent. In addition, maximal entropy may not be good enough for this kind of task. Therefore, we also plan to explore other powerful algorithms like large linear classification and tree CRF (Bradley and Guestrin, 2010; Ram and Devi, 2012) in the future.

Acknowledgments

This research was funded by HeNan Provincial Research Project on Fundamental and Cutting-Edge Technologies (No. 112300410007). We used the Amazon Elastic Compute Cloud (Amazon EC2) web service in our experiments. We thank Amazon.com for providing such great service for not only industrial applications, but also academic research.

References

Amit Bagga and Breck Baldwin. 1998. Algorithms for Scoring Coreference Chains. In Proceedings of the First International Conference on Language Resources and Evaluation Workshop on Linguistics Coreference.

Adam L. Berger, Stephen A. Della Pietra, and Vincent J. Della Pietra. 1996. A Maximal Entropy Approach to Natural Language Processing. Computational Linguistics, 22(1):39-42.

Joseph K. Bradley and Carlos Guestrin. 2010. Learning Tree Conditional Random Fields. In Proceedings of the International Conference on Machine Learning (ICML-2010).

Nancy Chinchor. 2001. Message Understanding Coference (MUC) 7. In LDC2001T02.

Nancy Chinchor and Beth Sundheim. 2003. Message Understanding Conference (MUC) 6. In LDC2003T13.

G.G. Doddington, A. Mitchell, M. Przybocki, L. Ramshaw, S. Strassell, and R. Weischedel. 2000. The Automatic Content Extraction (ACE) Program: Tasks, Data, and Evaluation. In Proceedings of LREC-2000.

Heeyoung Lee, Yves Peirsman, Angei Chang, Nathanael Chambers, Mihai Surdeanu, Dan Jurafsky. 2011. Stanford's Multi-Pass Sieve Coreference Resolution System at the CoNLL-2011 Shared Task. In Proceedings of the 15th Conference on Computational Natural Language Learning: Shared Task.

Xiaoqiang Luo. 2005. On coreference resolution performance metrics. In Proceedings of the Human Language Technology Conference and Conference on Empirical Methods in Natural Language Processing.

George A. Miller. 1995. WordNet: a Lexical Database for English. Communications of the ACM. 38(11): 39-41.

Sameer Pradhan, Eduard Hovy, Mitch Marcus, Martha Palmer, Lance Ramshaw, Ralph Weischedel. 2007. OntoNotes: A Unified Relational Semantic Representation. International Journal of Semantic Computing, 1(4): 405-419.

Sameer Pradhan, Alessandro Moschitti, Nianwen Xue, Olga Uryupina, and Yuchen Zhang. 2012. CoNLL-2012 Shared Task: Modeling Multilingual Unrestricted Coreference in OntoNotes. In Proceedings of the Sixteenth Conference on Computational Natural Language Learning (CoNLL 2012): Shared Task.

Sameer Pradhan, Lance Ramshaw, Mitchell Marcus, Martha Palmer, Ralph Weischedel and Nianwen Xue. 2011. CoNLL-2011 Shared Task: Modeling Unrestricted Coreference in OntoNotes. In Proceedings of the 15th Conference on Computational Natural Language Learning: Shared Task, pp. 1-27.

Vijay Sundar Ram R. and Sobha Lalitha Devi. 2012. Coreference Resolution Using Tree CRFs. In Proceedings of the 13th Conference on Computational Linguistics and Intelligent Text Processing (CICLing-2012).

Marta Recasens and Eduard Hovy. 2011. Blanc: Implementing the rand index for coreference evaluation. Natural Language Engineering, 17(4): 485-510.

Wee Meng Soon, Hwee Tou Ng, and Daniel Chung Yong Lim. 2001. A machine learning approach to coreference resolution of noun phrase. Computational Linguistics, 27(4): 521-544.

M. Vilain, J. Burger, J. Aberdeen, D. Connolly, and L. Hirschman. 1995. A model theoretic coreference scoring scheme. In Proceedings of the Sixth Message Understanding Conference (MUC-6).

Le Zhang. 2006. Maximum Entropy Modeling Toolkit for Python and C++. Software available at http://homepages.inf.ed.ac.uk/s0450736/maxent_toolkit.html.

Author Index